The Life and Times of Charles J. Belden Cowboy Photographer

Preface
By Mack Frost

Introductory Essay
By Brooks Roddan

The Photographs
By Charles J. Belden
From the Collection of
The McCracken Research
Library at the Buffalo Bill Center
of the West in Cody Wyoming
and the American Heritage Center
at the University of Wyoming in
Laramie

IF SF publishing

The Life and Times of Charles J. Belden Cowboy Photographer

First Edition

Photography credits: Photography by Charles J. Belden courtesy of The American Heritage Center at the University of Wyoming in Laramie and the McCracken Research Library at the Buffalo Bill Center of the West in Cody, Wyoming.

ISBN 978-1-7333864-9-4

Published by IFSF Publishing, San Francisco, California
www.ifsfpublishing.com

Cover and Book Design by David Barich, San Francisco, California

Printed by Bookmobile, Minneapolis, Minnesota

The Life and Times of Charles J. Belden
Cowboy Photographer

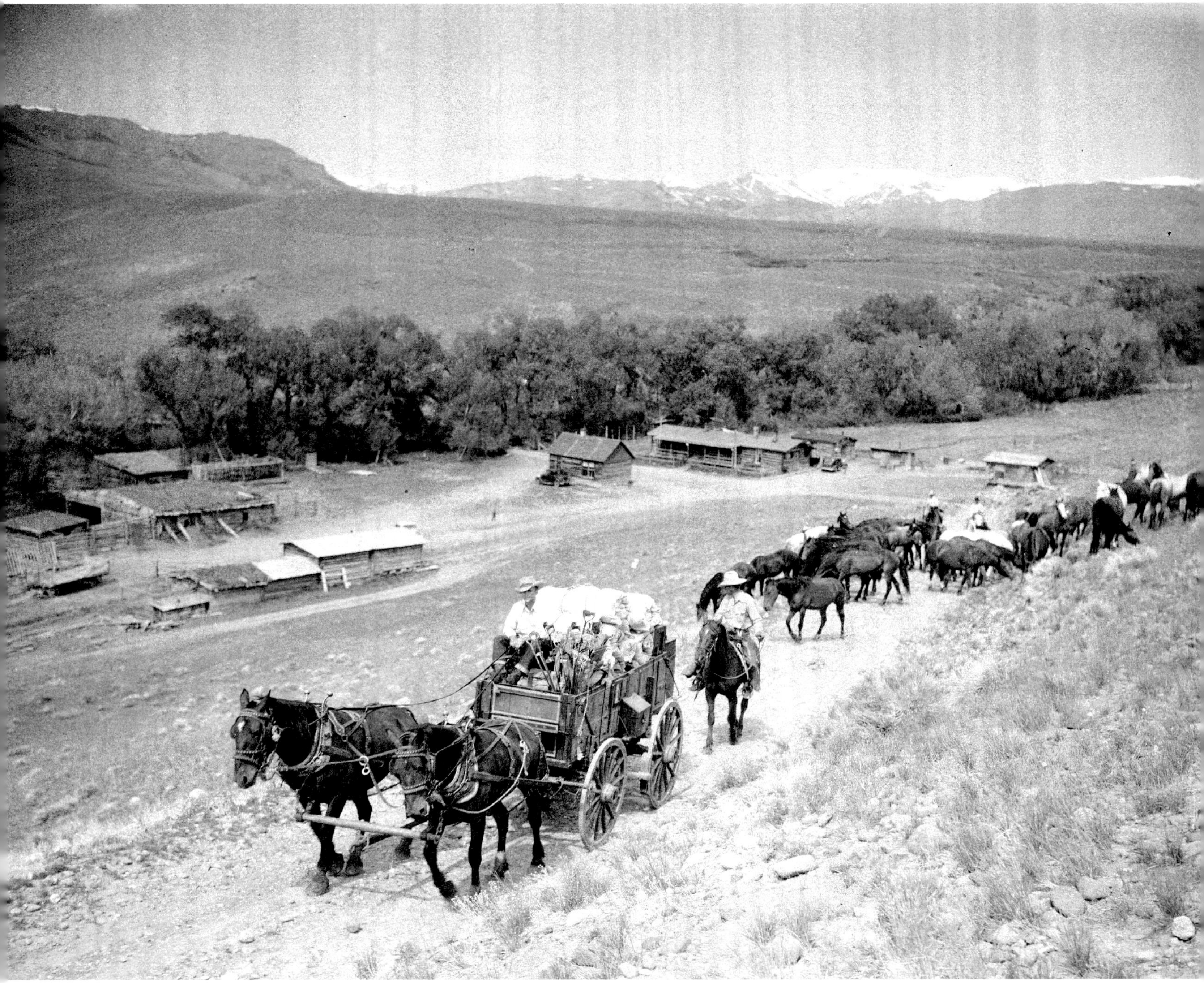

Contents

BIOGRAPHY

Brooks Roddan

Author and publisher Brooks Roddan spends part of each year at his home in San Francisco and part at a family-built straw-bale cabin in Wyoming, writing as well as directing the editorial activities of IFSF Publications. Roddan has published three novels, seven books of poems; he blogs irregularly, and has most recently taken up painting, a preferred pastime. He first became acquainted with Charles Belden's work while eating a sandwich at The Proud Cut restaurant in downtown Cody, Wyoming. From then on Roddan began noticing Belden images wherever he looked, in businesses and in public spaces, becoming convinced that a book devoted to his work as a photographer of the American west was essential.

MACK FROST

Mack Frost was born and raised in Cody, Wyoming. A graduate of Cody High School in 1969, Frost then earned advanced degrees in radio and television production, completing his Bachelor of Science degree at Montana State University in Bozeman, Montana. Inspired by his grandfather, Ned, a legendary outfitter and photographer, Mack developed an early interest in the arts, leading to a career in radio broadcasting, film processing, and movie exhibition. An accomplished photographer, Mack's work is often featured in galleries throughout the west. He currently works for the McCracken Research Library at the Buffalo Bill Center of the West, digitizing the photographic and manuscript collections, preparing them for on-line presentations.

ACKNOWLEDGMENTS

Making a book is always an adventure, so often beginning with a writer who believes, at least at first, he has some sense of where a book should begin, then coming sometimes painfully to acknowledge Pascal's observation that 'the last thing one settles in writing a book is what one should put first'.

Lili Turnell, Gloria Hedderman, and Lea Ann Roddan were in on the ground floor of the making of this book, each making a considerable investment of their time, interest, and energy to help get the thing off the ground and into the air—thank you all! Mack Frost of The Center of the West, a resource on all things Charles Belden and a fine photographer himself, was an extremely valuable consultant. David Barich, book designer, and Bill Barich, editor, helped guide this book forward to completion. Barbara Monday, pilot Billy Monday's grand-daughter, chimed in from Colorado, offering insights on Belden's relationship with the pilot and their exploits when airborne. Merrily Gumpel, Wapiti neighbor, took a real interest in the project, and other Wall Creek friends would stop by the cabin from time to time with encouragements or observations. As time went along a wider and wider circle of people interested in the Belden project developed as the book moved forward, and for them too I offer my sincere gratitude.

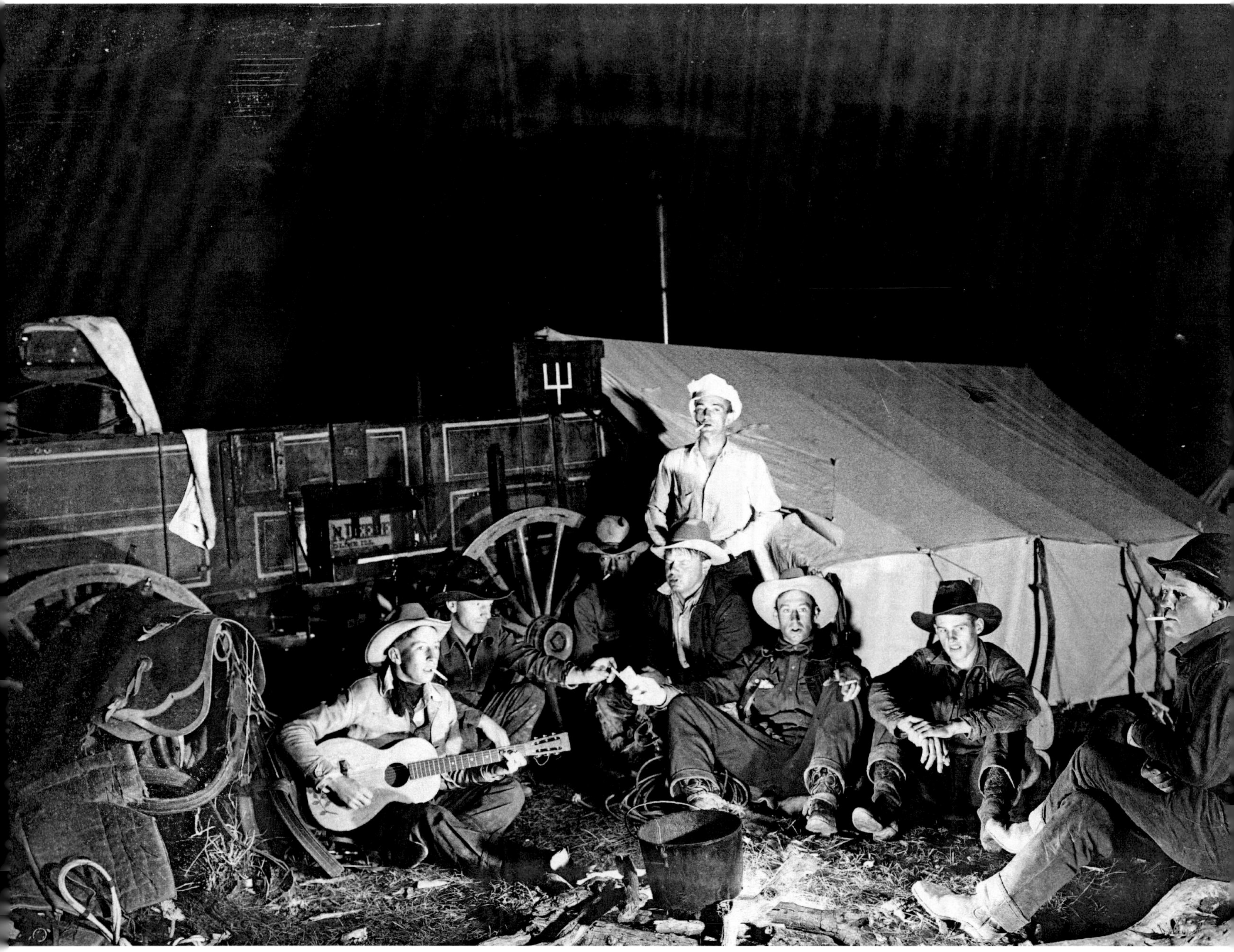

Charles J. Belden Cowboy Photographer

By Mack Frost

Charles Belden first became intrigued with photography as a boy on pack trips into California's Sierra Nevada, where an uncle showed him how to use a glass plate camera. "We invariably had two or three pack mules loaded down with cameras, plates, and equipment, and I doubt if more pains have ever been taken to photograph that region," he wrote to a friend, referring to the Kings and Kern River basins. No doubt those trips lingered in his mind as an influence when he started taking the photos of cowboys and the American West that made him famous.

Belden bought his first camera, a Zeiss Minimum Palmos, for twenty-five dollars after graduating from M.I.T. with a degree in mechanical engineering. He intended to take some pictures on a grand tour of Europe with some friends including Eugene Phelps, whose father owned the sprawling Pitchfork Ranch near Cody, Wyoming. Though the Palmos used 4 x 5 inch glass plates, it was small enough to be regarded as a portable camera at the time. It could withstand rough conditions in the field and, with its fast shutter speed, could take action shots.

The youths traveled in Belden's 1908 Packard. The highlight of the trip was a 3000-mile drive across Russia, where they posed for a photo at the Kremlin and were "feted and honored in all the larger cities." On his return, Belden held a lackluster job at an engine factory for two years, but it left him unsatisfied, and when he visited Phelps in Wyoming, his life changed radically. He'd seen ranches on those pack trips, of course, but the Pitchfork was on a different scale—actually seven ranches on some 250,000 acres, home to 10,000 Herefords and 20,000 Rambouillet sheep.

Belden fell in love with the Pitchfork and began courting Phelps's sister, Frances. They were married in 1913, and Belden eventually ran the ranch with Eugene. As a budding photographer, he'd stumbled on a trove of wonderful material that hadn't yet been documented. He would devote himself to photographing the cowboys at work and play, along with the life of the ranch through the various seasons, recording "the different phases and incidents of handling cattle on the range." The Pitchfork afforded an unforgettable setting for the images he hoped to capture.

Belden approached the task with considerable artistry. The Palmos was still his camera of choice. Although he could buy pre-packaged glass plates, he preferred to make his own, mixing emulsions in his attic darkroom to coat them and storing the dried ones in light-proof boxes until they were needed. His darkroom was unique in that he'd created a light source for his enlarger by cutting a tunnel-shaped hole in the roof and painting the interior white. That reflected northlight from the sky through his negative and enlarging lens onto photo paper.

He framed his images carefully, almost every detail planned in advance. He told the cowboys where and how to pose, staging the scenes as a movie director

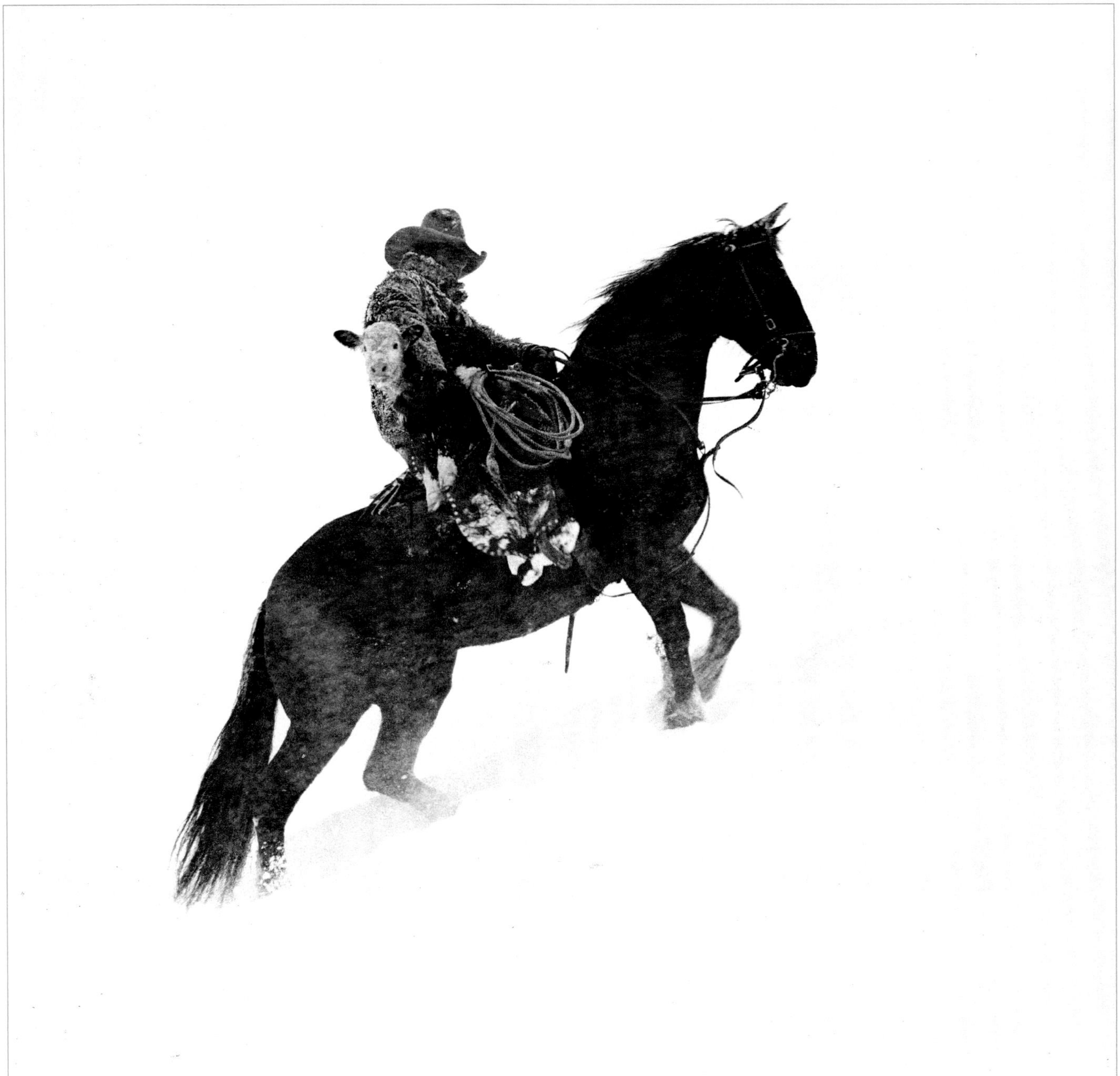

would, leaving nothing to chance. The cowboys might look as if they'd gathered casually by a campfire with their guitars, but Belden had arranged it all and insisted they hold the pose until he shouted, "Action!" The cowboys didn't seem to mind. A few probably joked about being "movie stars" on Saturday night at the local saloon. Some of Belden's photos were composites—a horse and rider, say, transposed to an alpine forest. In the absence of a telephoto lens, he attached his field glasses to the camera lens.

Belden stayed loyal to the Palmos, but he liked technology and invested in newer cameras such as the Zeiss-Ikon Contax T2 35mm Rangefinder as well. He owned several with a different lens mounted on each, so that he could quickly switch to the right focal length, a trick that news and sports photographers still employ. He enjoyed shooting home movies of the ranch and his family, the abundant wildlife in the Bighorn Basin, and the rodeos. He loved planes and gave aerial photography a whirl, following herds of elk, deer, and mountain sheep with a pilot friend. Belden charted their migrations with a Bell & Howell Eyemo at 32 frames a second to help with a government game census. Two spotters did the counting.

Already a master of natural light, Belden took full advantage when flashbulbs became available. A flash gave proper illumination to a scene and reduced the exposure time of the photo he was trying to create. He could set up and shoot interiors whenever he liked. Some of those scenes have a painterly quality, the sort of glow that recalls the Old Masters. Surely Belden would've visited the great museums of Europe on his grand tour, and might well have learned a trick or two.

Belden played a part in saving the pronghorn antelope. The herds were dying out due to poaching, harsh winters, and coyotes and other predators. Belden hit on a scheme to capture newborn pronghorns and bottle-feed them until the fawns were either strong enough to be released into the wild or sold to zoos and private collectors—a clever way for Antelope Charlie, as he billed himself, to look good and also make a little money. The pronghorns sold for $100 apiece.

Belden was his own best press agent. As his fame grew, he basked in the limelight. Celebrities like Will Rogers and Amelia Earhart visited and publicized the Pitchfork's dude ranch. But Belden wasn't much of a rancher, really, nor was Eugene Phelps. The Depression put an end to their struggles to stay afloat. Discussions about selling were held, but the ranch wasn't sold at this time.

Belden headed to Florida with his second wife, leaving behind a huge inventory of images that established him as a premier photographer of the American West.

Belden's work continues to live on through the online digital collections of the American Heritage Center at the University of Wyoming in Laramie, and the McCracken Research Library at the Buffalo Bill Center of the West in Cody, Wyoming.

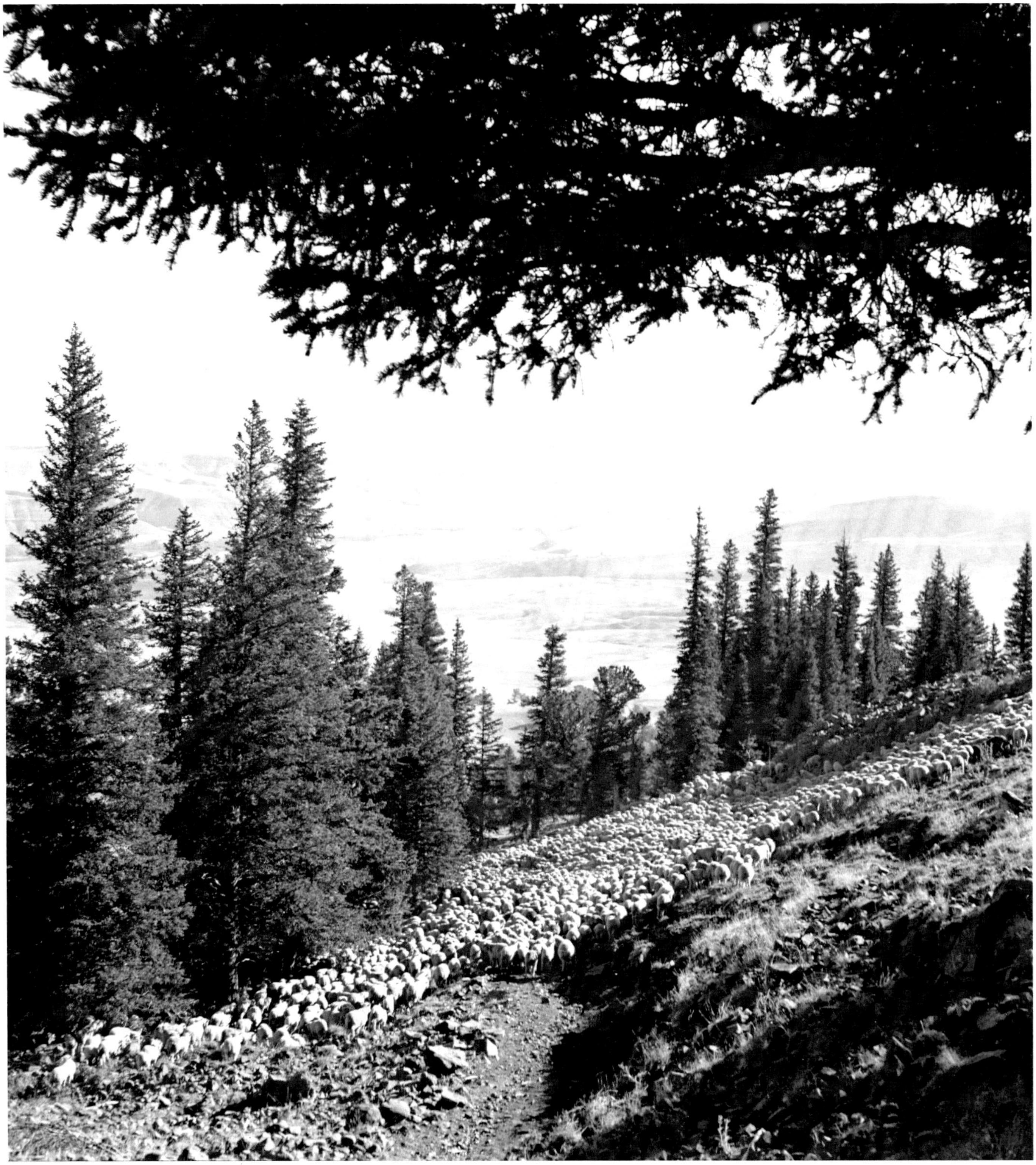

The Photograph as Adventure Story

by Brooks Roddan

I saw my first Belden photographs in the early 1970s, having hitchhiked from Los Angeles, in love with a Wyoming girl who would become my wife, not realizing at the time or until some years later they were Belden photos, or that I'd seen so many in or near the place they'd been taken—the Pitchfork Ranch in Meeteetse, Wyoming.

My own western adventure began then. I spent more and more time in Wyoming, so often making the long car trip from California, now married with two young sons, our new family exploring *upstate Wyoming* as I came to call it, the northwest part of the state. I saw Belden images wherever I looked. I hiked Belden mountains, fished Belden streams, drifted alongside Belden clouds, rode a Belden horse, saw Belden cows cross a stream. Stopping at a roadside diner I'd run into a Belden or two, framed and mounted on a wall, knowing by then it was indeed a Belden, as if it were there to greet us all.

A Belden image resonates, shimmers; most Belden photographs are black-and-white yet so vivid they often create the sensation of being printed in color. His subject is the American West with the highest mountains and fastest rivers, the tallest trees and the greatest deserts, spaces so wide open that the most outrageous tales could be told whether they were true or not. The West waves a magic wand on the imagination, the scenery often larger than life, even supernatural, making it possible to make up almost any sort of story about what you are seeing. No wonder photographers came west a moment or two after the camera was invented—Edward Muybridge, William Henry Jackson, Edward Curtis, Timothy O'Sullivan, the forefathers of American photography.

. . . . .

Charles Belden never had to go 'out west', he was already as far west as he could be in the continental US, California--a rich kid born in San Francisco in 1887 to a prominent and fantastically wealthy family. His grandfather Josiah Belden had been a member of the Bidwell-Bartleson Party, 1841, the first significant attempt of American emigrants to make a wagon crossing from Missouri to California, a pioneer. Josiah Belden would become one of San Francisco's original developers. There's still a Belden Place in San Francisco, a street named in his honor, with upscale restaurants and boutiques.

. . . . . .

Nothing in Charles Belden's upbringing would necessarily point to photography becoming a career. Rather, I've come to see his life as a series of adventures, a 'Grand Tour' of a life with great highs and lows, all quite promising personally and professionally, some thrilling I'm sure and some not, always improbable.

. . . . . .

I don't identify as a historian; I don't pretend to be one. I'm a relative newcomer to Wyoming in thrall to Belden's photographs, and this telling is a series of

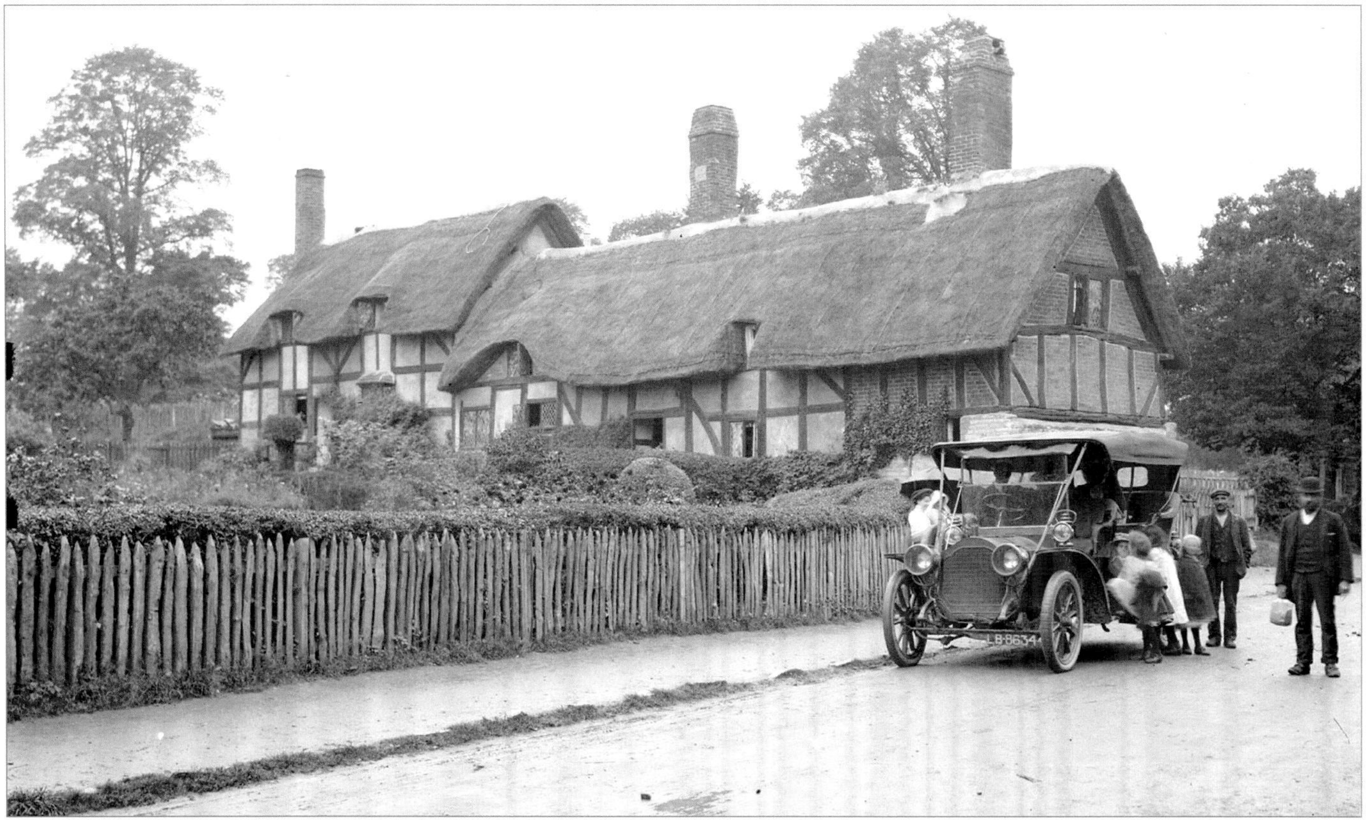

impressions written long before I knew his life story. So much of biography is unreliably anecdotal, a tale told over a campfire one night and remembered very differently in the morning. And by now the Belden bio is full of holes that can't be filled, like the back-country silence and open spaces Wyoming specializes in. He lived most of his life on a remote ranch named the Pitchfork near a tiny town with a big name that sounds small—Meeteetsee—population 327. The ranch, however—unlike most of its neighbors who didn't go electric until the passage in 1936 of FDR's Rural Electrification Act—had its own power plant built in 1918. Still, 'social media' then amounted to a phone call at best, placed through a local operator who often stayed on the line to listen in. Belden left some letters behind, most dealing with business concerns, and thousands of photographs, but otherwise it's almost as if he vanished once he left Wyoming.

. . . .

The Pitchfork Ranch, a somewhat ominous name for a wonderfully scenic property, was established by a German count named Otto Franc in 1878. Franc was an accomplished outdoorsman who died on the ranch in 1903, tangled up in a barbed wire fence, his shotgun 'accidentally' going off and killing him. Foul play was suspected though never proven. Otto Franc kept a daily journal all those years, some of the most tumultuous in Wyoming history; it's still worth reading. Francs Peak, 13,000 plus feet, the highest point in the Absaroka Range, is named in his honor, a kind of beacon visible from every aspect of the Pitchfork.

. . . . . .

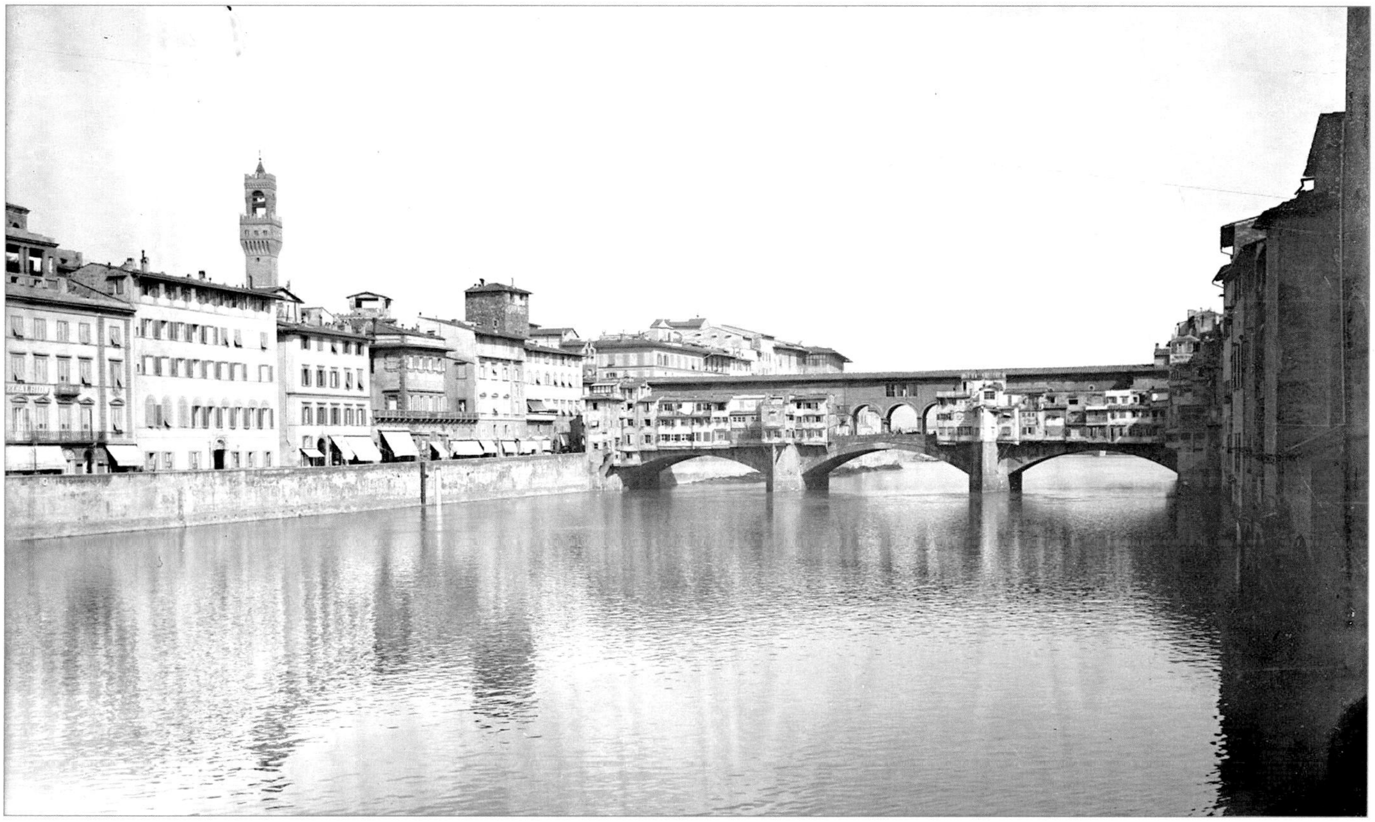

Imagine Charles Belden driving up to the Pitchfork Ranch, 1912, just returned from his European motoring adventure with his best friend and college roommate, Eugene Phelps whose father owns the ranch. Belden gets his footing immediately, arriving with instant status, the best friend of the ranch owner's son, a young a man who appears to already know what he wants to do with his life, committed to living a much different one than the life he'd been born into, hoping to become his own man *for better or worse.* Belden falls in love with Phelps' sister, Frances, and they soon marry, raise a family, off on a brand-new adventure in a place he must feel he has, more or less, all to himself

. . . .

Vast isn't too great a word for the Pitchfork; the ranch still lives up to that description today. Wyoming must have seemed like a magical kingdom to the 25-year-old Belden, a candy store stocked with brilliant subject matter—a spectacular, mostly unexplored realm ready to have its picture taken, where next to no one having taken pictures there before, certainly no one with Belden's background, training, and enthusiasms. Of the 3,000 plus images Belden left behind, the vast majority were taken on the ranch. Belden had found a world large enough to "contain multitudes" as another primary American artist, Walt Whitman, wrote in his poem, "Leaves of Grass."

. . . . . .

You can't be dull in Wyoming, dull is not allowed. The extremes always wake you, the weather, the

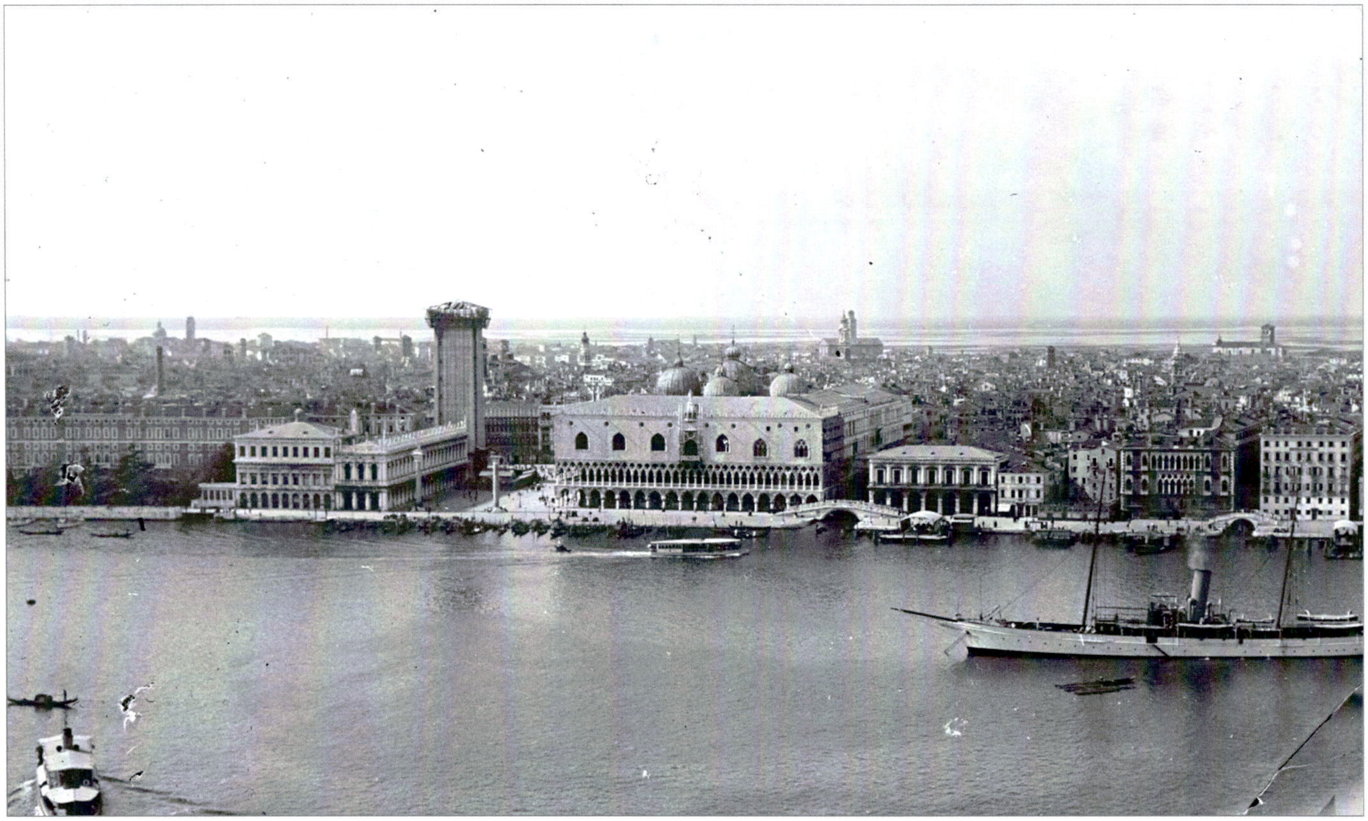

wind, the sky, the mountains. In Wyoming I often go to sleep at night with the question, *'I wonder what will happen tomorrow?'* suspecting that whatever does happen is likely to be the unexpected. I'm reminded of the narrator of Owen Wister's classic novel, *The Virginian,* asking when he first sets eyes on Wyoming, 'Does this same planet hold Fifth Avenue?'

. . . . . .

Looking at the pictures of young Charles Belden's post-college trip through Europe, one considers the possibility, however unlikely, that Belden might've encountered Eugene Atget, the legendary Parisian street photographer, whose mission at the beginning of the 20th century was "to document all of the architecture and street scenes of Paris," while realizing they were in the act of disappearing. On his business card Atget described himself as, "Creator and Purveyor of Photographic Views of Old Paris," doubling down on the irony, most likely lost on him, of using a relatively modern invention to preserve the past. Atget received little recognition in his lifetime. Only in 1930 when American photographer Berenice Abbott bought up all Atget's negatives in order to preserve his work—and the Surrealists made him one of their heroes—did Eugene Atget become celebrated as the dogged genius he was.

A case can be made that Charles Belden was the first site-specific American photographer. Belden came to work the Pitchfork much like Atget worked every arrondisement in Paris, often taking the same photograph over and over, sometimes with almost imperceptible changes in angle or perspective, as did Atget.

. . . . . .

Photography at the turn of the 20th century wasn't a particularly accessible practice, and not yet considered an art; to be a photographer was not necessarily to be an artist. Photography was technical and cumbersome, producing images captured by a machine, not something that showed the hand of the artist like a painting or a sculpture.

The history of photography seems to have evolved at the speed of light. Charles Belden was right there, near the beginning, one of its poster boys, coming of age when certain cultural agreements made it legitimate for a machine to produce an image first formed in the imagination. The new emergent technologies could support that aim. Belden not only accepted technology, he embraced it! Belden hurtled through life—faster, speedier, higher from the saddle of the horse to the car to the airplane. Kipling was famously quoted as writing, "Transportation is civilization," though he might as well have written, "Technology is civilization."

. . . . . .

By the time Belden enters the conversation, the floodgates in favor of welcoming photography as a legitimate art had opened. Old prejudices petered out; photography was finally admitted to the canon. Andre Malraux, a Frenchman like Atget and an avid traveler like Belden, would write mid-20th century, "For the last hundred years, art history has been the history of that which can be photographed." And Walter Benjamin in his landmark essay, *The Work of Art in the Age of Mechanical Representation,* quotes the French poet Paul Valery:

> Our fine arts were developed, their types and uses were established, in times very different from the present, by men whose power of action upon things was insignificant in comparison with ours. But the amazing growth of our techniques, the adaptability and precision they have attained, the ideas and habits they are creating, make it a certainty that profound changes are impending in the ancient craft of the Beautiful.

While the French were the first to set the foundation for photography to be taken as seriously as other arts, they are prone to be contrary. Charles Baudelaire, the poet, dismissed photography as a "brutish aping of nature," and "the refuge of every would-be painter too ill-endowed or too lazy to complete his studies."

. . . . . .

Many of the photographs Belden took in 1910 during his car trip through Europe are impressionistic enough to convince a viewer he'd looked seriously at fine art, perhaps even studied the paintings of Monet, for instance. Many of his pictures taken for their documentary value often seem to wear an impressionistic veil—Anne Hathaway's cottage in England, an unpaved road in the Alps, his college roommate and traveling companion Eugene Phelps changing a tire on the Packard—ordinary subject matter seen as the passing of time, the sudden shifting of light that creates a new image as if captured by a passerby.

It's also fair to say of Belden's approach to photography, even of this early period, that it was part intellectual exercise—he was, after all, formally educated as an engineer, wanting to take things apart so they could be reassembled, if only to know how things worked—and that his art-making instincts gradually took over.

. . . . . .

Scrolling through the images that survived the European trip, it appears Belden was a visual omnivore, gobbling up scene after scene as if he couldn't get

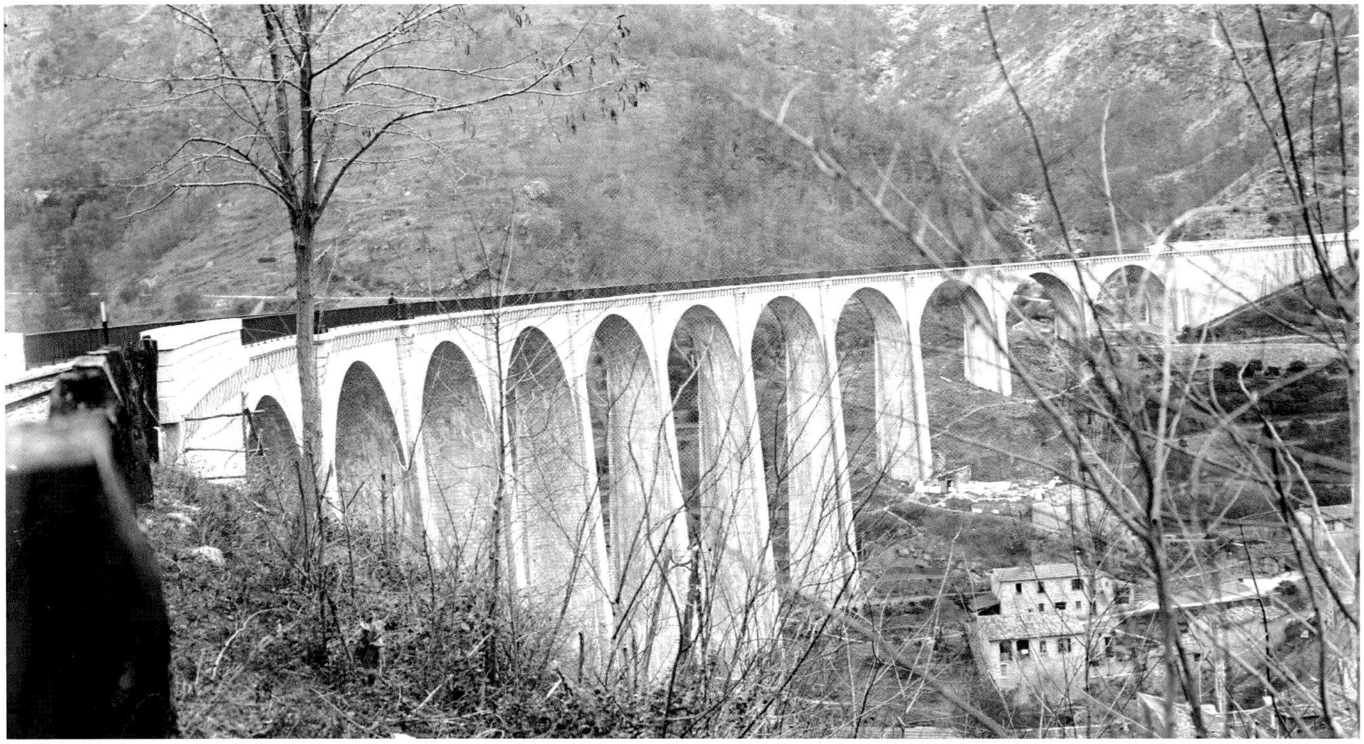

enough of them: you can feel the force of his curiosity! To look at the pictures is like looking through the notebook of a gifted young writer, an apprentice eager for experience, on an adventure that would guarantee new sights. To paraphrase one of Anthony Trollope's admirers, "He noticed everything." That admirer was Henry James, whose time in Europe was certainly well spent.

. . . . . .

It was the American Alfred Steiglitz, photographer and tireless promoter of photography, whose gallery in New York City, An American Place, launched the careers of the photographers and painters Paul Strand, Arthur Dove, John Marin, Marsden Hartley, and Georgia O'Keeffe among others. Steiglitz advocated for the elevation of the photographer to the stature of artist. "Photographers must learn not to be ashamed to have their photographs look like photographs," Steiglitz wrote in 1910, an astonishing statement then and now.

It's worth noting too, as Jordan Stein in San Francisco writes in his book *Rip Tales,* that photography emerged around the same time as the formal study of archeology, and "both disciplines concern an artifactual relationship with the past and the establishment of a firm fixity in time."

. . . . . .

If one becomes familiar with Belden's work and looks closely at thousands of photographs, one can't help but come away with the feeling that he was fascinated by the Pitchfork and already deeply connected to the people who helped manage it, but that he also had a great need to establish some sort of order in an environment that could be harsh, capricious, ornery, and merciless. Some of his landscapes are bleak, beautiful in their stark delineations, but bleak. Anyone who's experienced a Wyoming winter knows the score. As a Meeteetse man once said to me, "Wyoming summers can be pretty nice all right, but winter brings out the best in all of us."

A poet might write about the 'splendid isolation' of nature, but it's a whole other matter to be rounding up cattle in a minus 30–degree snowstorm or living alone in a sheep wagon in the mountains for weeks at a time where, when you speak, you're speaking to yourself. Men went days and days without saying a word and then, when engaged again with other people, would answer questions monosyllabically, "yep" and "nope" and "maybe." Such a response was often enough to cover the situation. Why waste energy on words when your energy might be needed elsewhere?

. . . . . .

Another passage from the novel *The Virginian* still resonates: "The romance of American adventure had drawn them all to this great playground of young men, and in their courage, their generosity, and their amusement at me they bore a great resemblance to each other."

The main female character in the book, Miss Wood, leaves the east for Wyoming, "craving the unexpected."

. . . . . .

Charles Belden, by this time as far away from San Francisco and the 'art world' as can be imagined, helping run a ranch in Meeteetse, Wyoming, seems to be in the right place at the right time. Life is bountiful in the big stone ranch house, filled with family and friends, and scenery that provides stimulating, ever-changing subject matter the serious photographer craves. Ranchers in Wyoming are highly regarded, the equivalent as one local put it "of royalty." Both the Beldens and the Phelps dressed for dinner, the organization of family life was in some sense formal, a reflection of their privileged upbringing.

And yet it's difficult to imagine Belden waking up one morning, looking in the mirror and saying to himself, "I am Charles Belden, artist," as difficult as it is to imagine him asking, "Is this really the kind of world I want to live in?" Rather, taking pictures was his way of being in the world. Robert Frost's definition of poetry as "a momentary stay against confusion" is an even better fit.

. . . . . .

By the early 1920s Belden was busy making photographs, doing what he loved doing, sending his work out to meet a growing demand. Publications from The New York Times to National Geographic and Saturday Evening Post snapped up his images, often featuring them in multi-page spreads. A Stetson hat was named in his honor—The Belden. During the late 1920s, Charles Belden became nationally known as "the Cowboy photographer."

However, being a photographer and making art is one thing, and running a ranch is another.

. . . . . .

It's unsettling to read Belden's correspondence from the late 1920s and early 30s, mostly typed, sometimes hand-written, a flurry of pleas for work he'd done or money owed him. Another kind of adventure, perhaps, but not the kind he'd hoped for.

The Great Depression took its toll. Money was tight, beef and sheep and grain prices were way down, disagreements between the partners occurred almost daily—it seems to Phelps that all Belden wants to do is make pictures, and it seems to Belden that all Phelps wants to do is to play around with mechanical projects that catch his fancy. The rich boys are suddenly 'up against the wall', as the saying goes. They'll try anything, even running a dude ranch on the Pitchfork. Belden starts a campaign to save the antelope, and Phelps draws up a plan to 'electrify' the little town of Meeteetse. Tension between the two men mounts. According to family lore, Belden would suddenly disappear from the once happy get-togethers, walking up to his office-darkroom on the third level of the house, his sanctuary. I've seen Belden's studio there. It surprised me how small it is. It has all the earmarks of a sanctuary, a monk's cell.

. . . .

A parsing of Belden's immense catalog suggests that his images of the American West create a new type of mythology. The cowboys on horseback in wide-open spaces herding cattle along otherwise empty trails take root in the public imagination as romantic symbols of still achievable, still accessible frontiers. That's especially true in the increasingly urbanized USA. Wherever you live, whether in Manhattan or San Francisco or Tokyo, the power of Belden's images has such a strong emotional appeal it's easy to imagine yourself as a pioneer in the westward expansion. Belden's photographs of certain western landscapes and the cowboys who occupy them were wildly popular. He portrayed ranch hands, shepherds, and day laborers at work, very often men with no formal education but skilled in the arts of 'making do,' often creating something out of almost nothing at all, sometimes simply surviving, who performed physically demanding and dangerous jobs, hardly glamorous and, for the most part, not particularly well paid. Images of this version of the west poured out of Belden's camera; he was able to present the reality and satisfy the fantasy with each image. A friend in San Francisco, a scholar and connoisseur of western films of the '30s and '40s, is convinced that certain scenes in the movies of John Ford and Howard Hawks were lifted straight out of Belden's oeuvre.

. . . . . .

It seems worth noting too how many of the photos that became recognizable as a Belden were taken in the late 1920s and early '30s, a time of extreme personal and professional duress. There still remains a squadron of legendary photographers who did their best work early—not unlike lyric poets, who often believe they only have a year or so of productive time before the spark is gone and the poetry dries up—but Belden had a long, productive career. To his credit, he seemed to have flourished during those lean years despite the tension, uncertainty, and the ranch mismanagement of the partners. Instead he was determined to scramble around for assignments, shooting photograph after photograph to make a little money.

. . . . . .

Was Charles Belden religious? Forced to speculate, I'd say no—there's too much pantheism in his portfolio. I'm not saying anything here I wouldn't say to Belden's face, but I doubt he went to church. I could be mistaken; I just can't picture him there. If Belden did go to church his heart probably wasn't in it; he was probably thinking of other things. Was he a drinker? (At one time bars outnumbered churches and markets in Meeteetse). Perhaps, but not to excess, his life was too full with family, worries about the ranch, how the next photograph might turn out.

. . . . . .

When critics accused Belden of 'staging' some of his pictures, he most likely found the accusation amusing. The legendary Carleton Watkins, whose pictures of Yosemite in 1860 encouraged lawmakers in D.C. to create the national park system, once ordered that a tree be cut down because it "interfered with the scene I tried to create." Yes, Belden art directed cows and cowboys, sheep and shepherds, even a supposedly wild coyote that was actually stuffed. He often arranged people and props for the benefit of the image he was attempting to present. Yes, Belden carefully composed his scene as every real artist does.

. . . . . .

Samuel Johnson in his rollicking travelog of a book, *Journal of a Tour to the Hebrides* (1775) writes:

> A landscape or view of any kind is defective, in my opinion, without some human figures to give it animation.

. . . . . .

Often overlooked are Belden portraits of people and how many photographs of them he took—regular ranch hands and cowboys at work and play, townspeople, portraits, candid photographs of railroad workers and mail-carriers and truck drivers.

Also, the many searchingly lovely portraits of his family—Frances his wife, and his daughters, Margot and Annice—bring to mind Picasso's great drawings of his wives and children, also made when they were young. Tender, hopeful, pensive, filled with life.

And yet another surprise from his vast portfolio: Belden photographs of both domesticated and wild animals—cattle and sheep, antelope, bears, elk, coyote as if they were human beings.

. . . . . .

Were Belden a writer, I'm convinced he'd write his best stuff in winter. Every season in Wyoming belongs to Wyoming, every season shows the writer a different sight or sound or feeling, the profound differences between winter, spring, summer, fall. I believe that Wyoming showed Belden all its 'colors', but winter must have looked to him best in black and white, the truest colors of them all.

And what was Charles Belden's relationship with color? I'm allowed to guess—I'll guess he loved color; color was life, just as certainly as is black and white. The pink clouds, a blue moon in overdrive above the ridges of a purple mountain, deep shadows in the creases of a cowboy's face.

More colors Belden might have loved: egg yolks in a skillet with bacon grease, hay bales, clouds whiter than white, the blue scarf his wife wore, the smiles of his children, herds of antelope with their high-desert tonalities.

The horse Belden rode, his favorite horse, a horse from which many of his most famous pictures were taken was named "Pinky," and there are many affectionate black-and-white pictures he took of his young daughters bottle-feeding wild antelope.

. . . . . .

When Charles Belden started flying in the later-1930s it's as if he couldn't wait to fly! I can almost hear him saying, *Let's get up in the sky as soon as possible.*

An airfield was cleared on the Pitchfork—there's ample room on the ranch for take-offs and landings. The psychological aspect of flight—freedom and escape, an untethered rising with the promise of new adventure—can't be overlooked. Flying is pure fun; it seems to have given Belden a new perspective and even some commercial benefits. The contemporary artist James Turrell, an avid pilot, considers the sky as his "studio, material and canvas."

Belden partnered with his good friend and pilot, Bill Monday, a commercial aviator, dreaming up project after project. It's a serious lark, an adventure with practical benefits; from the sky Belden's able to inventory livestock, images he could once only imagine, rescue a stricken hiker lost in the wilderness, help save endangered antelopes, one adventure after another, get images he could only imagine, rescue a hiker in the wilderness, help save endangered antelopes, one adventure after another.

. . . . . .

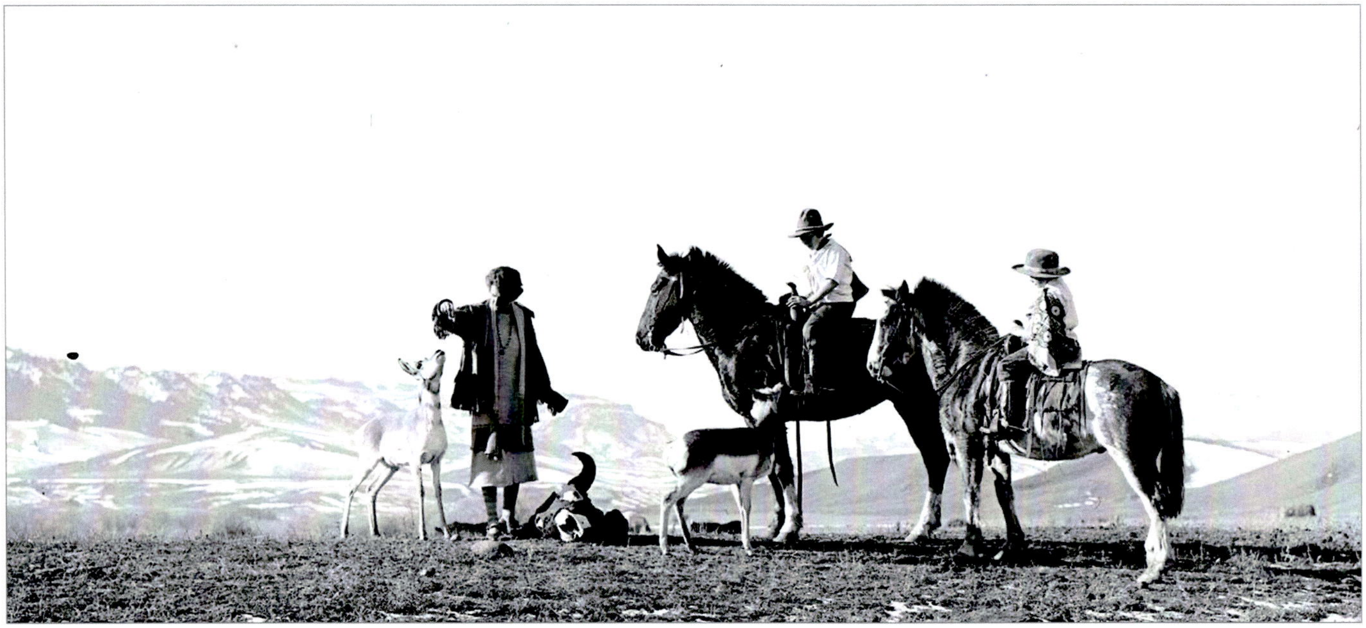

What's in a name? Charles or Charlie?
Charles Belden: pledged by the ethos of a privileged upbringing to make things better and if not better, then certainly not worse; never squander what's been given; live with purpose and if that purpose was to take photographs, take the most beautiful, original pictures as you possibly can. Leave your mark.
Charlie Belden: a complex carbohydrate, a combine of curiosity, energy, ambition, affability; 'Charlie', not Charles; always ready for a good time, an adventure; industrious, not because he ever felt the extreme pressure of providing, of making a living. Instead, he made photographs because, as Wallace Stevens wrote of a poet he admired, "He writes his poems as if he had to write them."

. . . . . .

Questions I'd like to ask Charles Belden:

1) What do you remember about the first time you saw the Pitchfork Ranch?

2) Do you consider yourself an artist?

3) If you lived your life all over again, would you live any differently?

I'd ask too: Were you aware of the modernist art of your time? Have you ever seen a Picasso? Did you know Duchamp? Man Ray? What about Ezra Pound's famous exhortation that the artist's job is to "make it new?"

. . . . . .

Even exhaustively researched, a biography remains a strange brew of the known and the unknown. A photograph can outweigh an anecdote, and can last as long as a memory. What remains from Belden's prodigious output besides the pictures he made? Some magazine and newspaper articles, a student's master's thesis from The University of Wyoming, little scenes remembered here and there. Who knows what really happened on the Pitchfork, what day-to-day life on the ranch was like in the 25-plus years Belden was running the place, in the prime of his life, with his college roommate and business partner, Eugene Phelps. Was it playful? Difficult? Lonely? Isolated? All of the above? None of the above?

. . . . . .

Charles Belden, always the adventurer, left the Pitchfork Ranch in Meeteetsee, Wyoming in 1940 for Clearwater, Florida, a new wife in tow.

Someone asks a family member, "Why did Charlie move to Florida?"

"To be as far away from Wyoming as he could be," was the answer.

It must have been a strange, even sudden departure from northwest Wyoming to arrive in central Florida near the Intracoastal Waterway, 2,291 miles from the ranch. Florida of all places, where it so rarely, if ever, snows.

In Florida, Charlie keeps 'shooting,' no longer the Cowboy photographer; instead he bills himself as "Seahorse Charles Belden" and takes pictures of sailboats, beaches, women in bathing suits. He has resources. The Belden family owned significant real estate holdings in New York City and beyond, and his new wife had been married to a Wyoming oilman.

A series of adventures ensue. A trip to Europe in the late 1940s and a meeting with Josef Tito, the Yugoslavian dictator; a series of assignments for local newspapers, including a photo documentary of snakes indigenous to the Everglades; and print ads for apartment buildings. The work never catches on no matter how he tries—some 130,000 images are now inventoried. They seem stale, chamber-of-commerce exercises, his heart not completely comitted to what he's doing. Suffering from Parkinson's Disease, unable to hold a camera steady, Charles Belden dies of a self-inflicted gunshot wound in 1966.

. . . . . .

Having looked and looked again at so many of Charles Belden's photos, I've come to believe I'm seeing something of him in almost every image. Belden is a force, a whirlwind, as if he's still bent on walking out into the backcountry, hungry to discover a new world. The energy of these remarkable images is still on the move! Relentless, vigorous, they show a constant awareness of and engagement with people and places; his best photographs are both an examination and a revelation. Belden rode horses, drove cars, flew in airplanes, always eager to see the next astonishing thing, to take the next photograph that would so often tell a brand-new story.

Belden photographs keep telling stories. Some of the stories have become our own, we hold on to them, they lodge in our actual lives and in our imaginations. The best of Belden's work remains a big-hearted invitation from the American West, open around the clock—Just Look Around You, There's Still So Much To See!

To live in the American West is to see a Belden image every day.

The Photographs

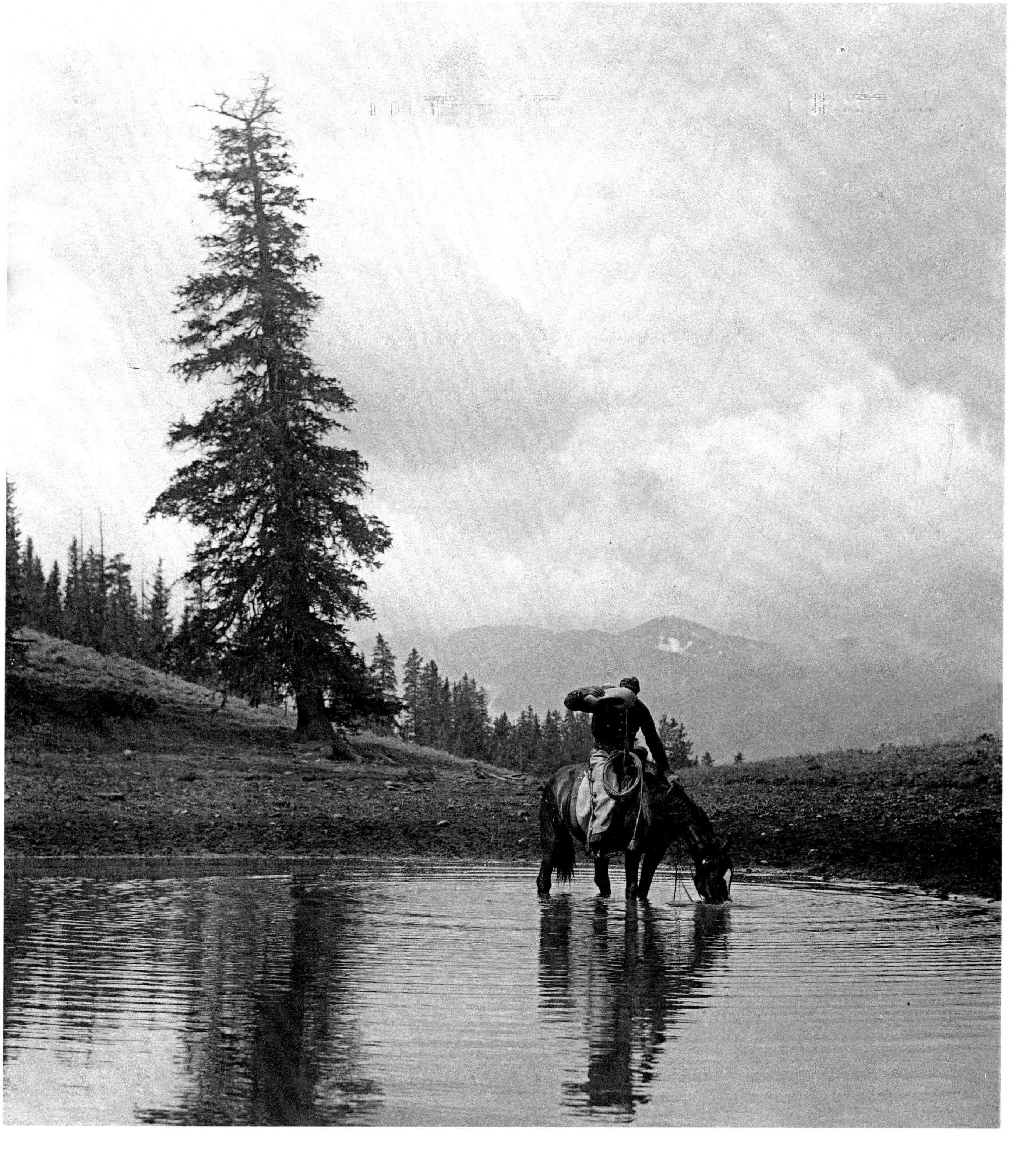

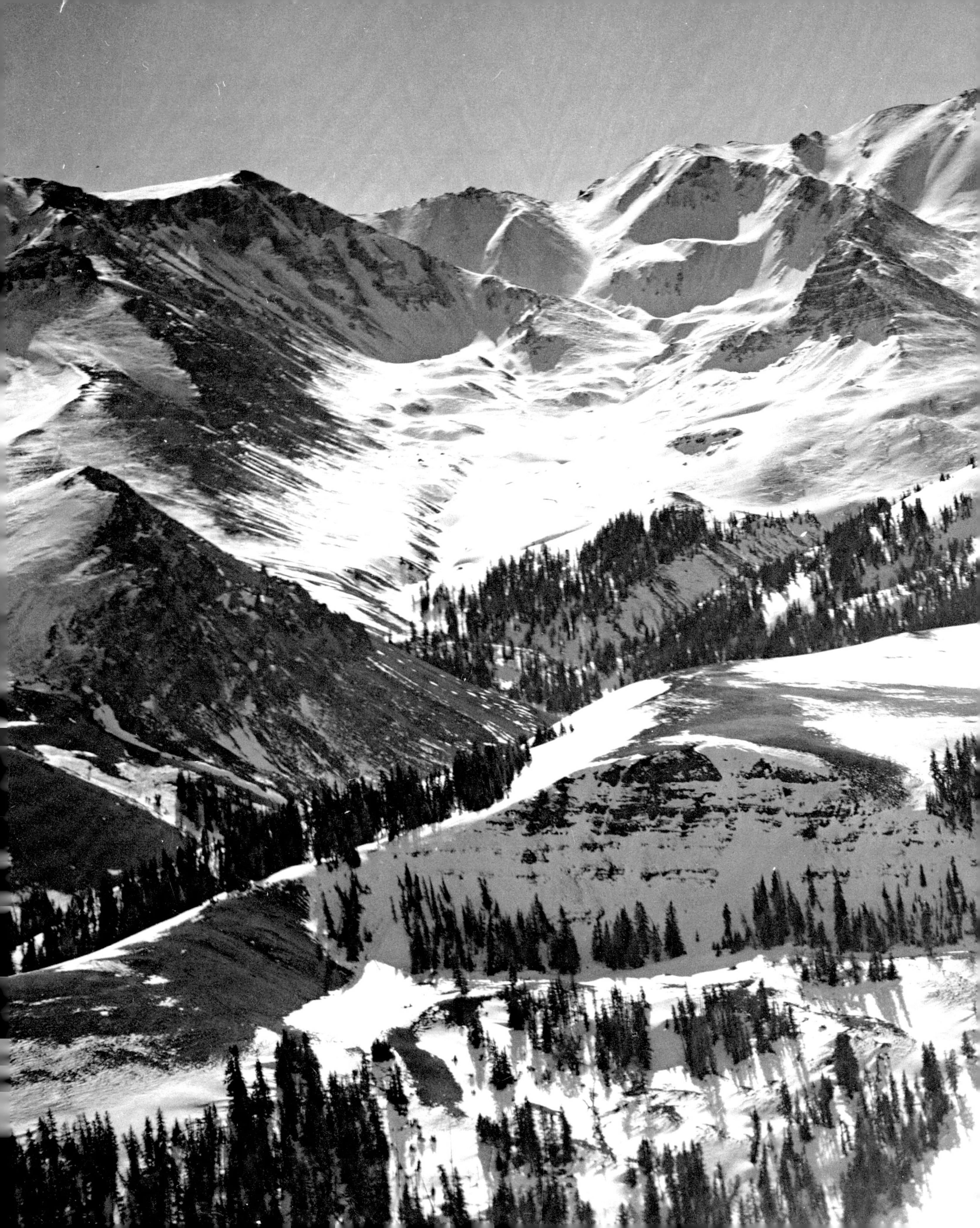

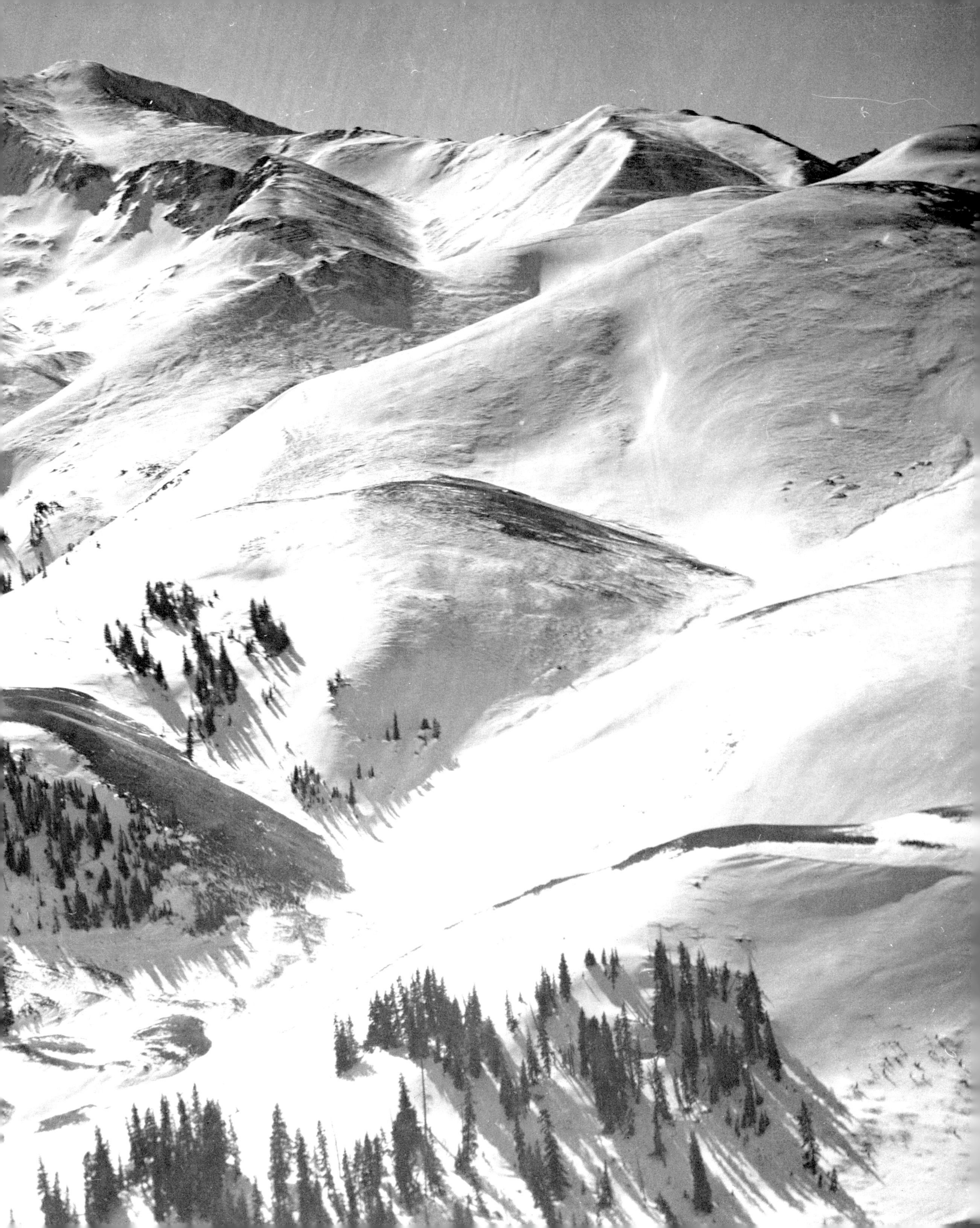

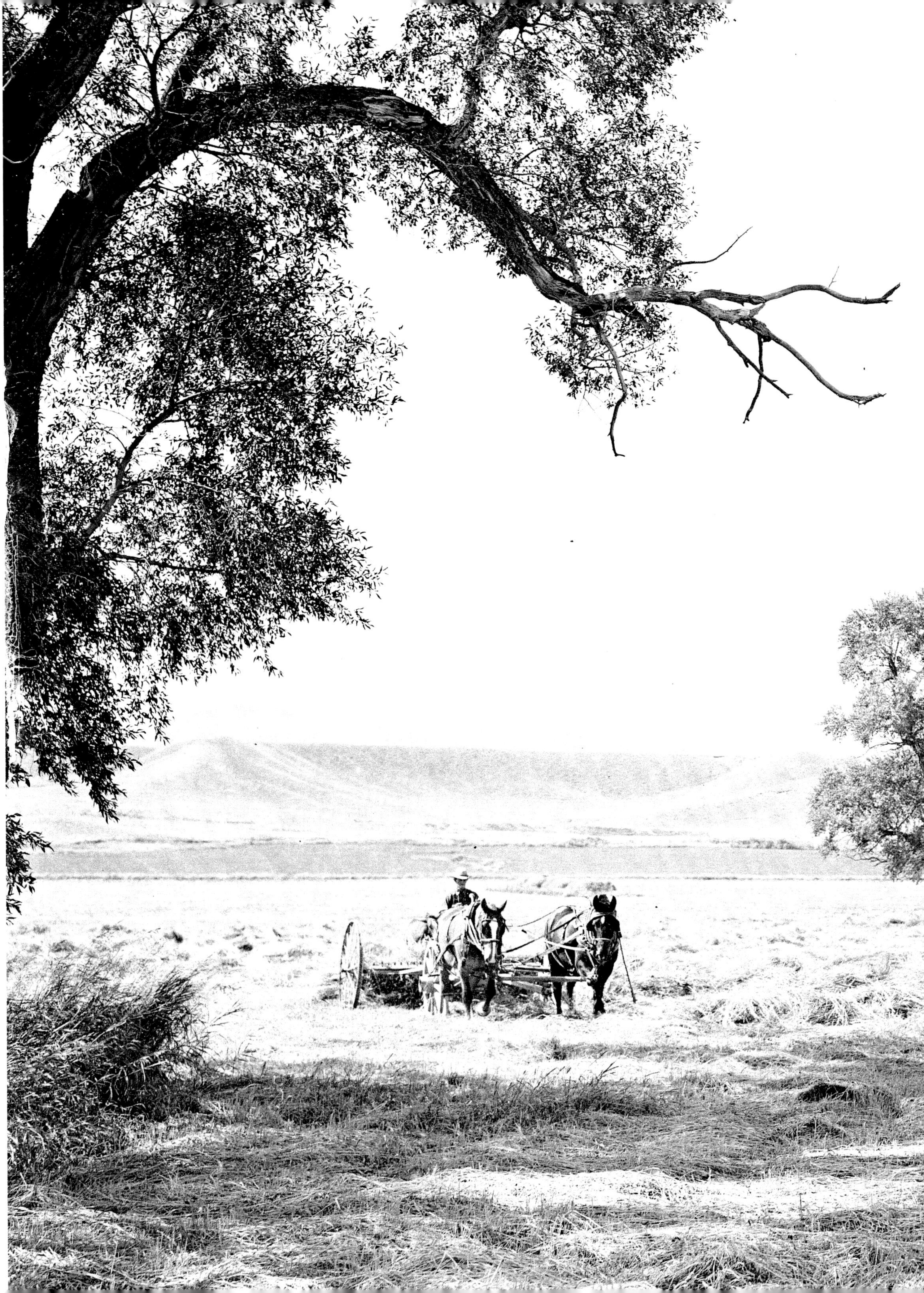

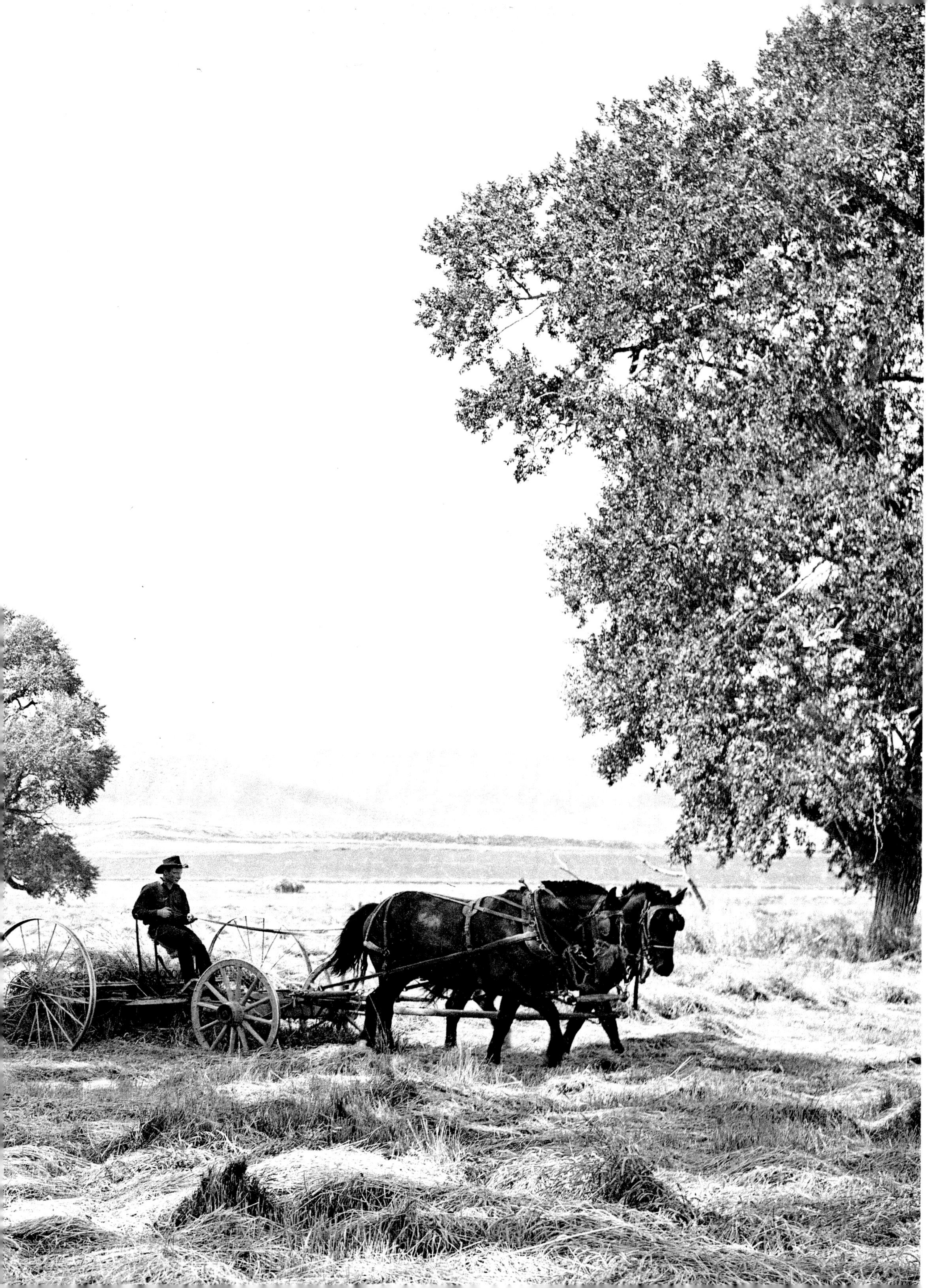

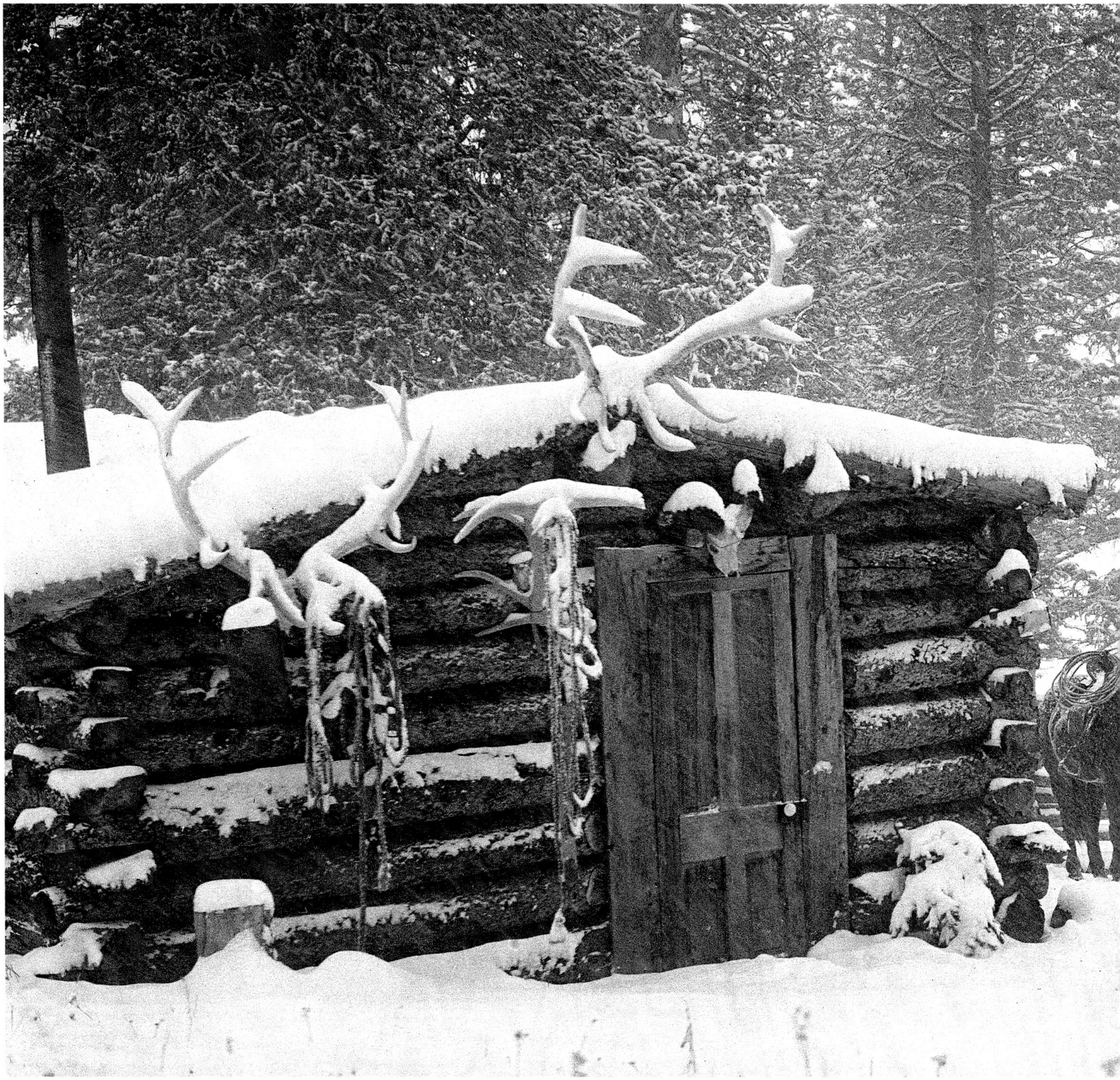

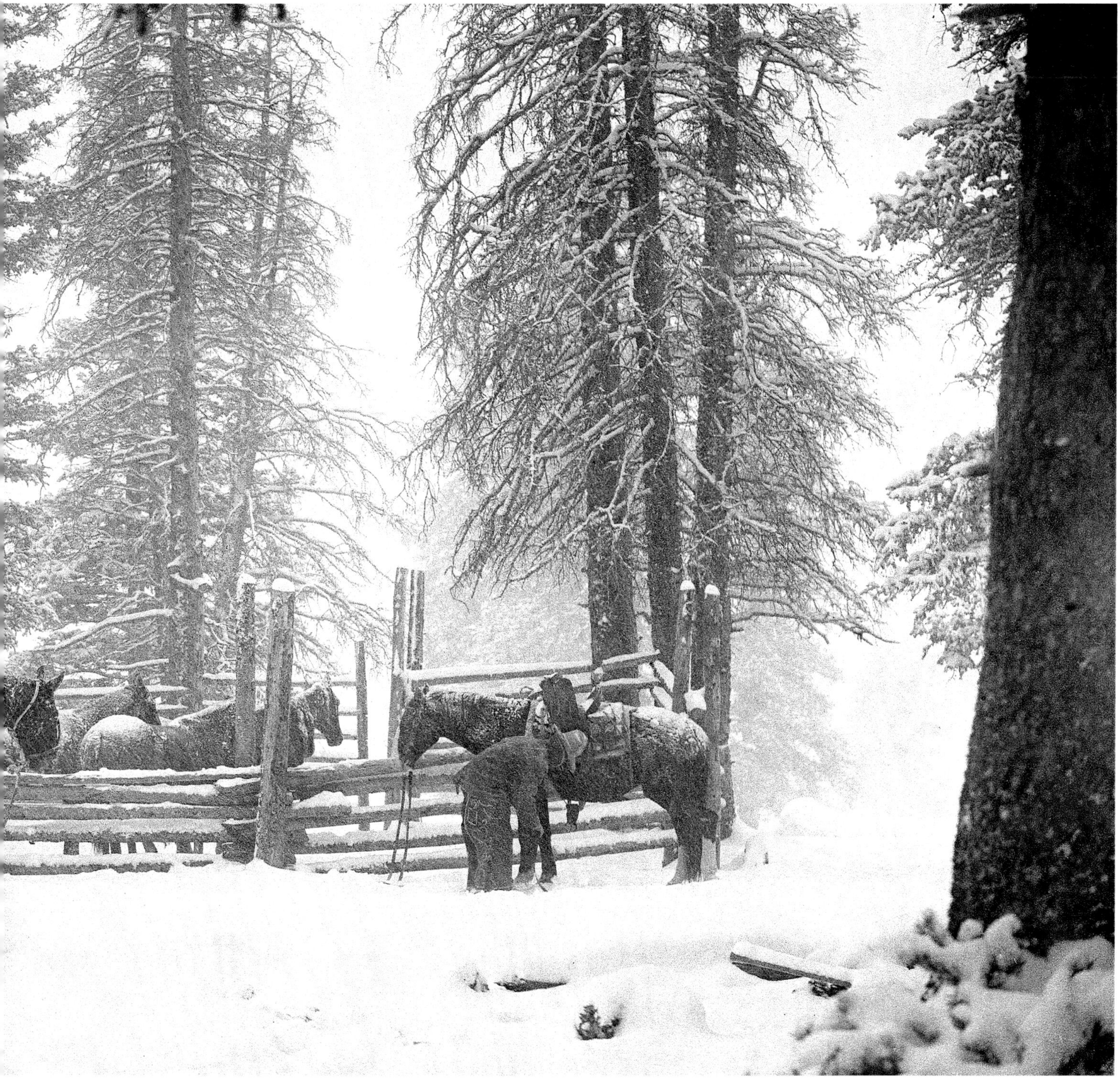

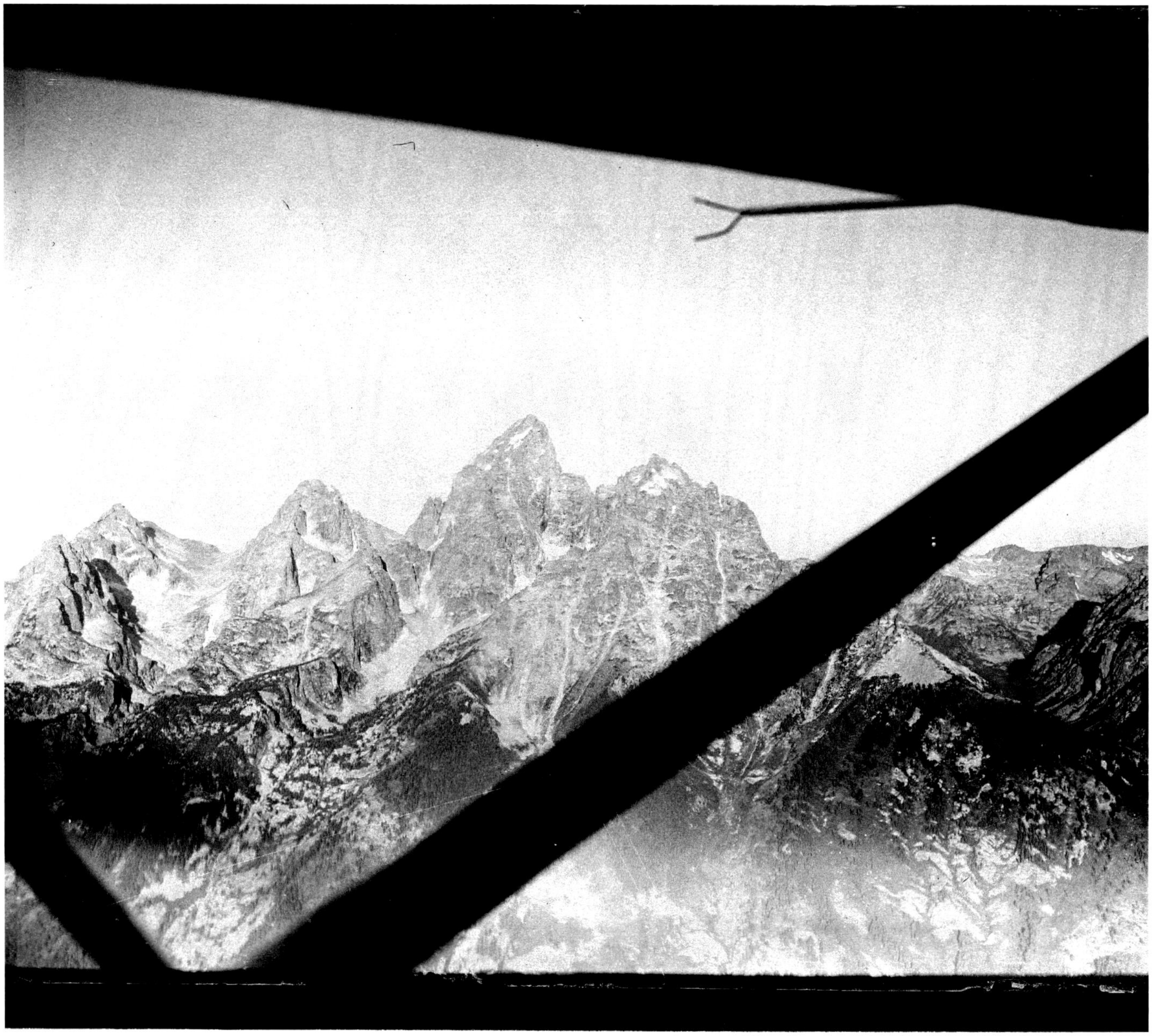

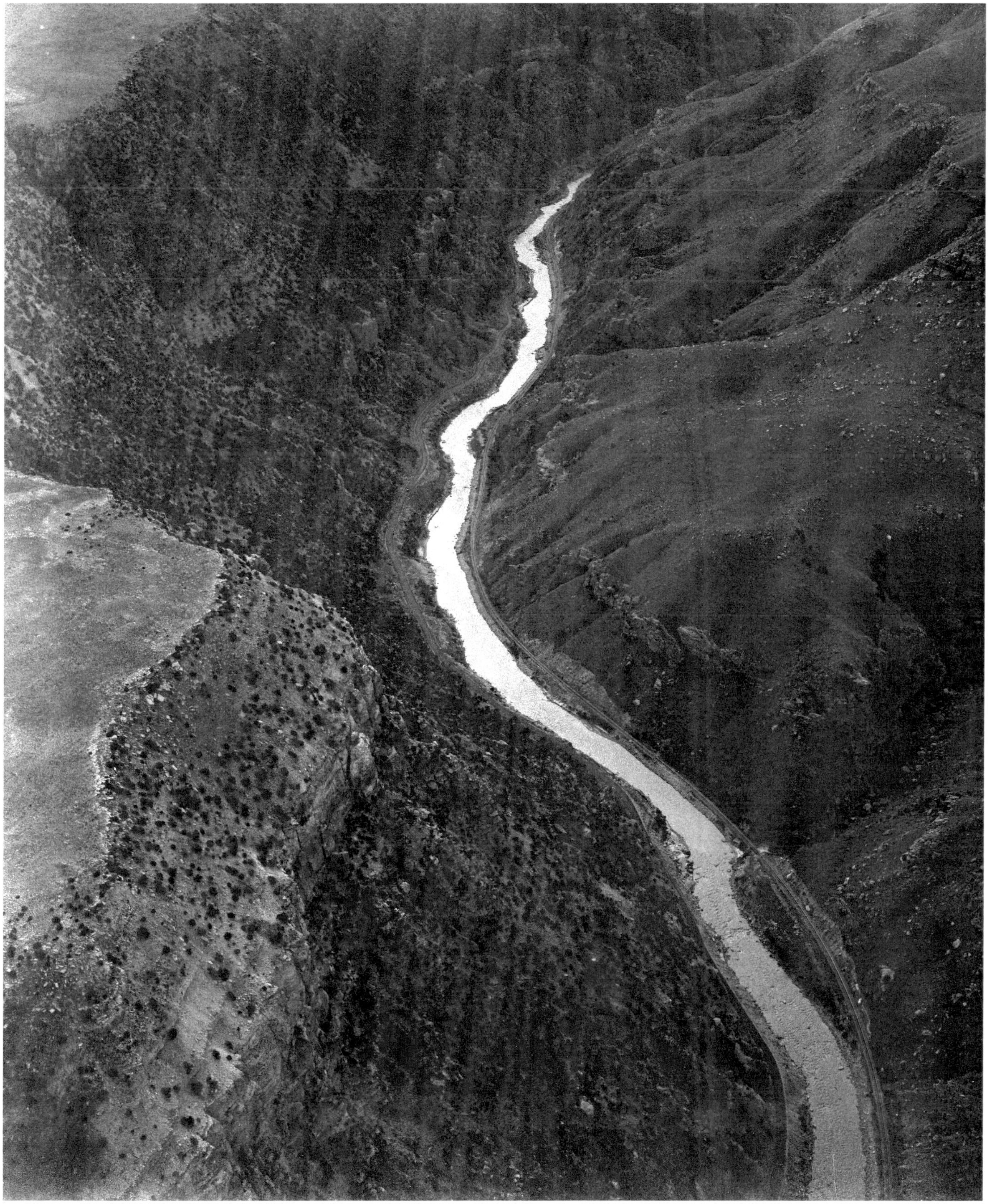

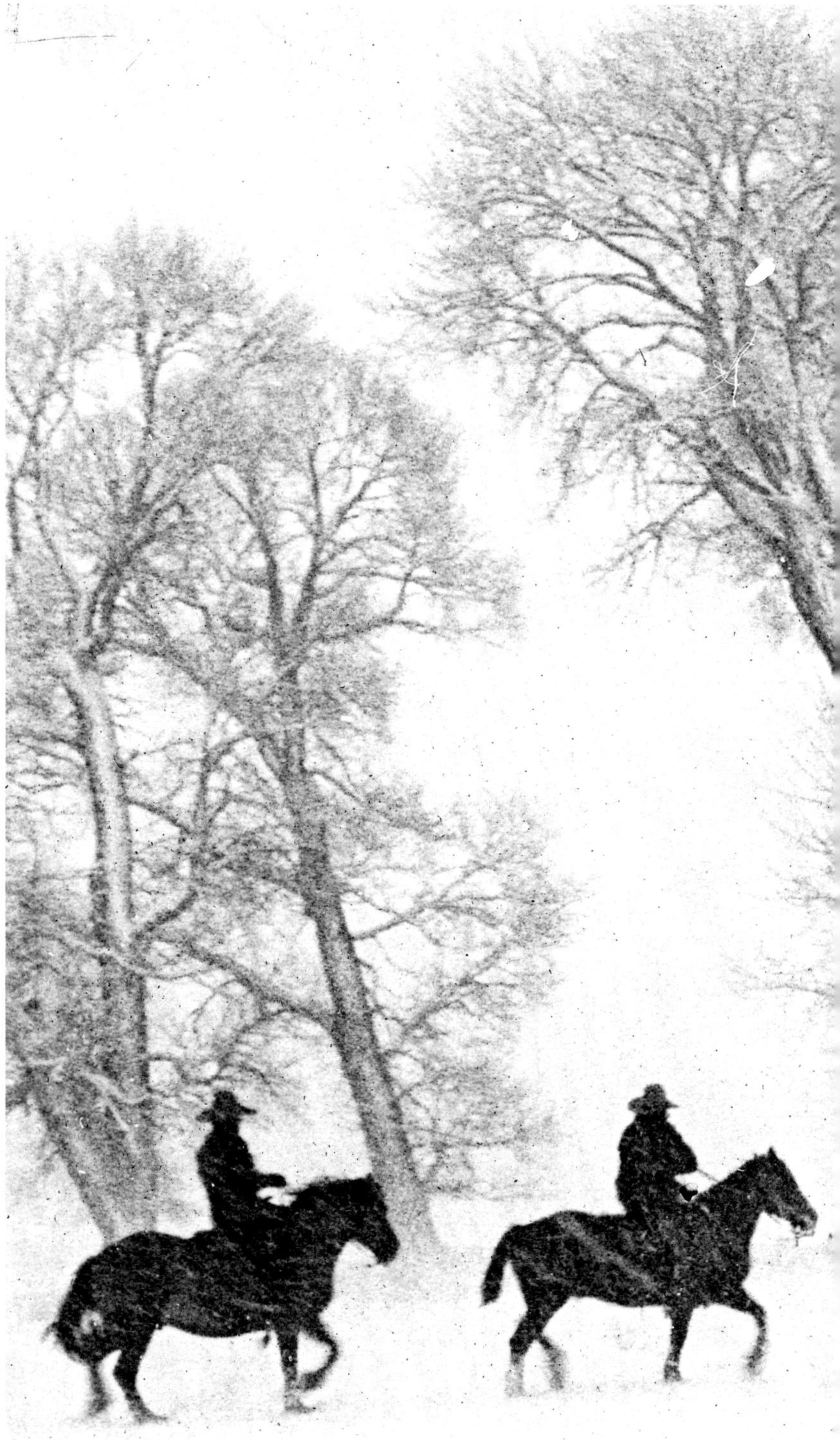

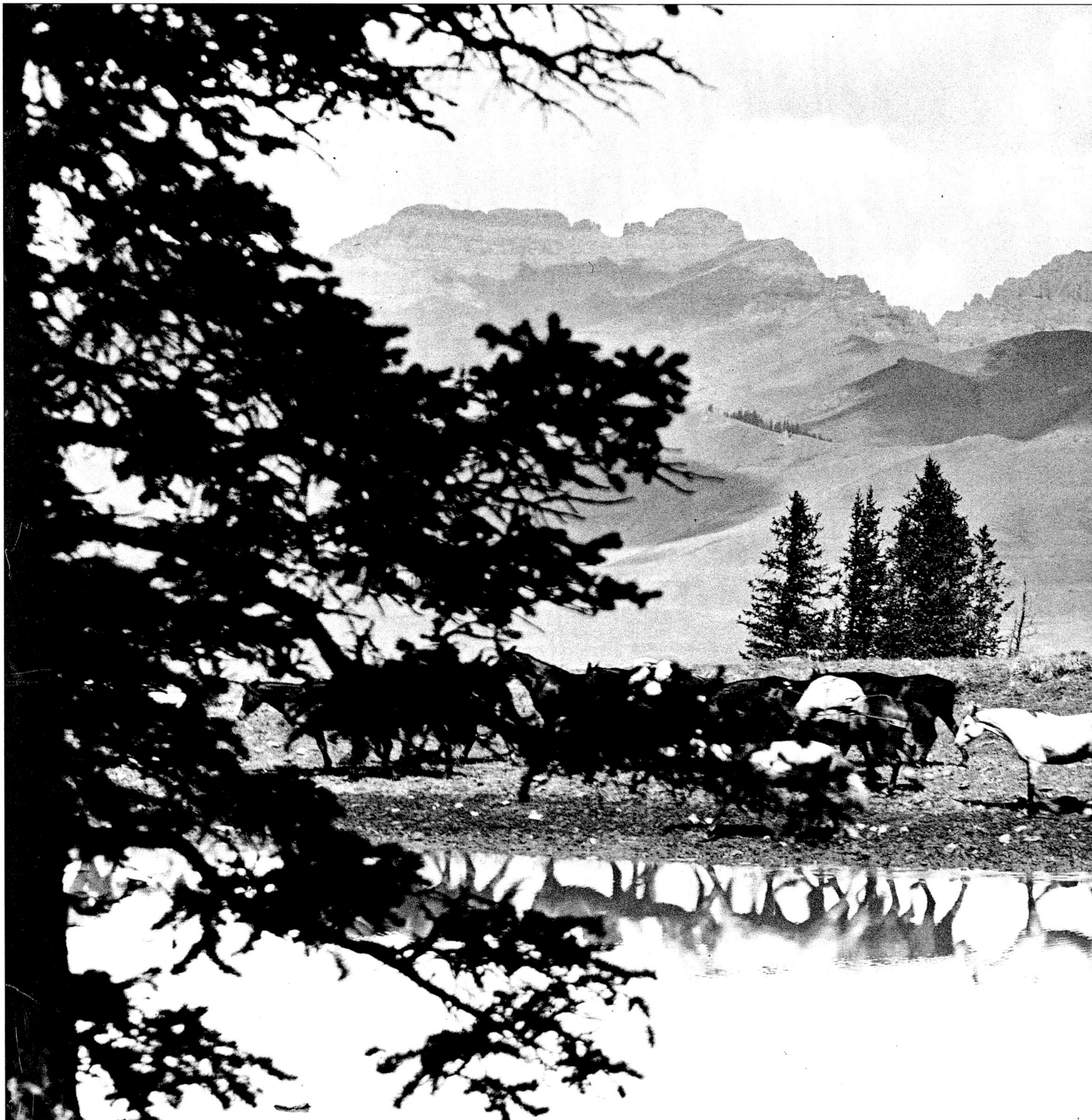

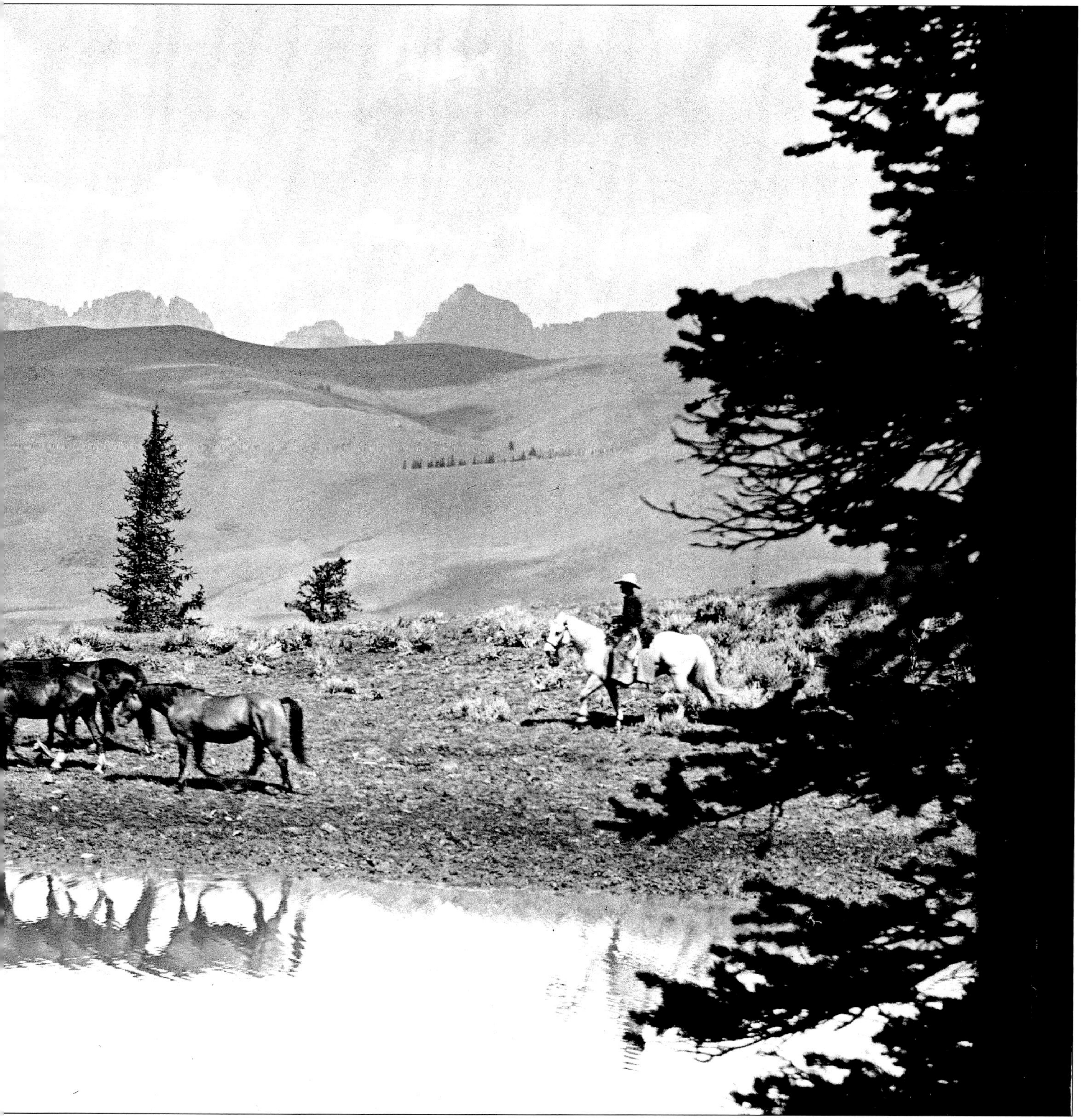

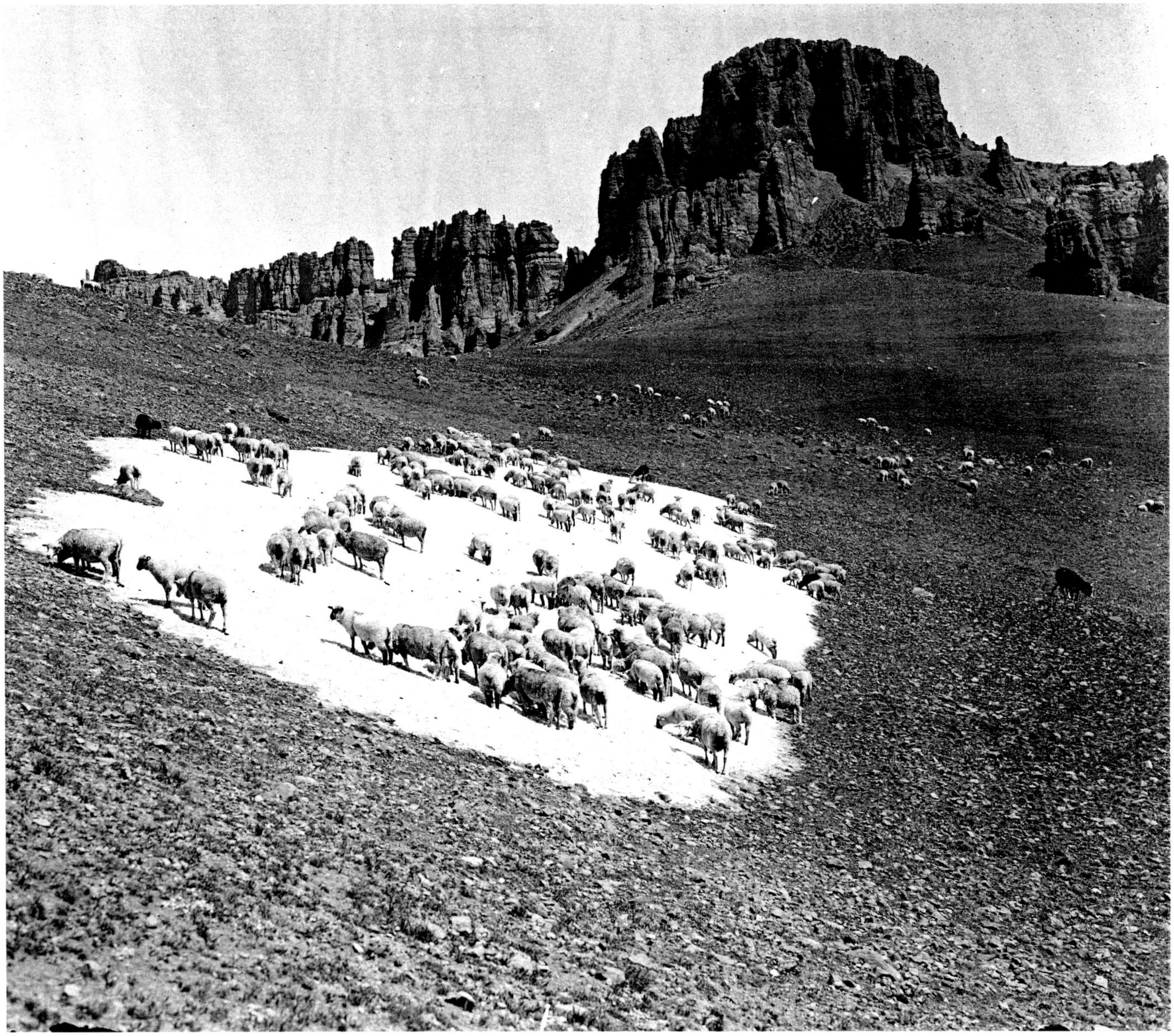

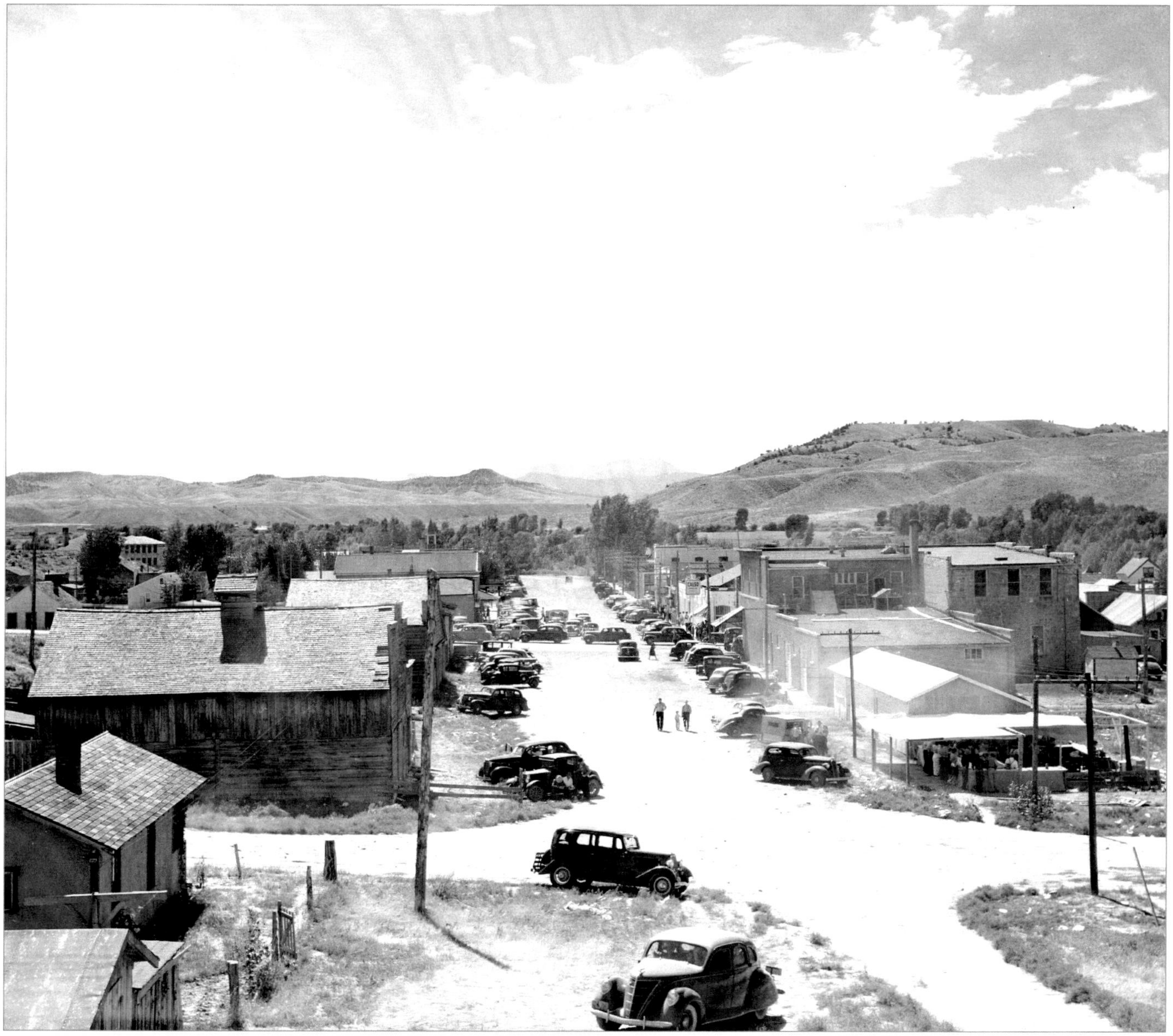

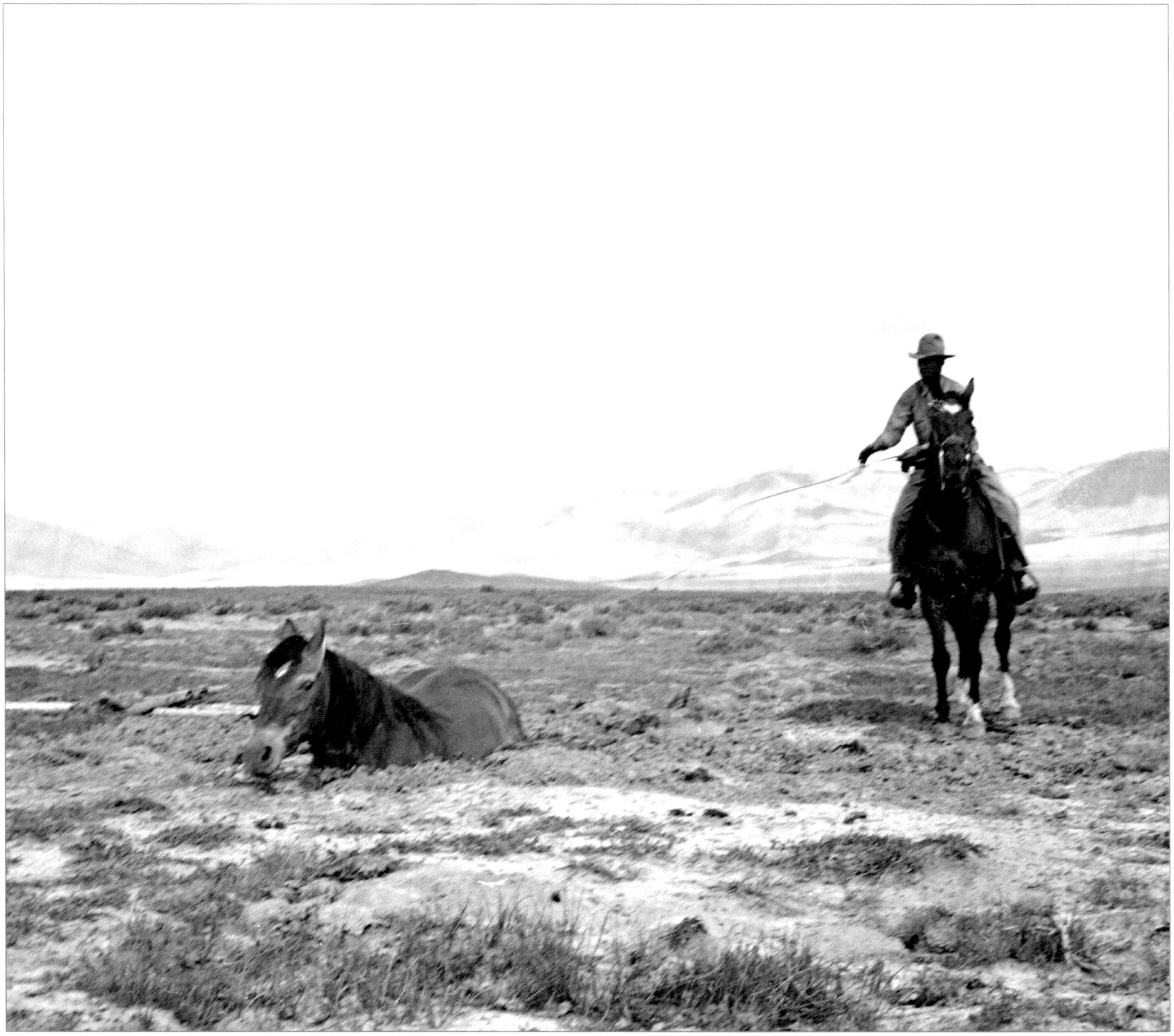

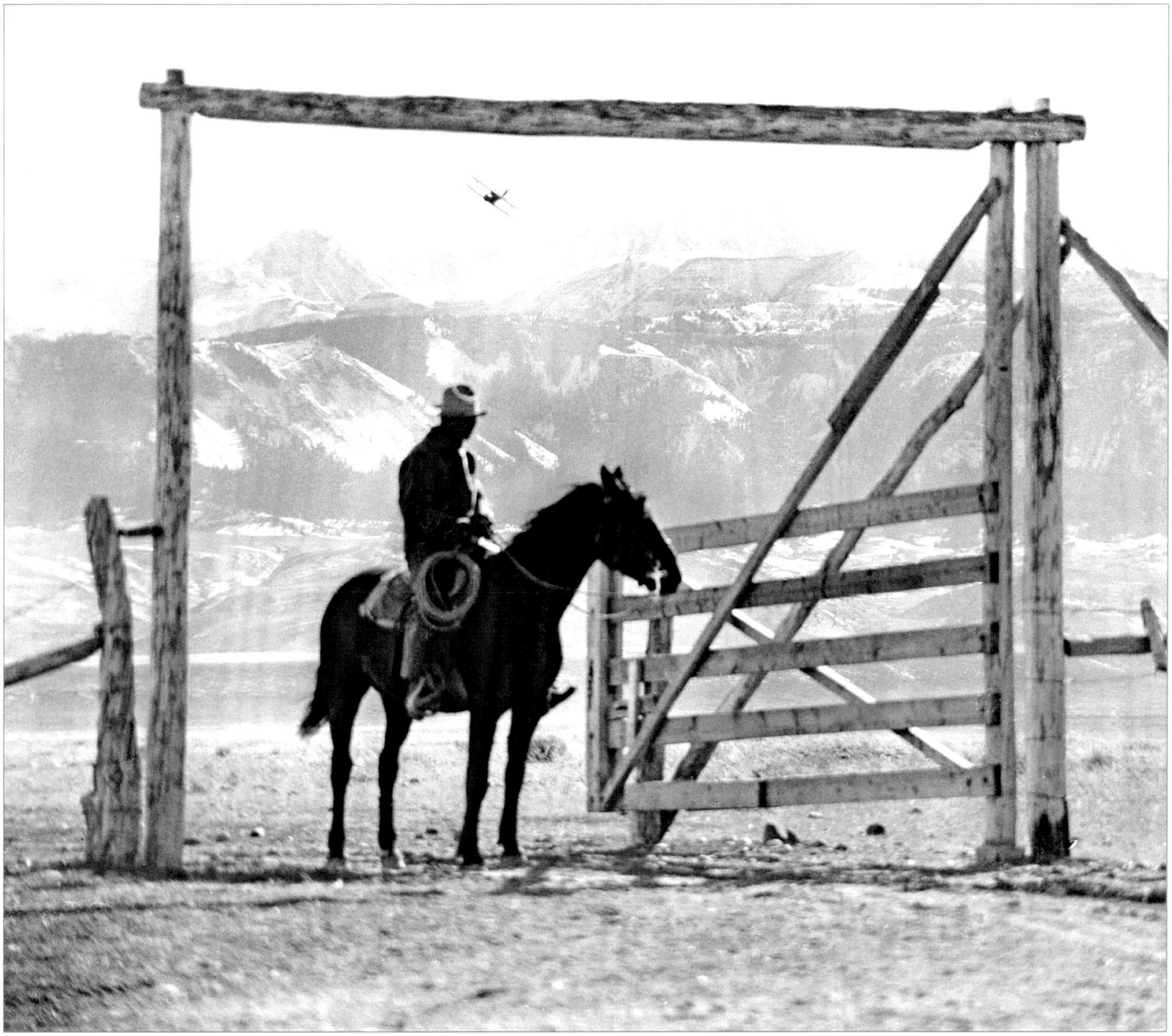

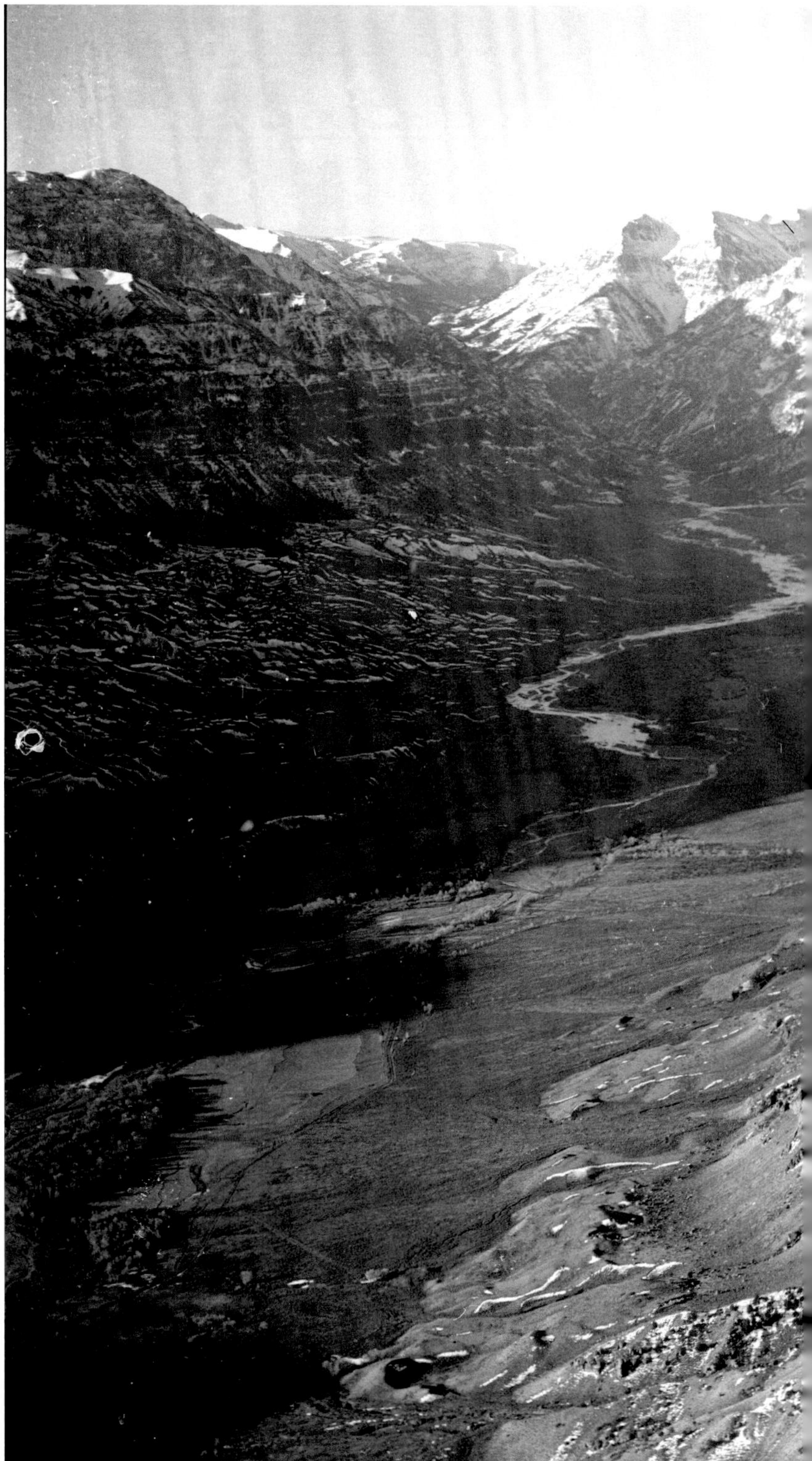

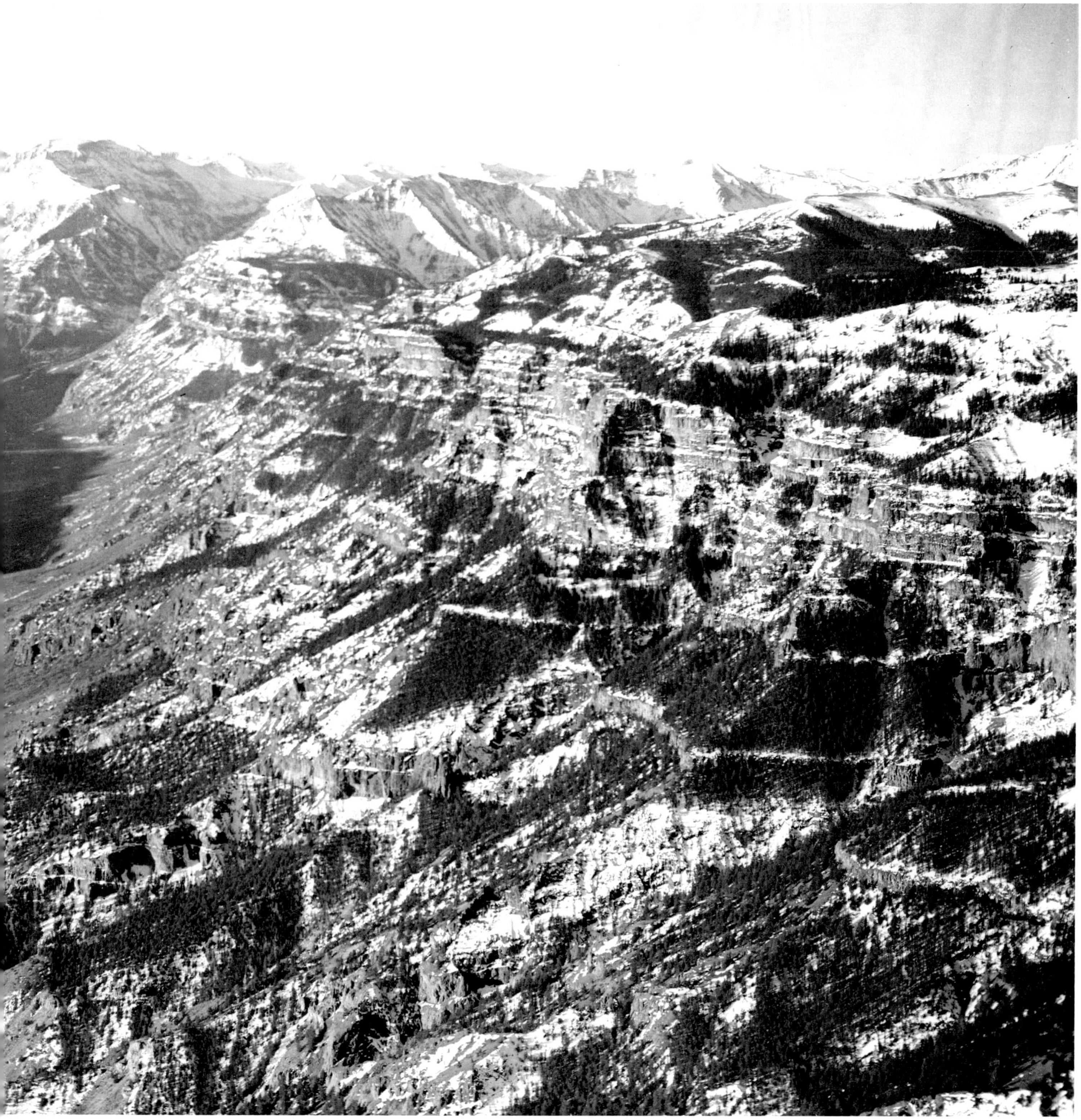

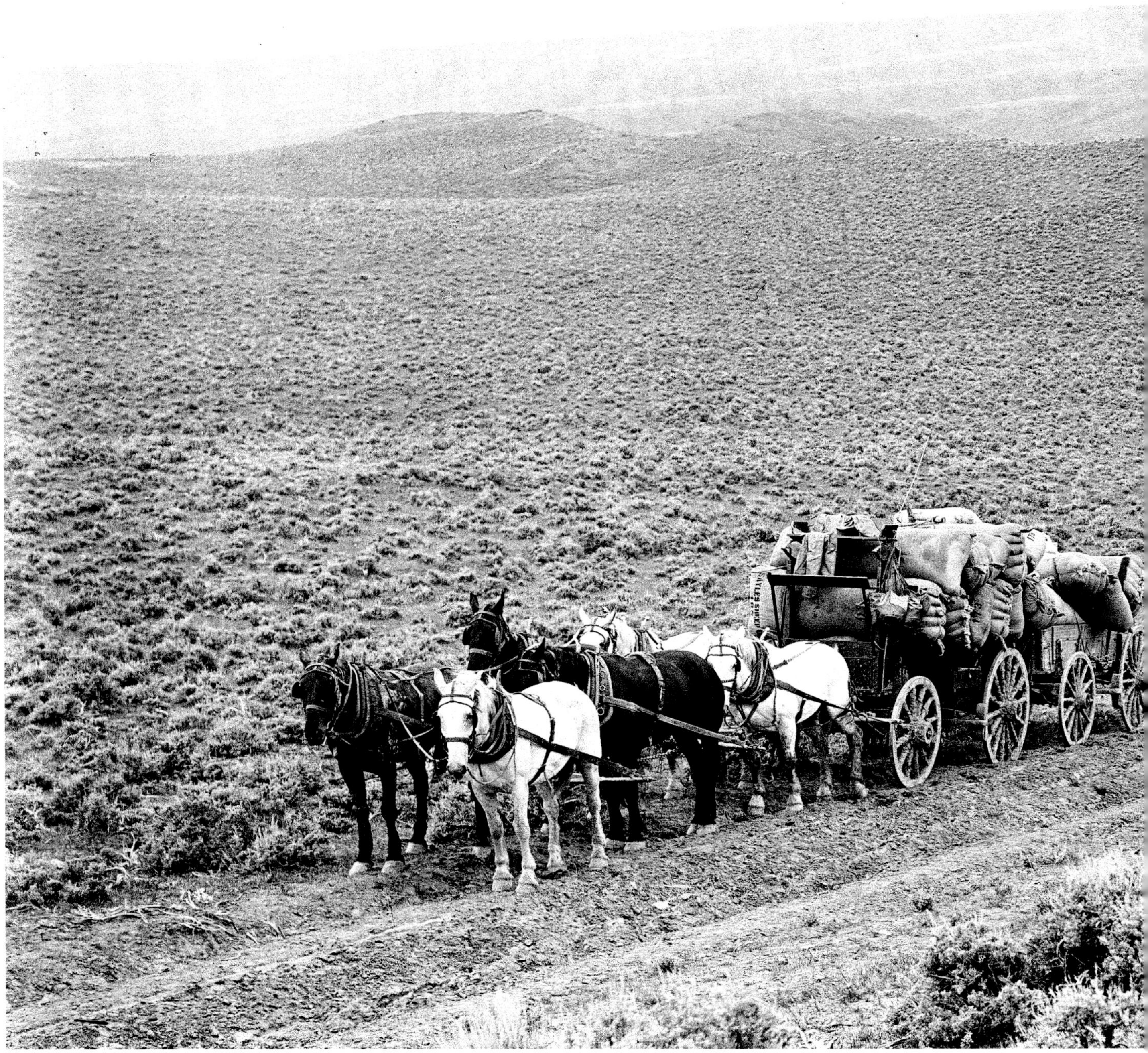

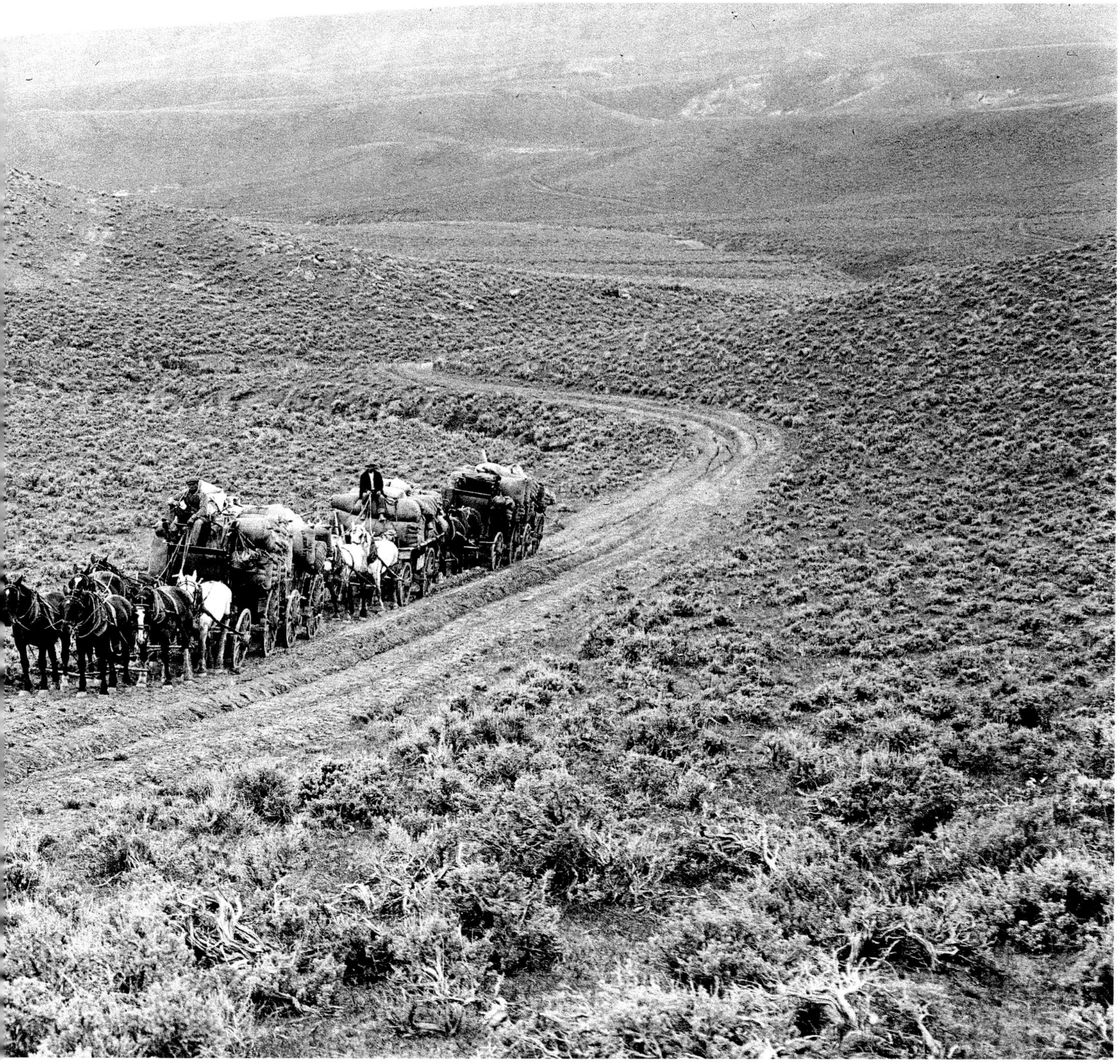

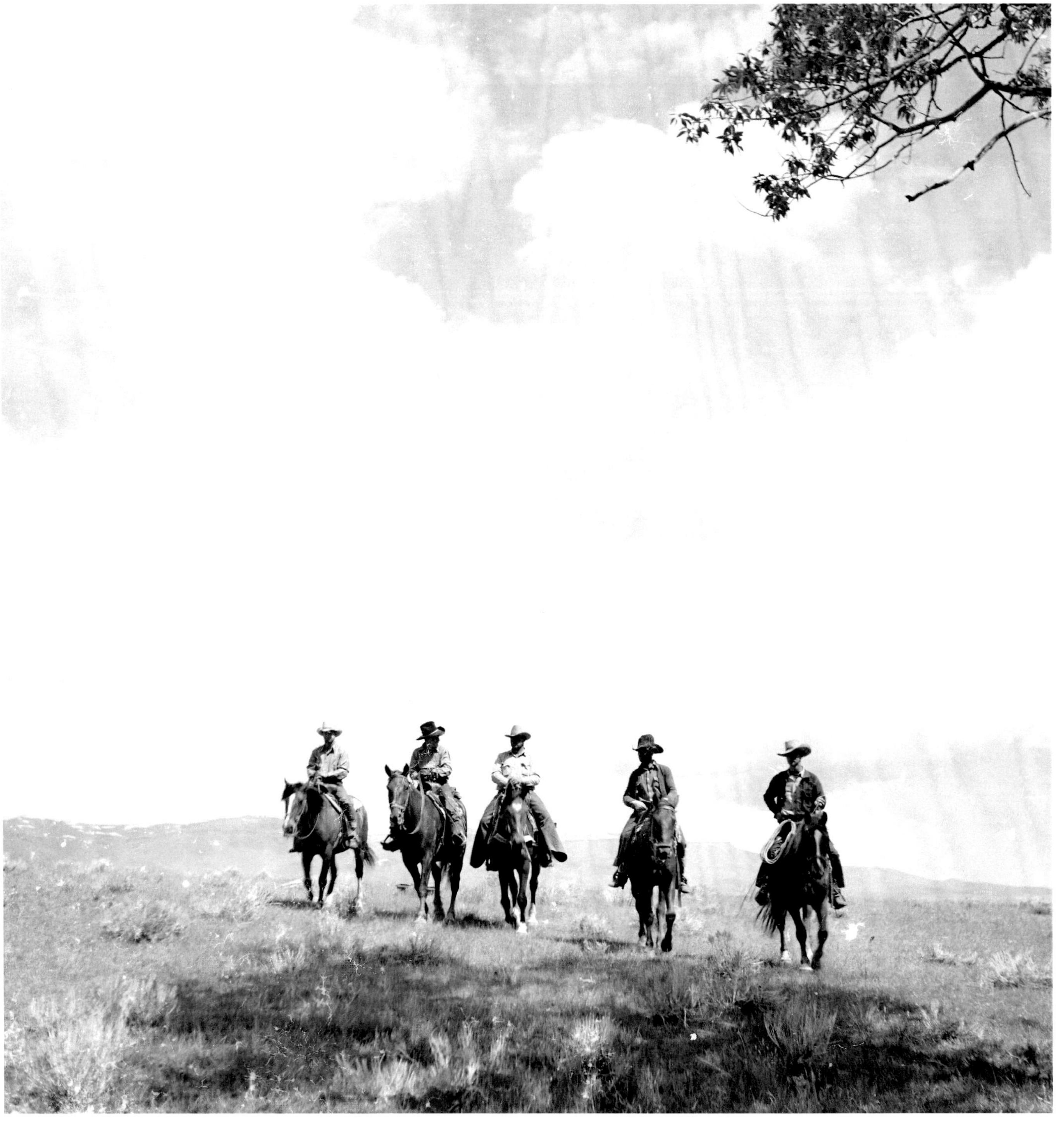

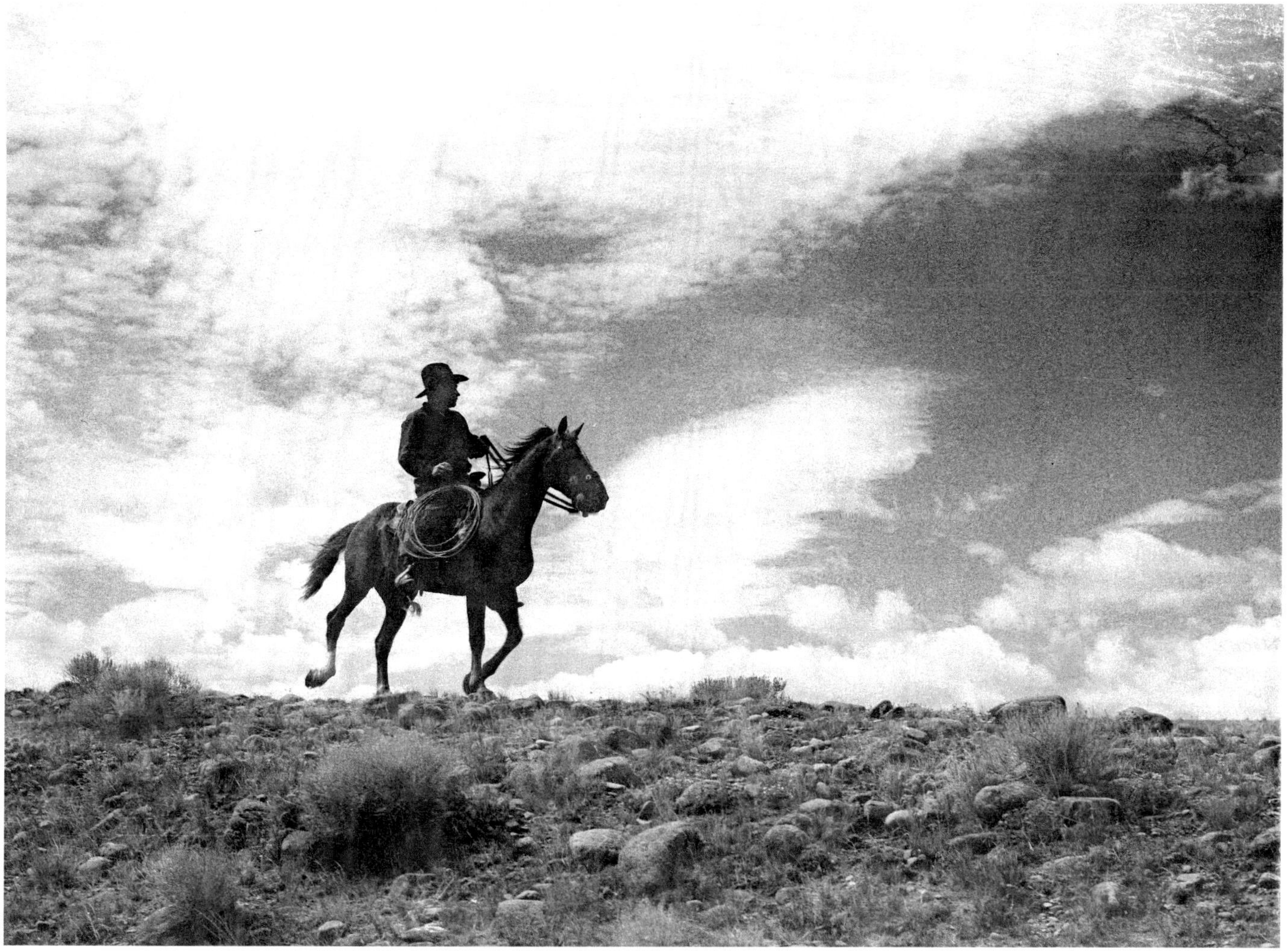

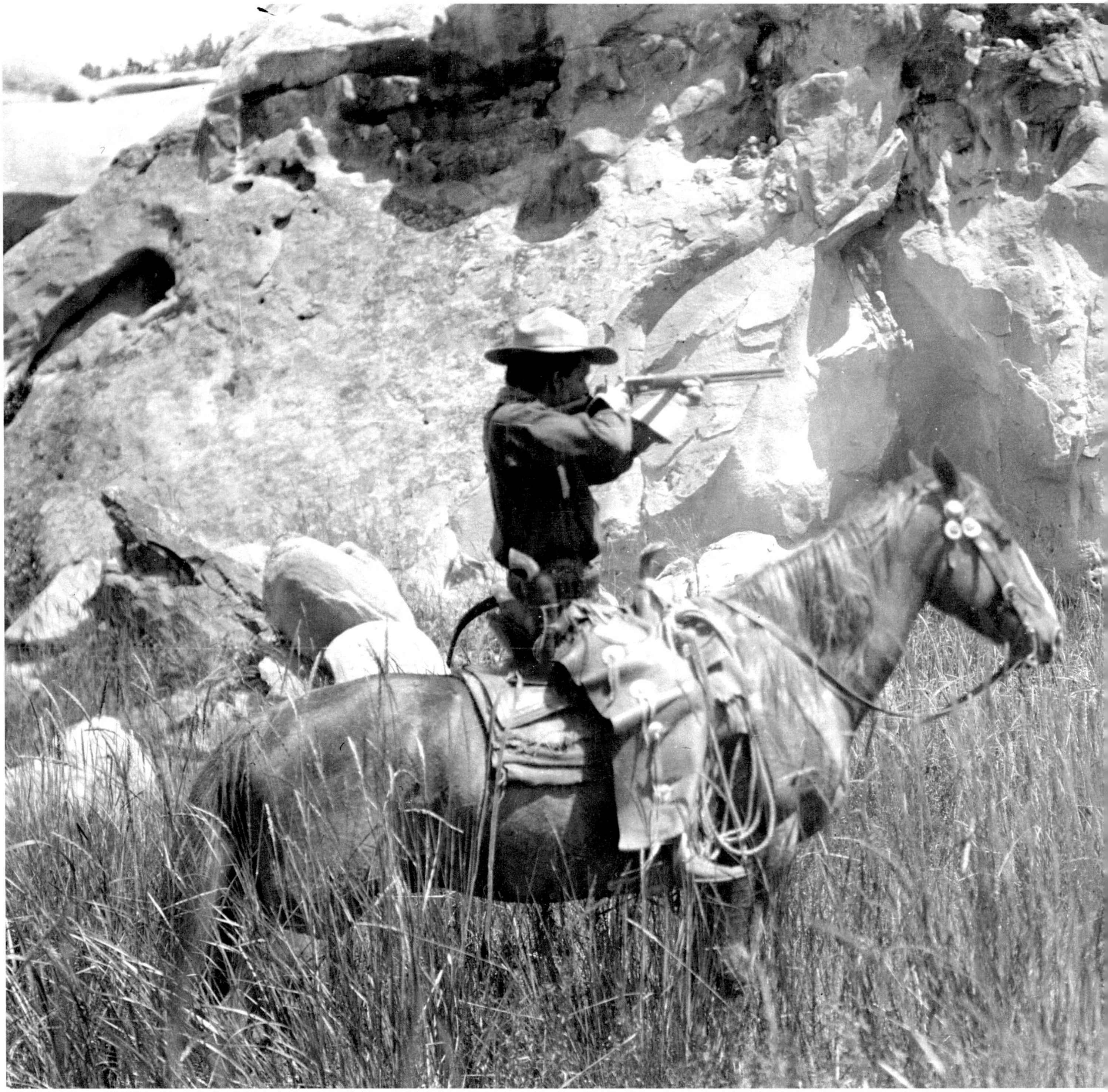

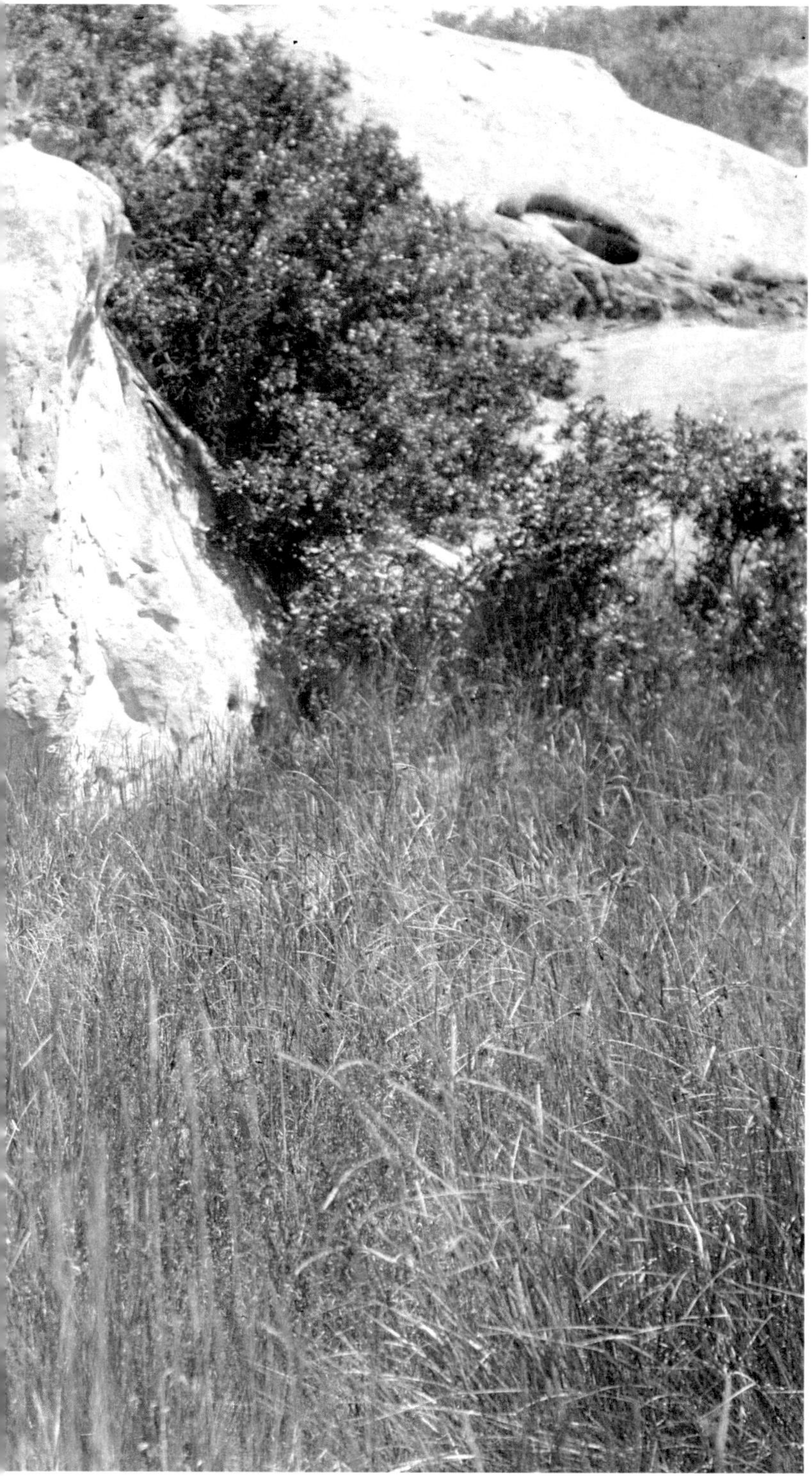

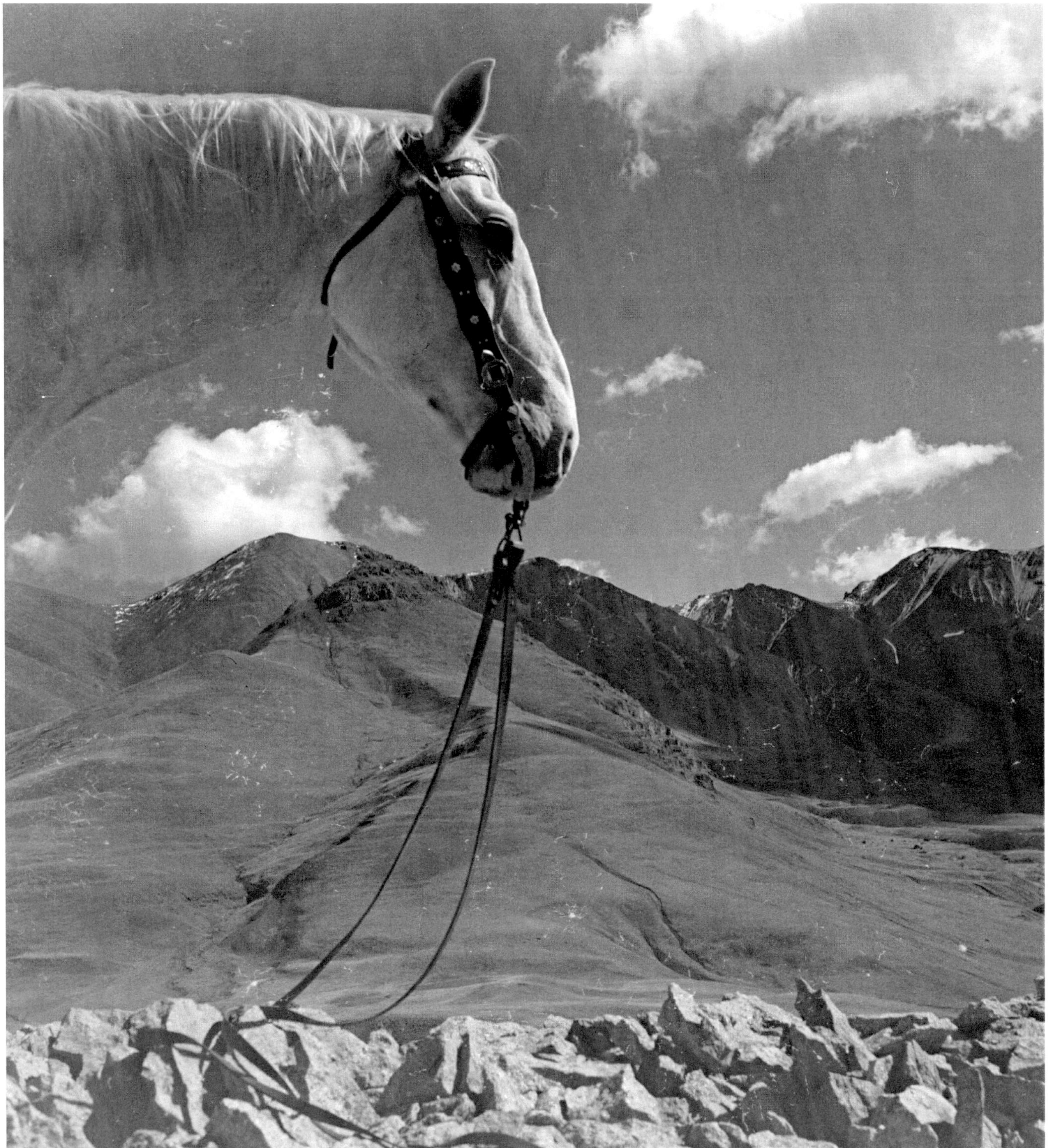

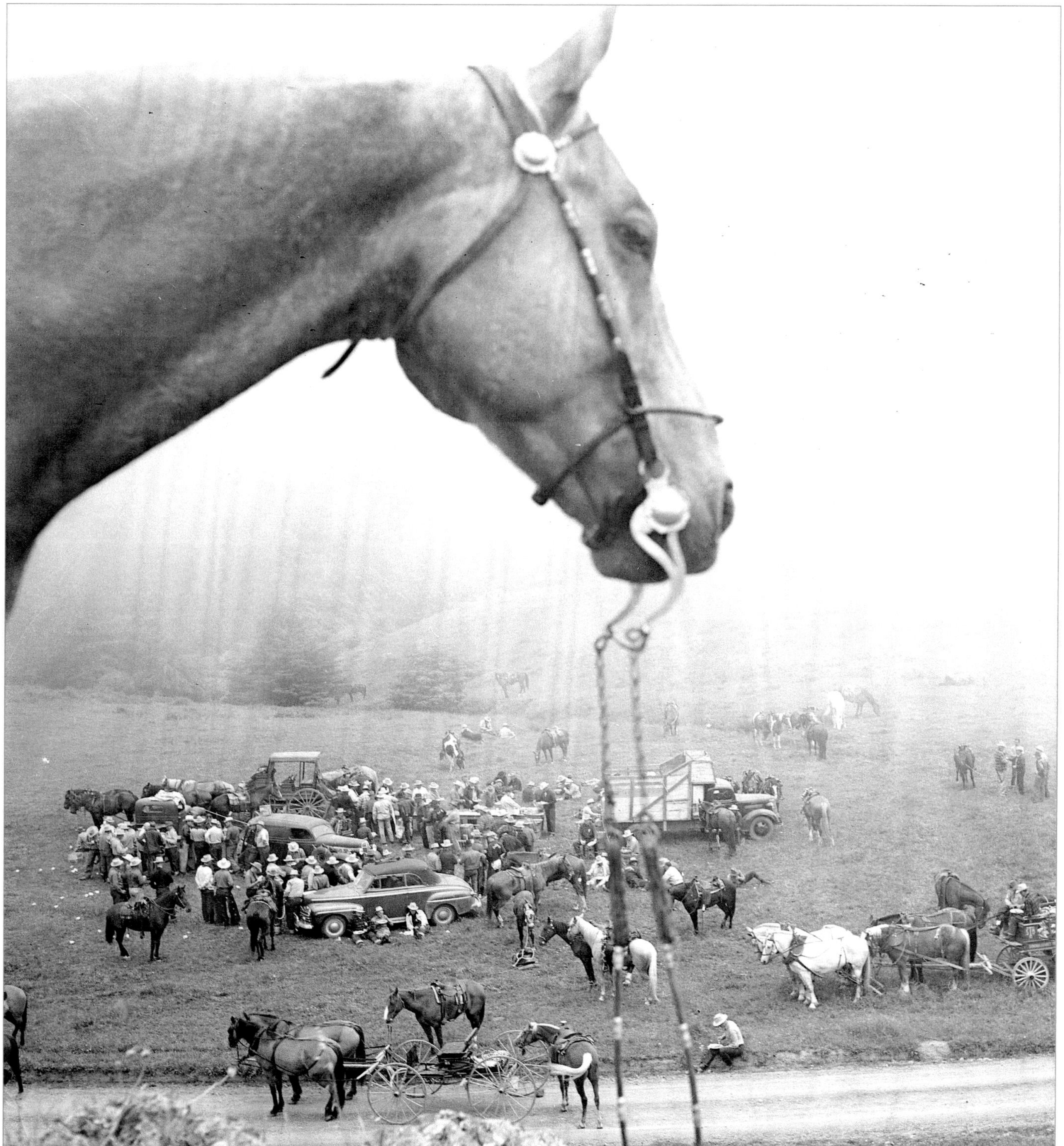

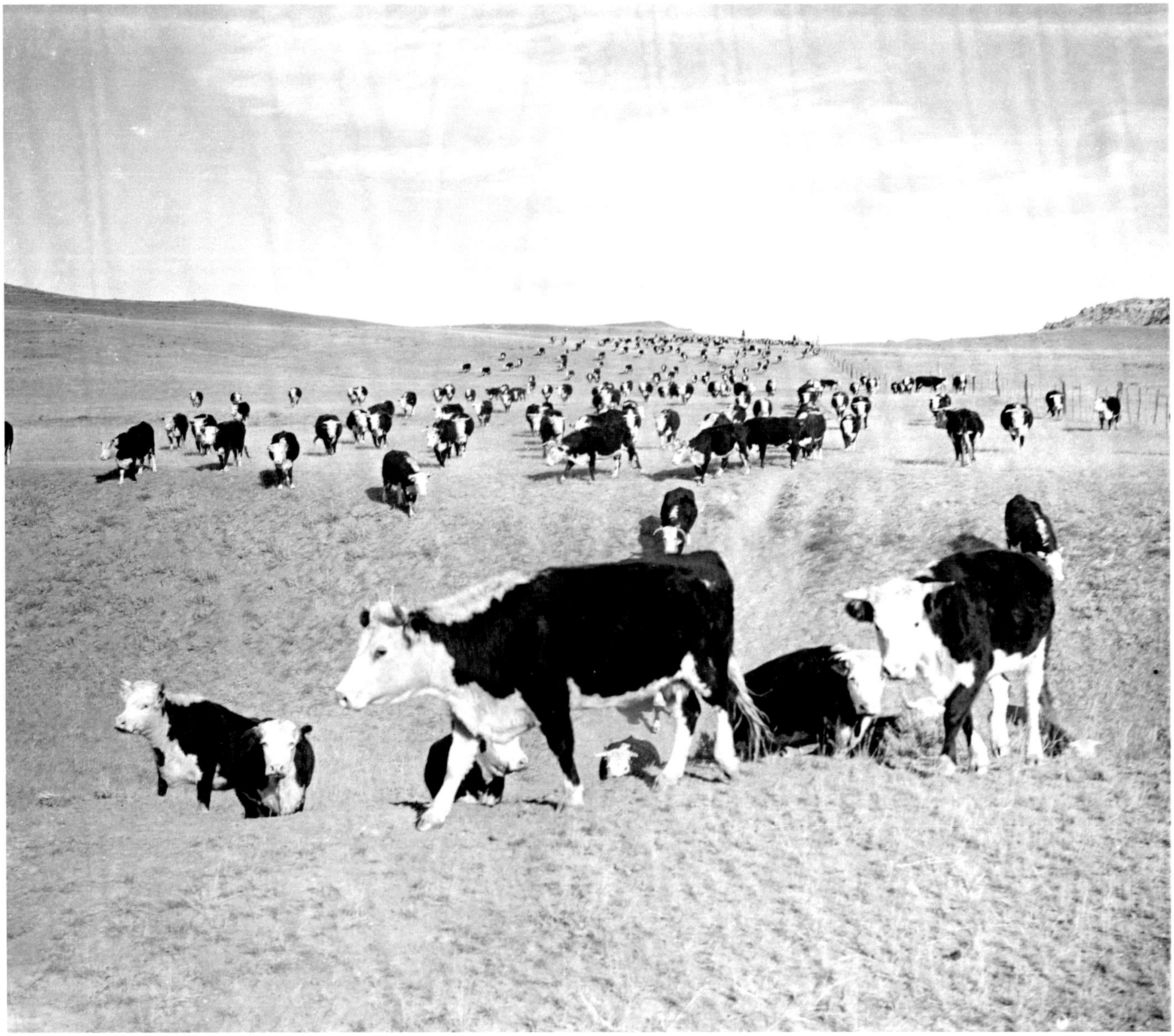

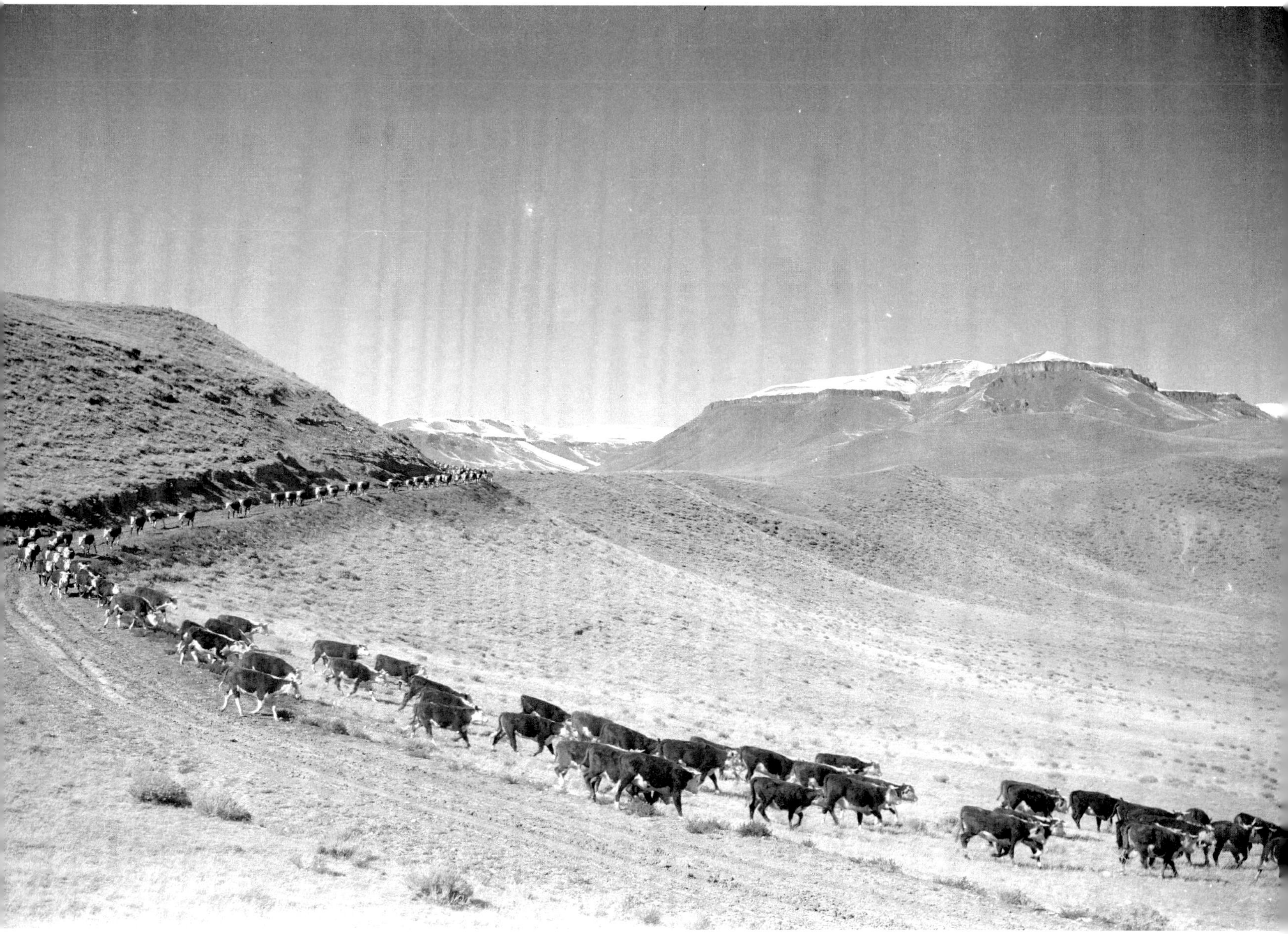

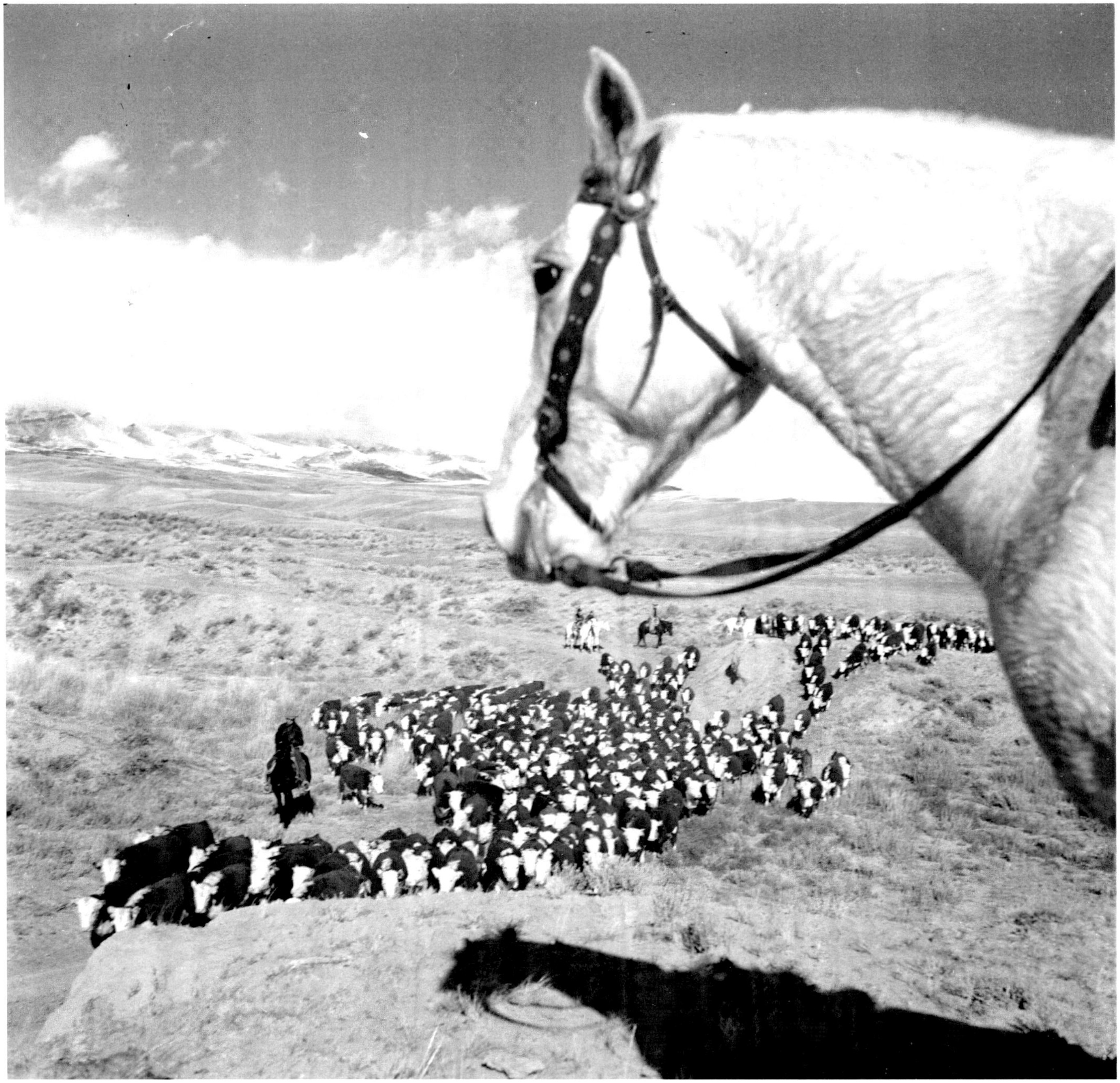

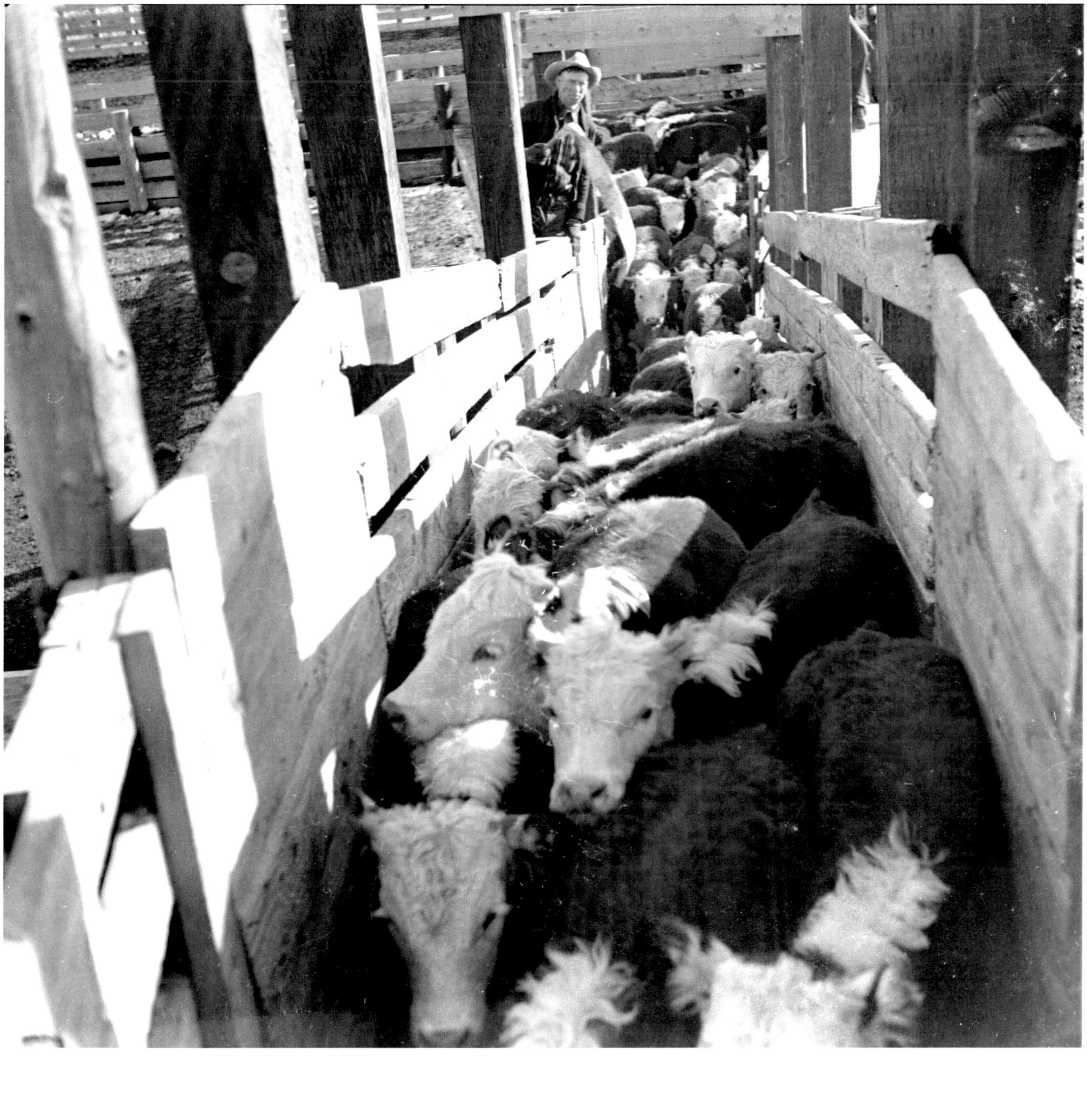

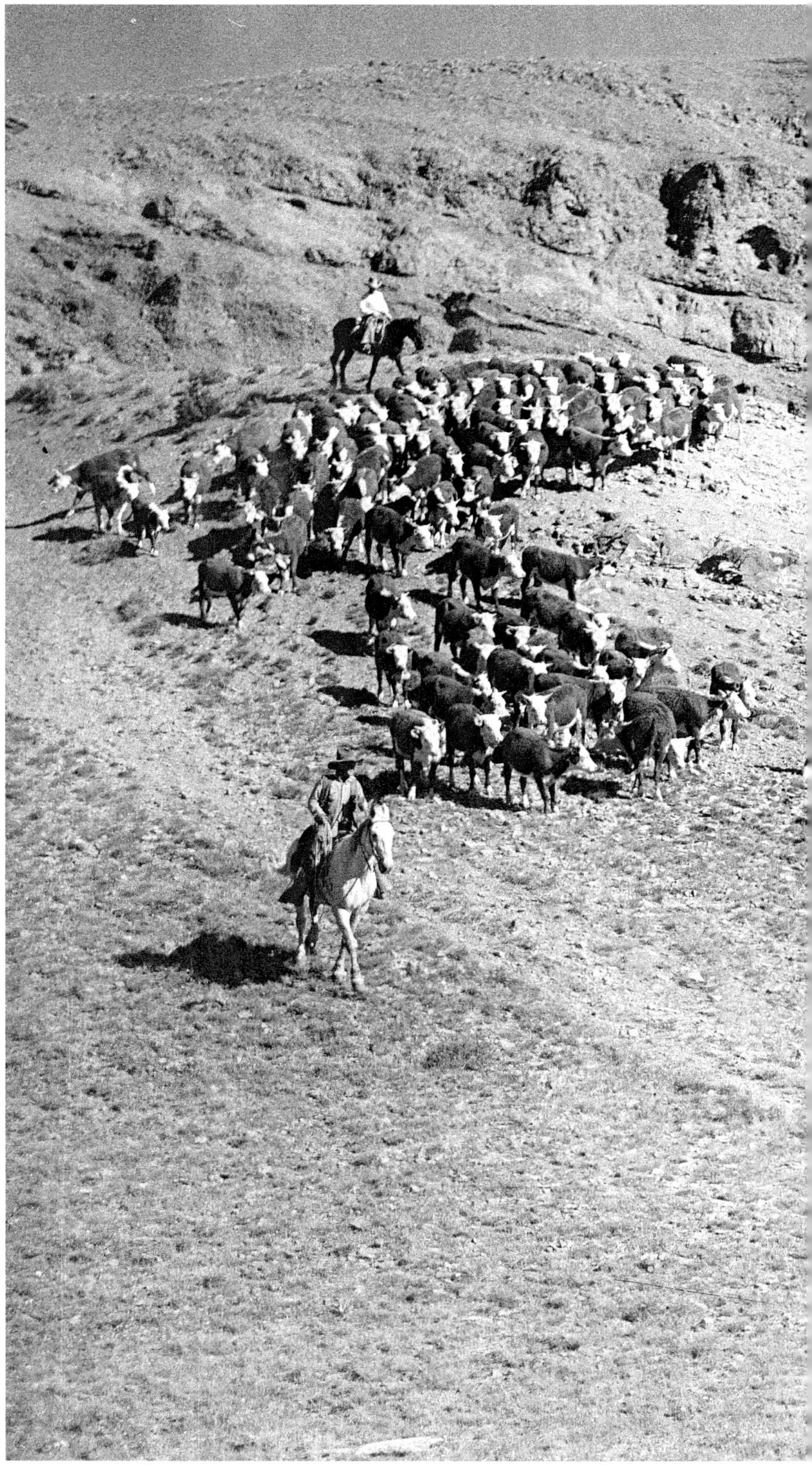

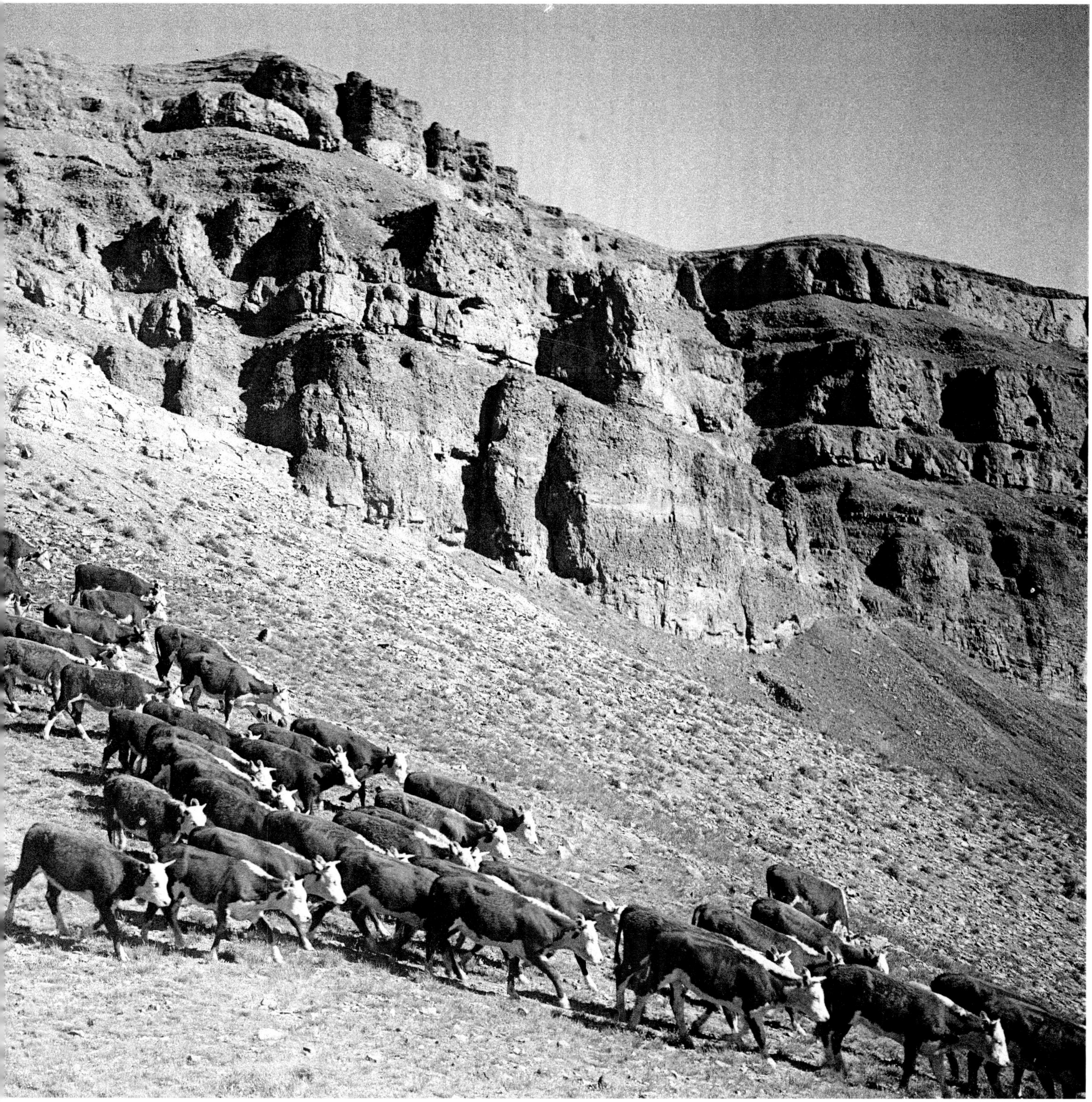

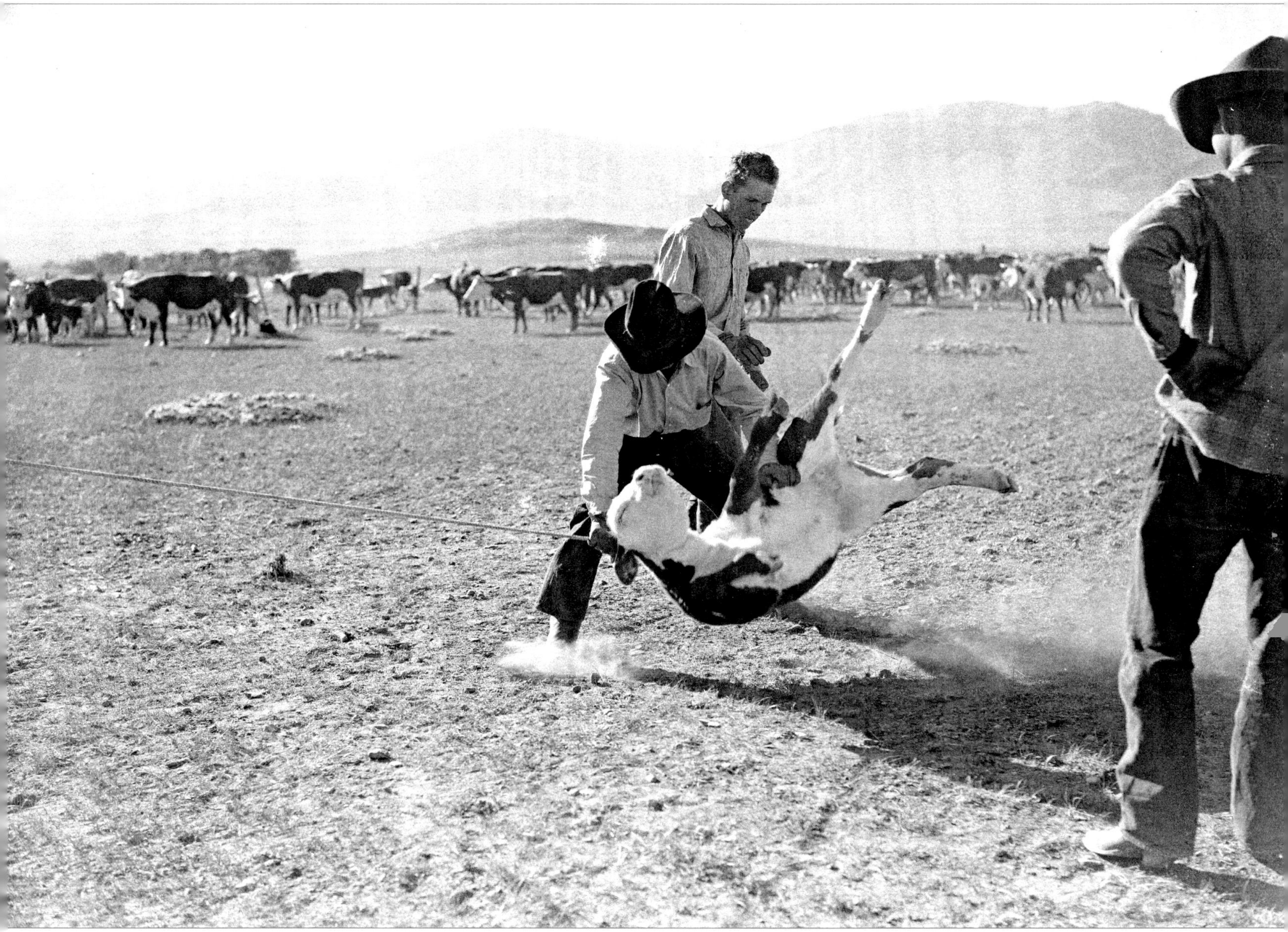

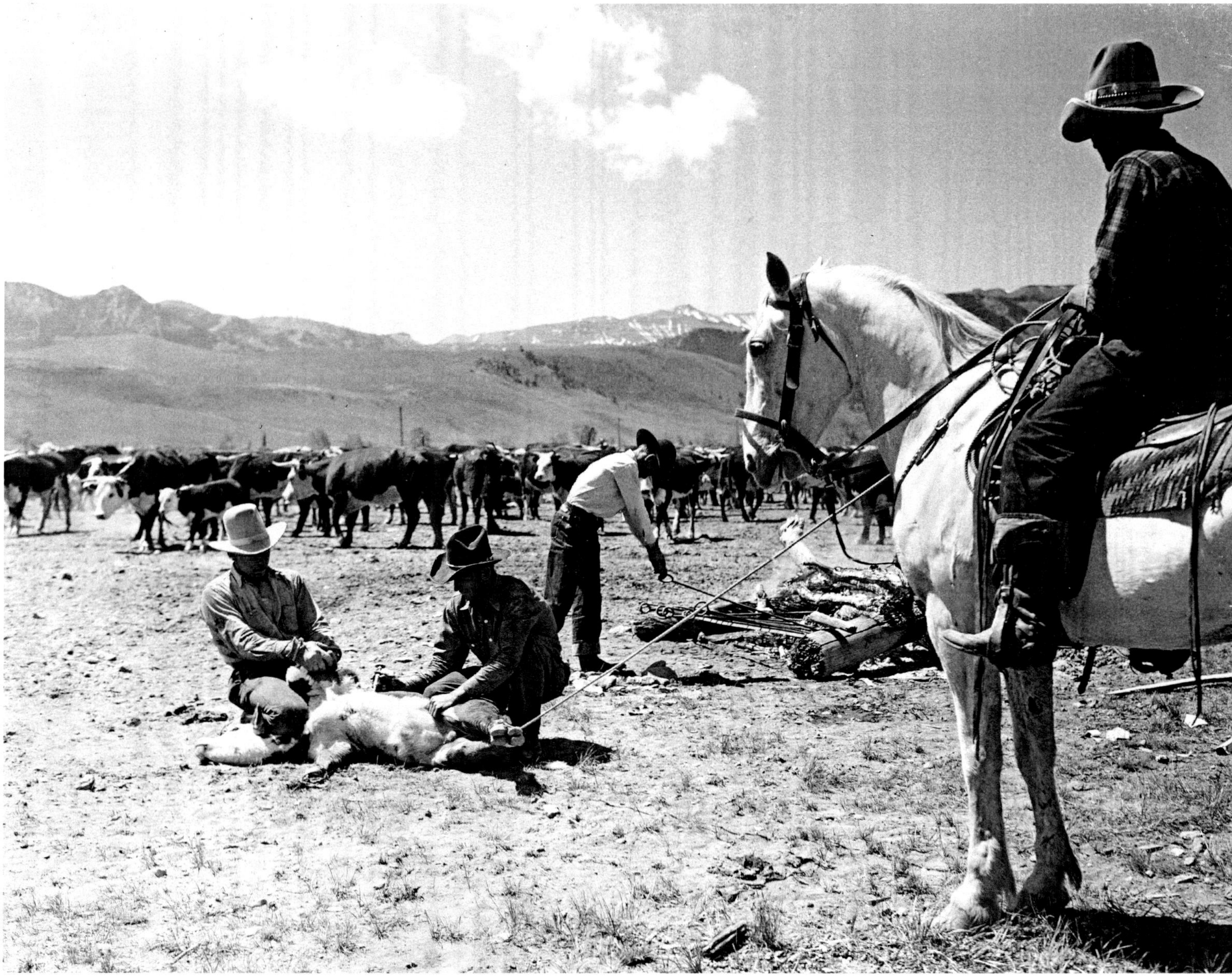

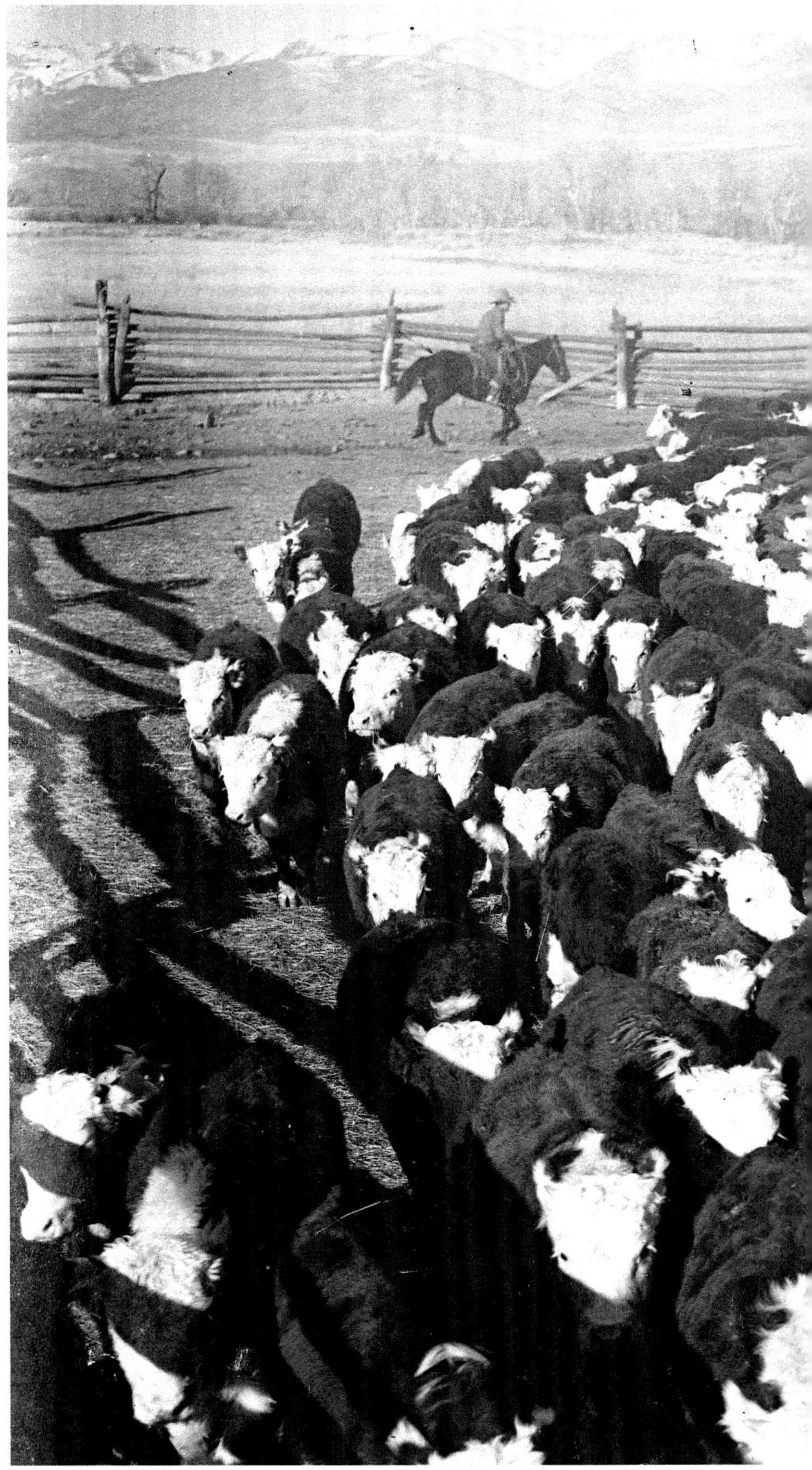

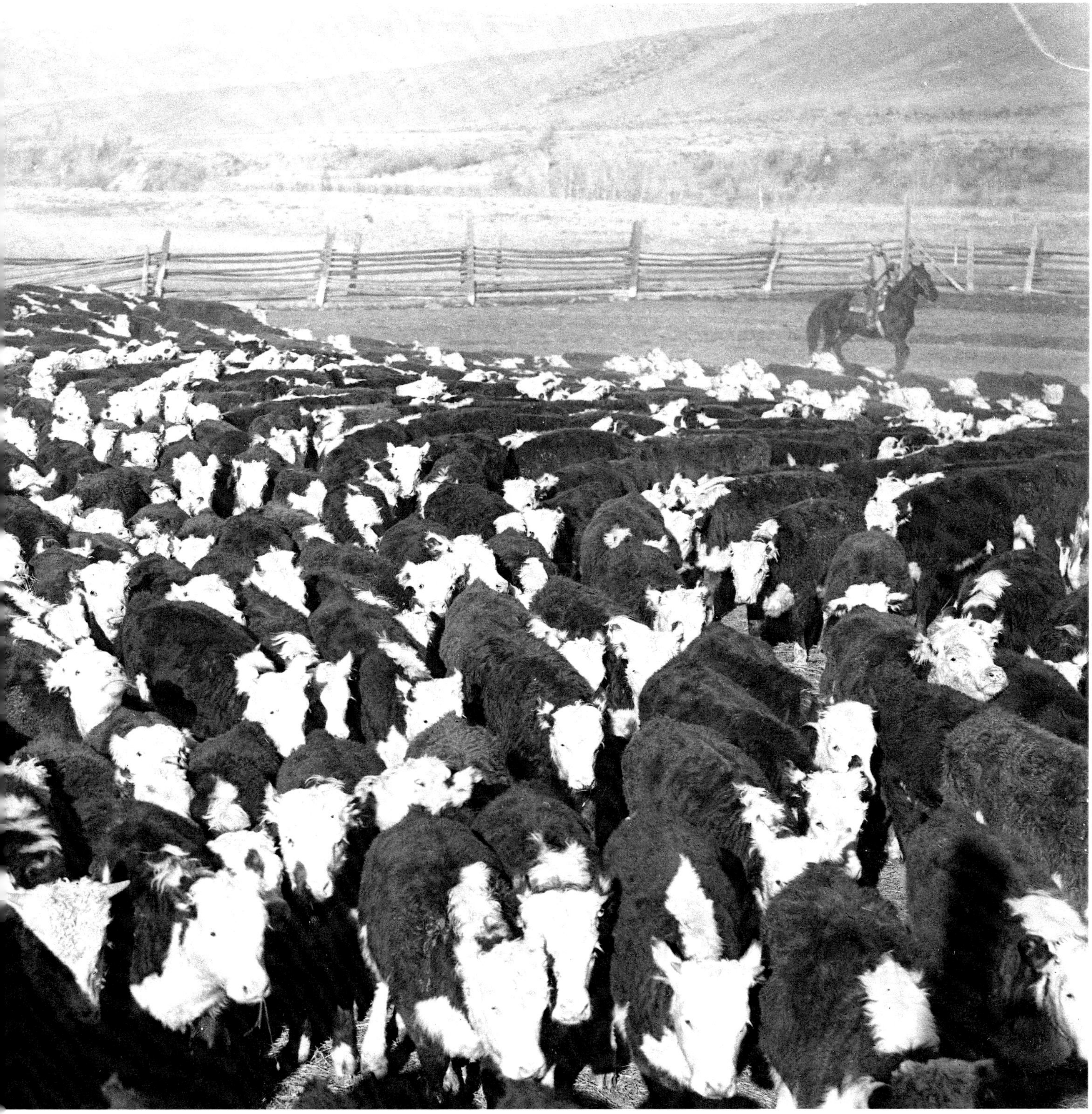

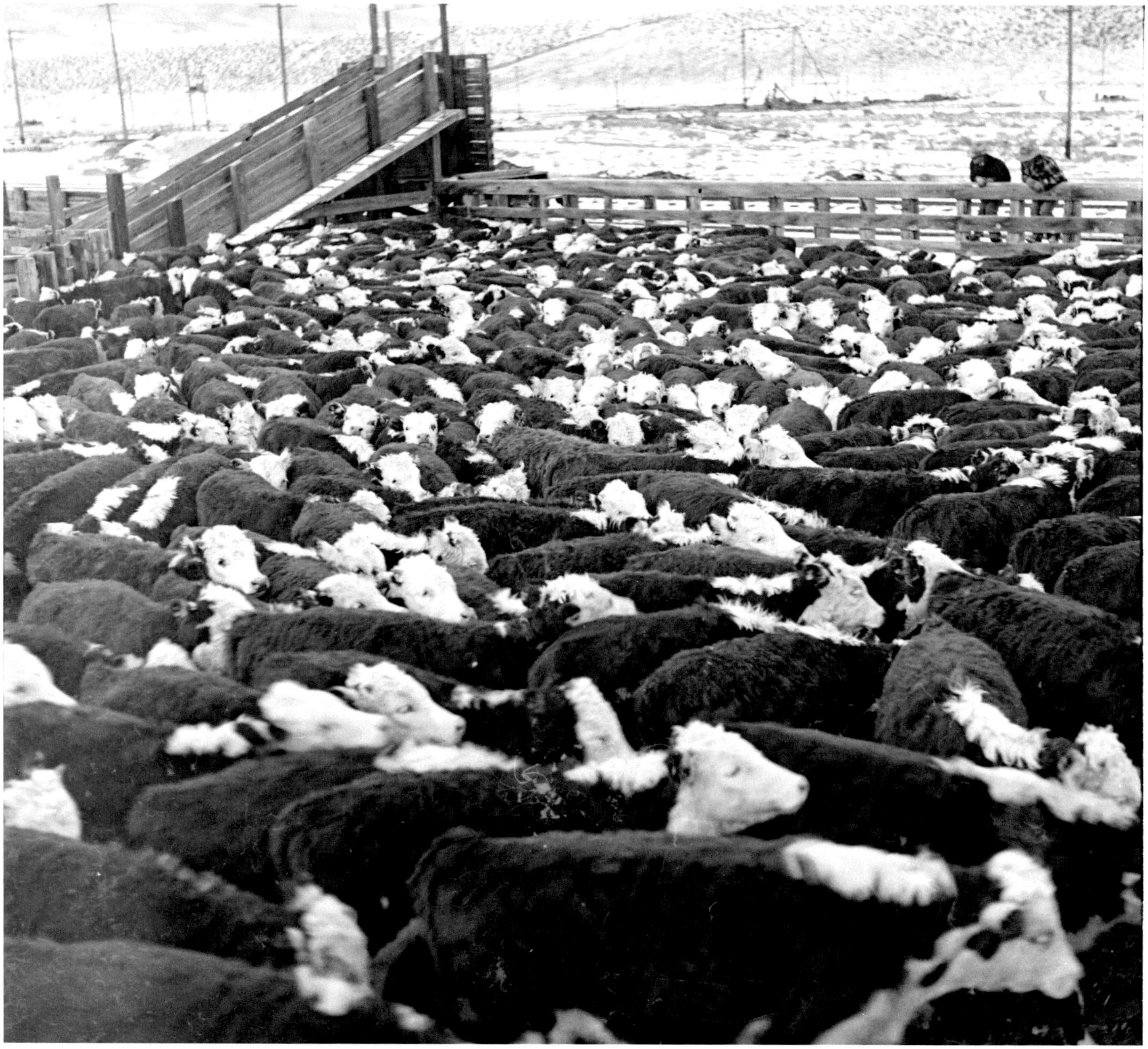

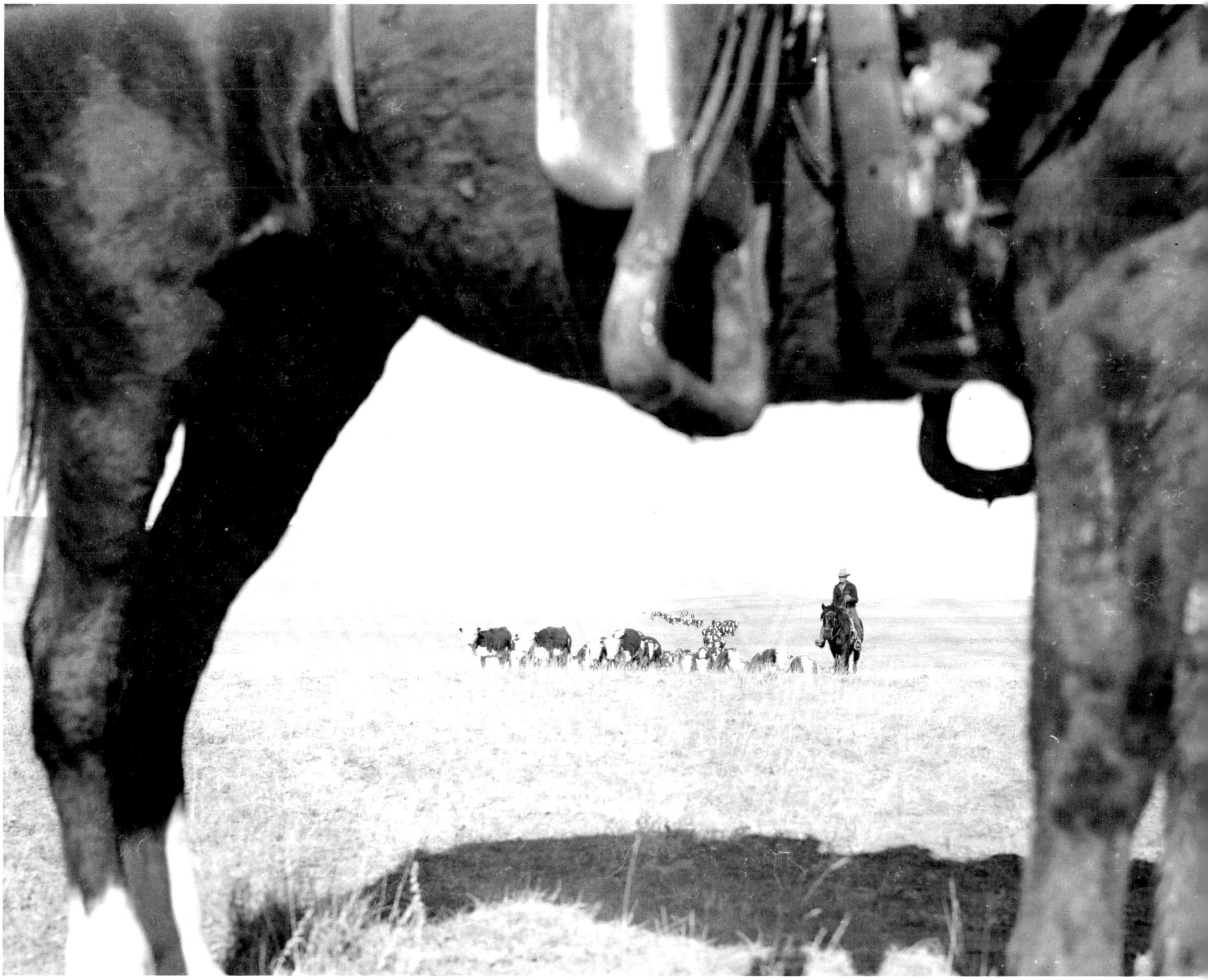

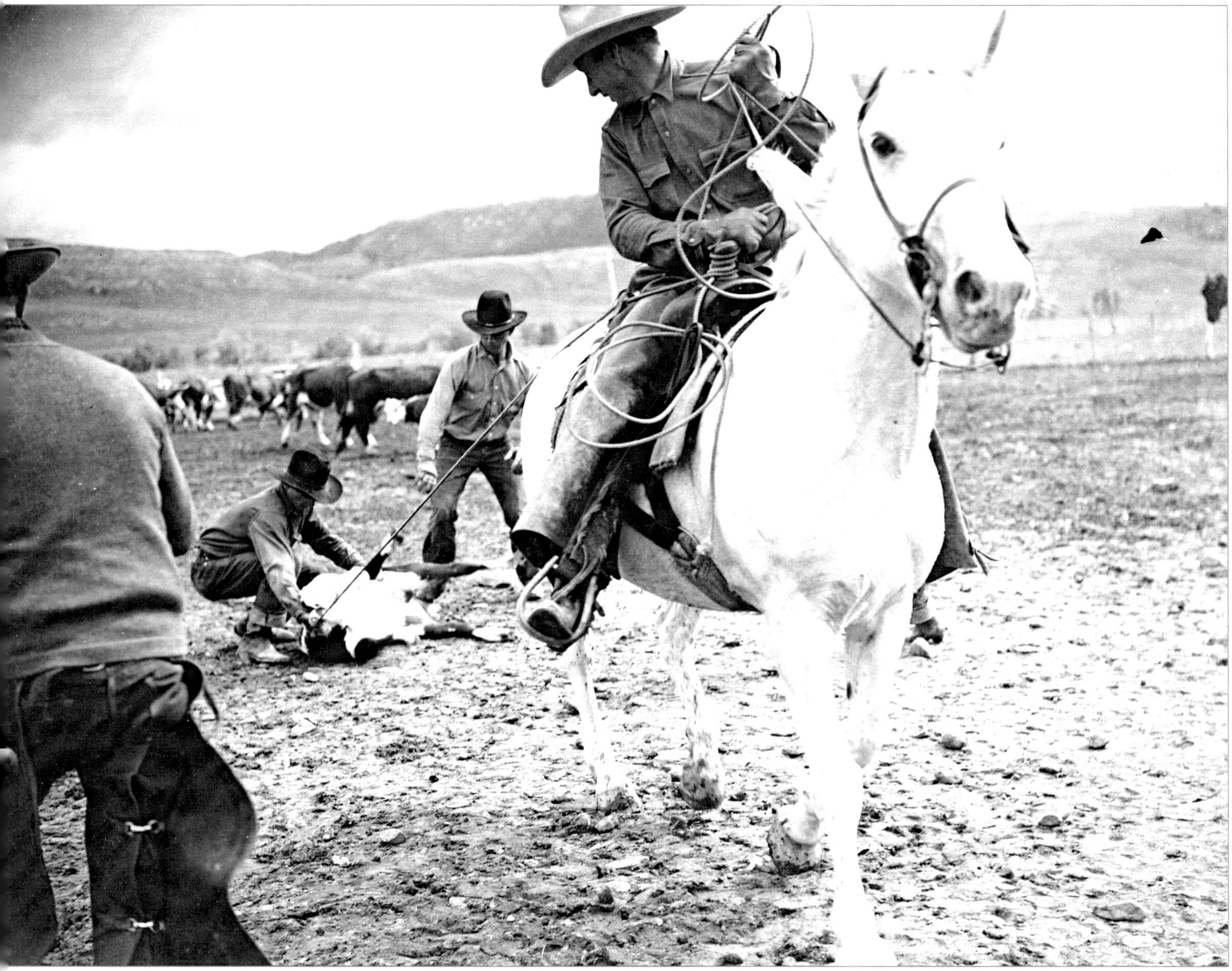

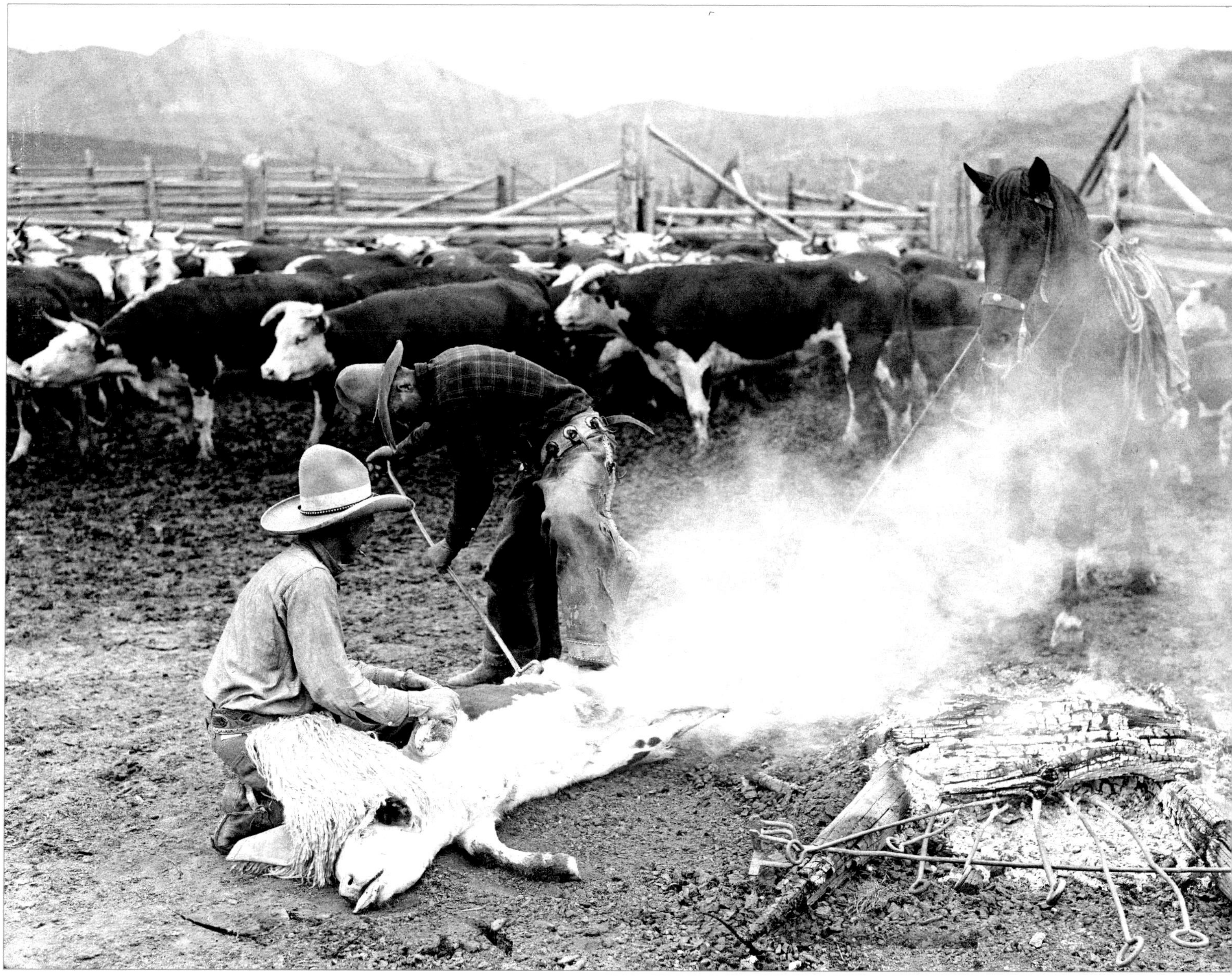

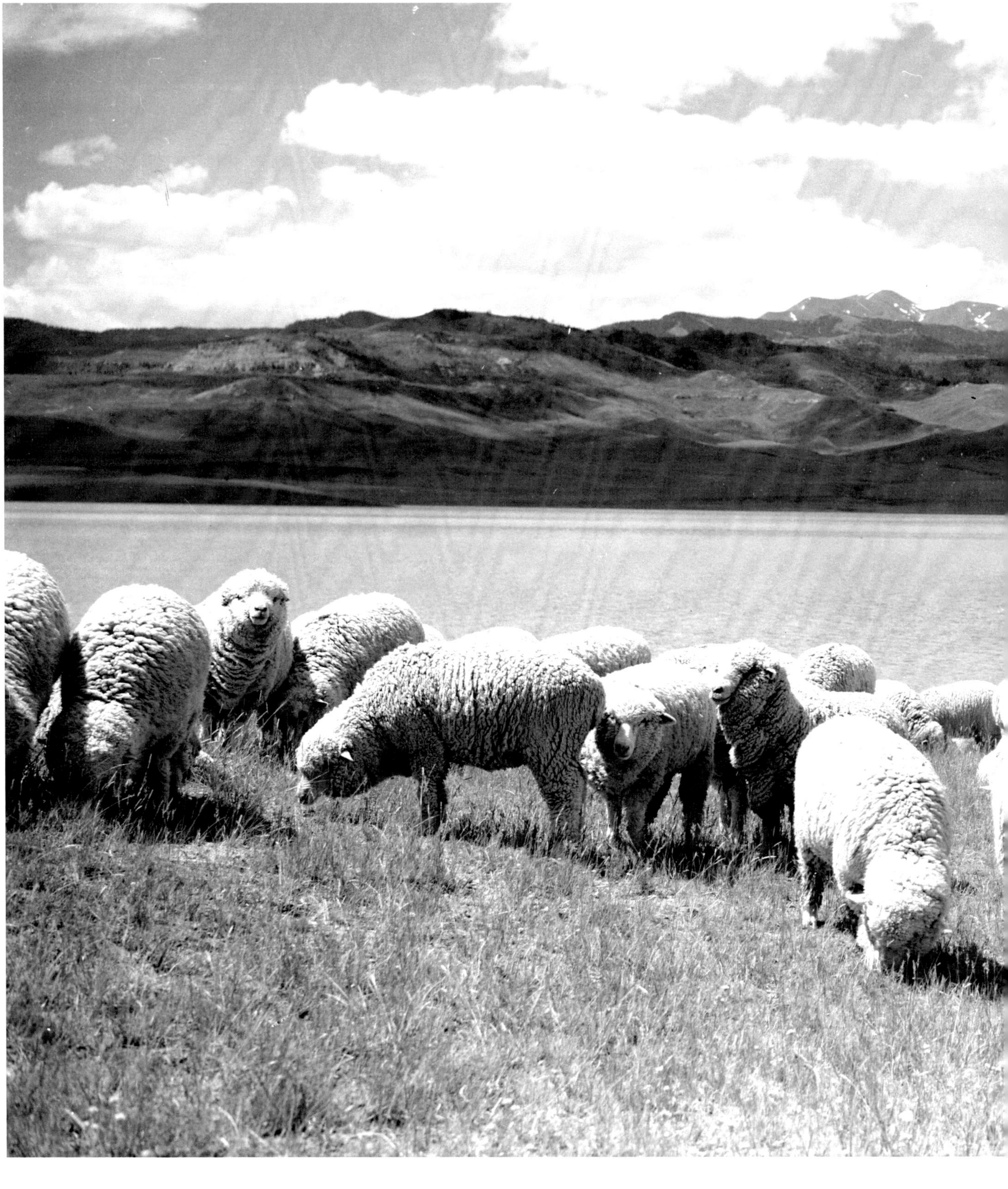

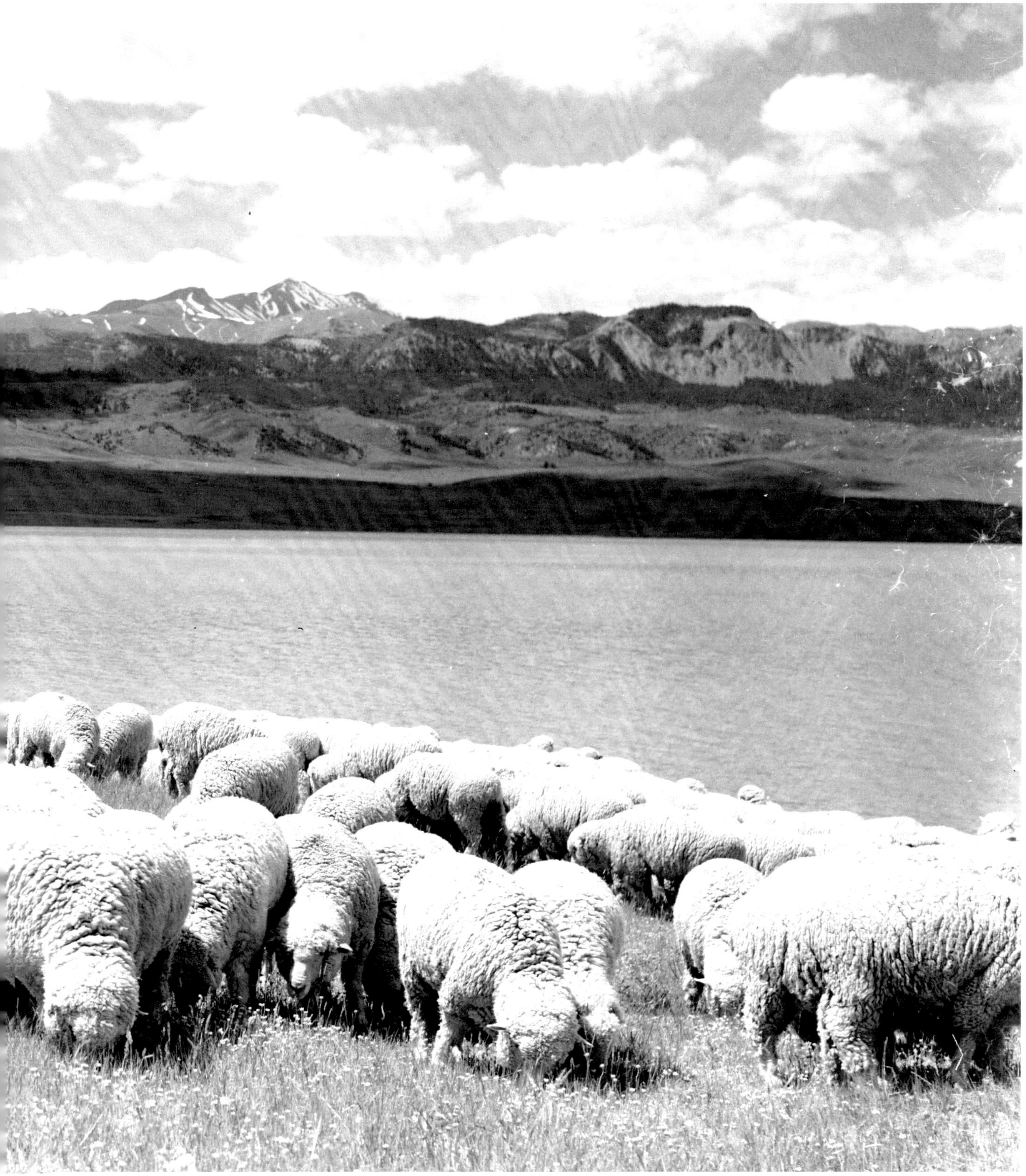

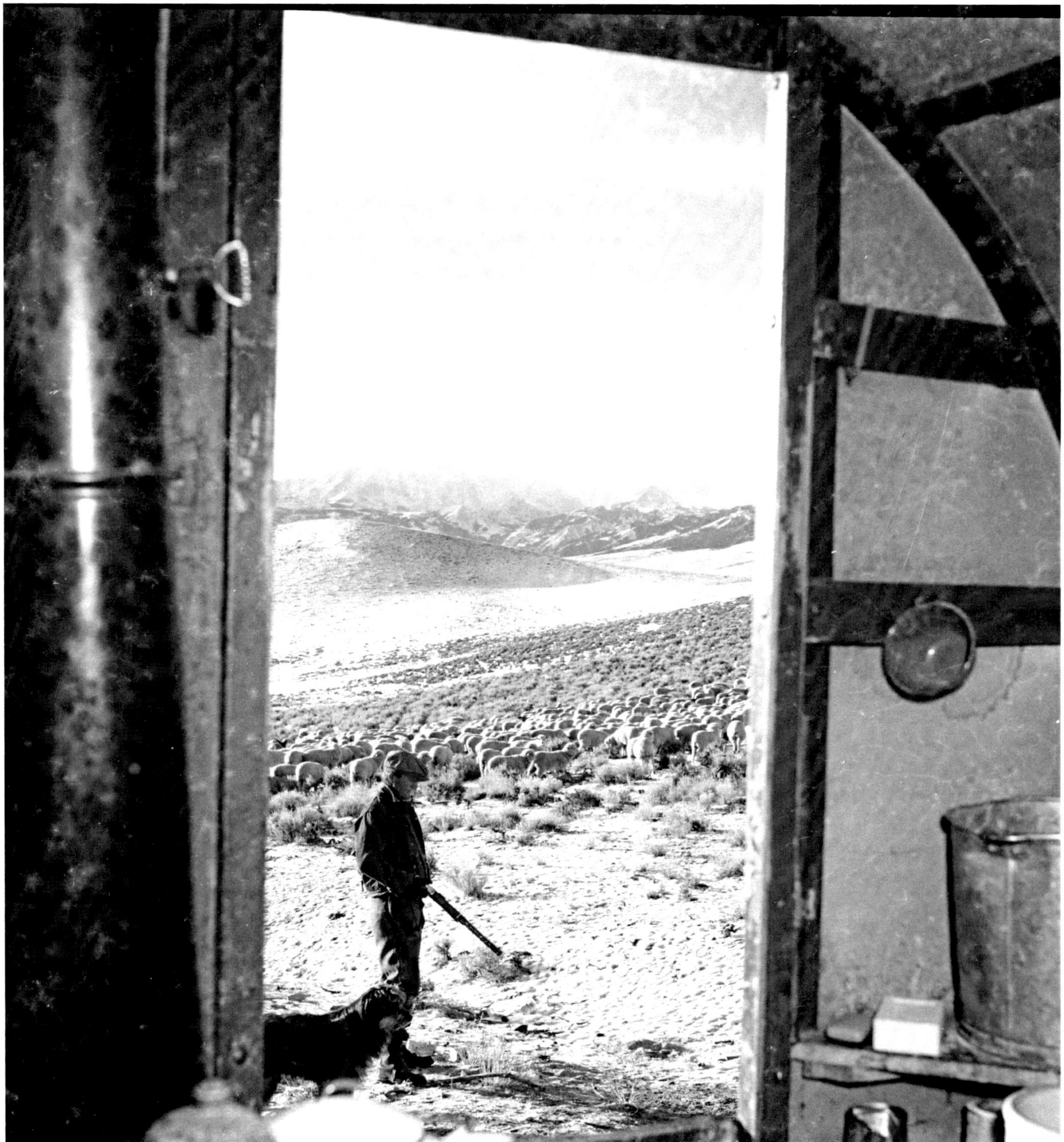

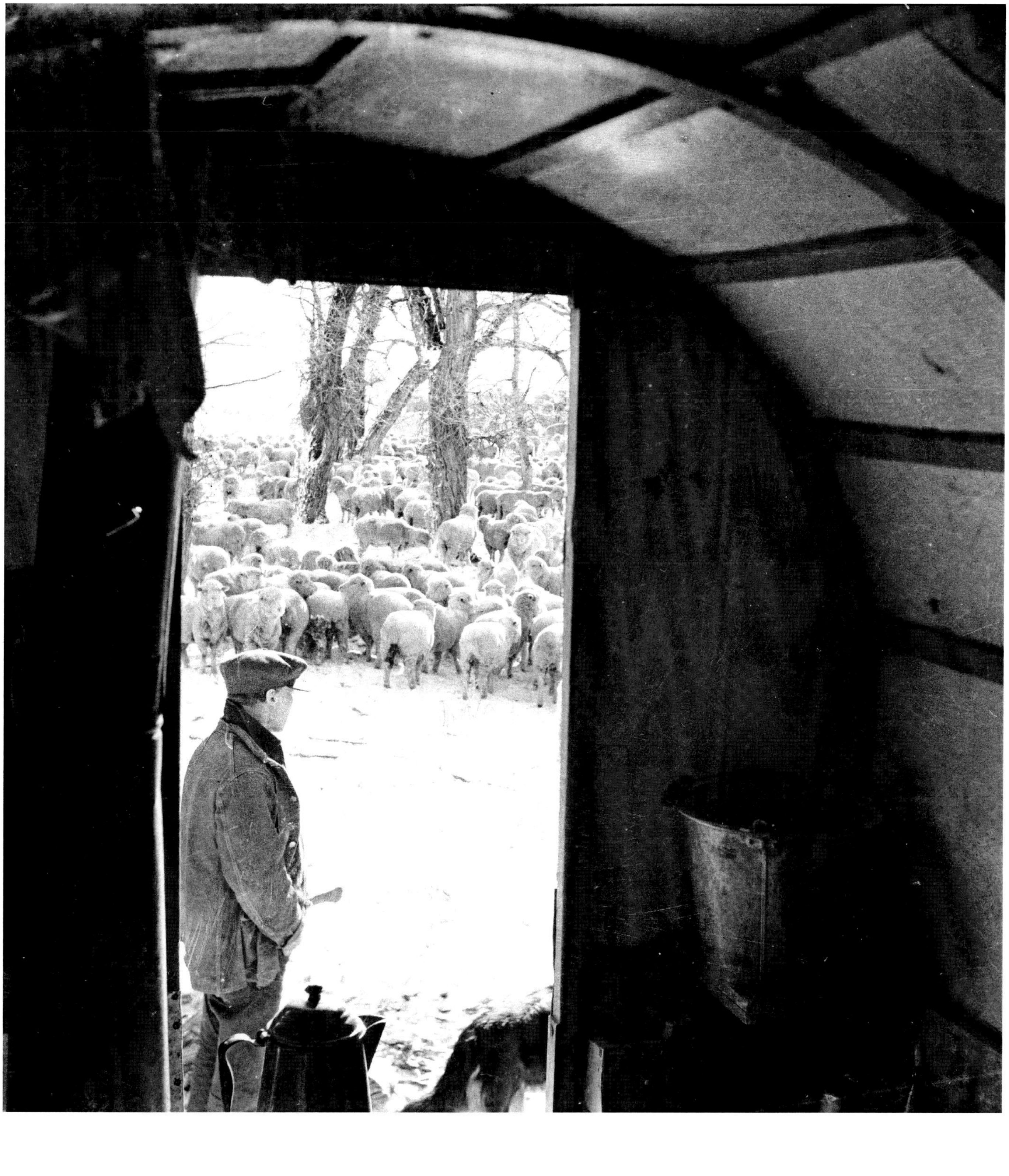

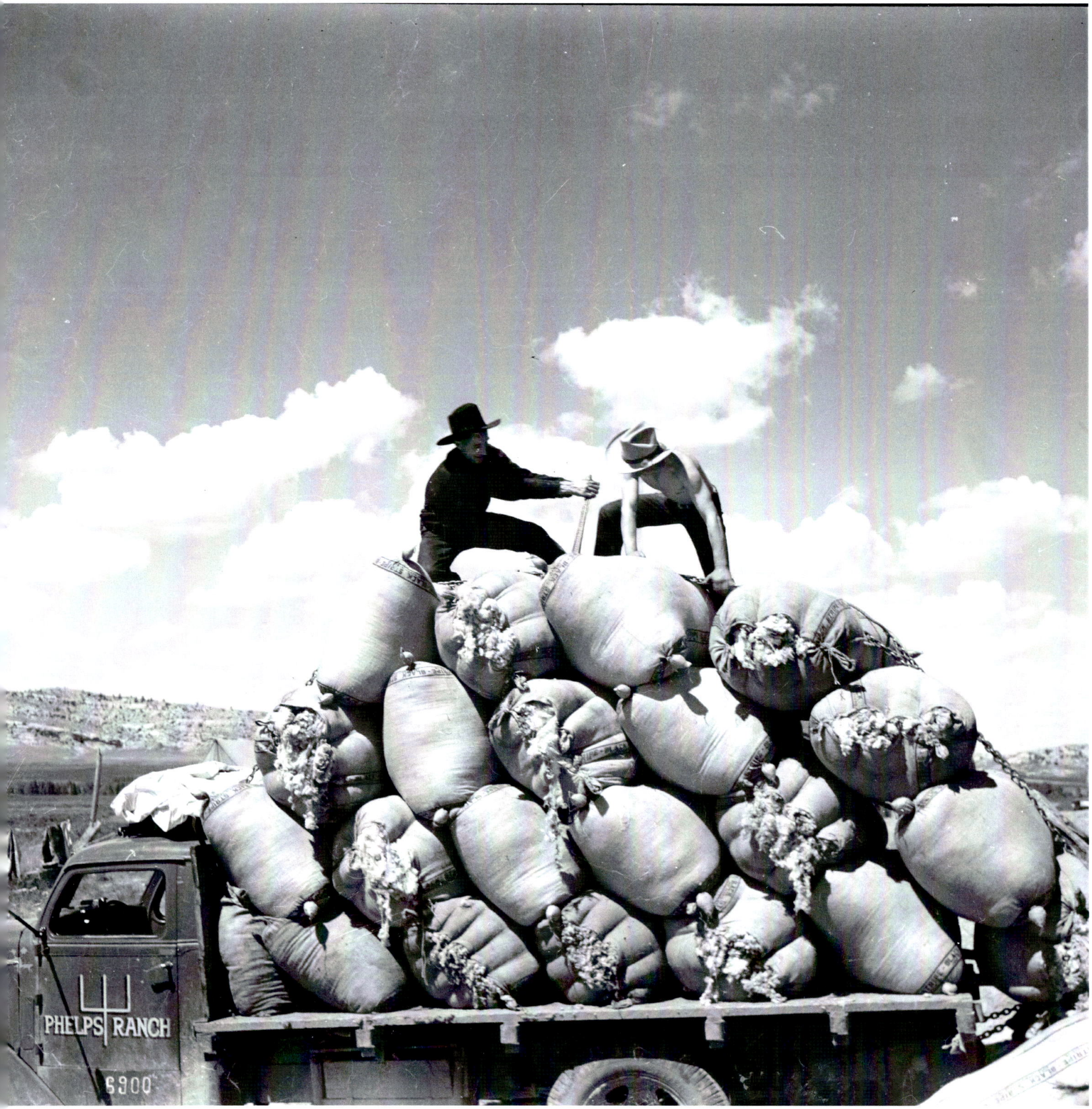
PHELPS RANCH
6900

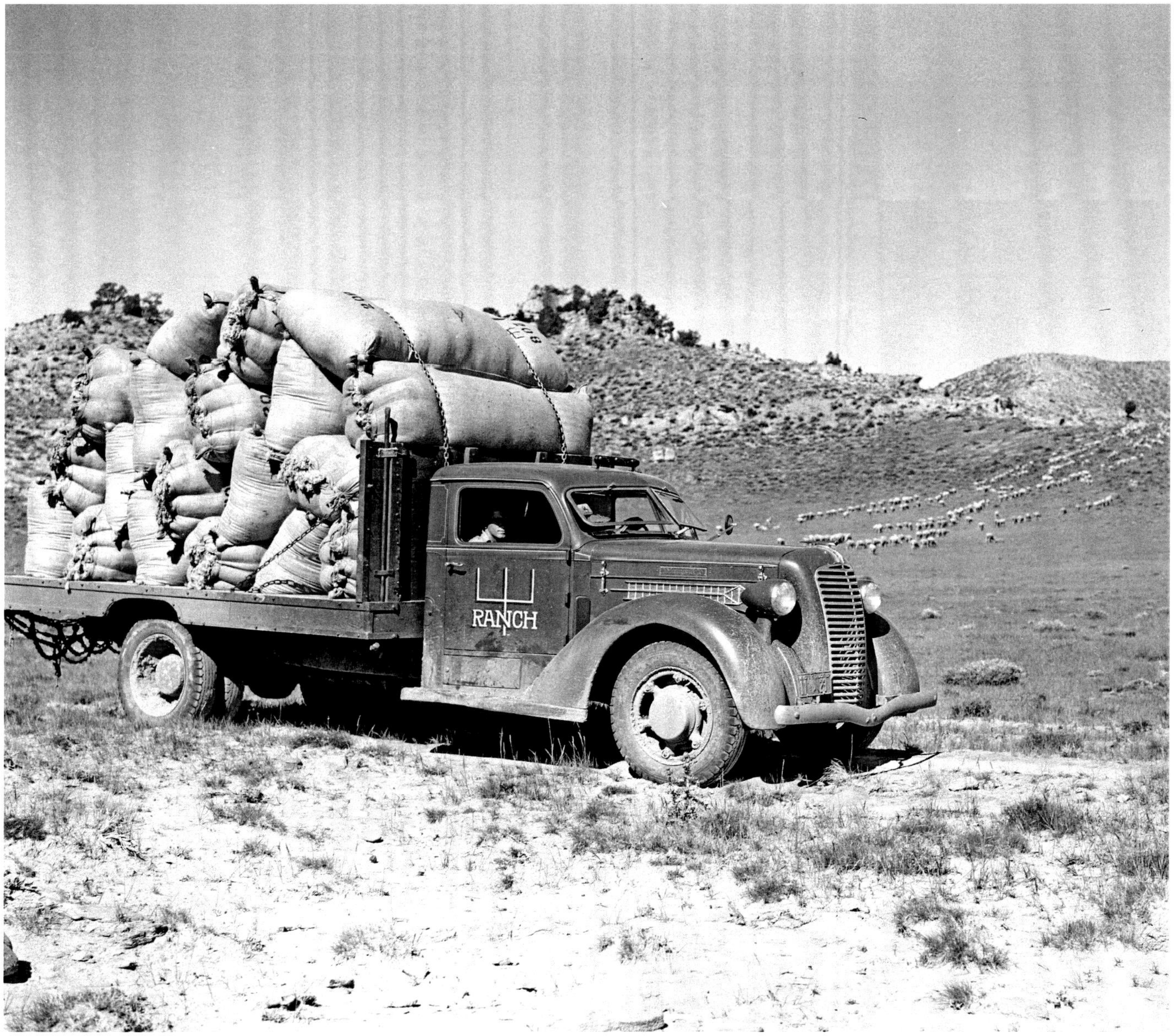
RANCH

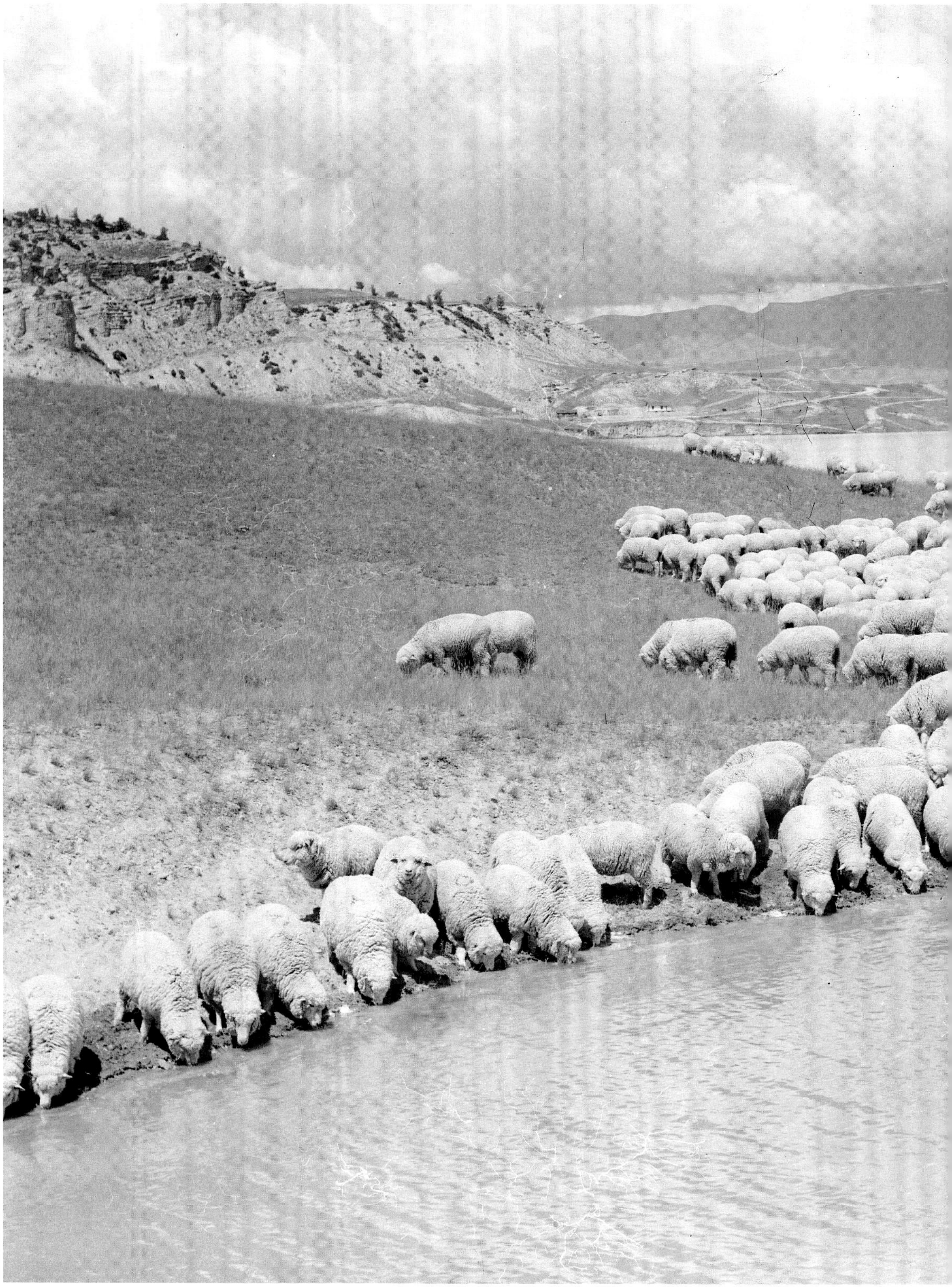

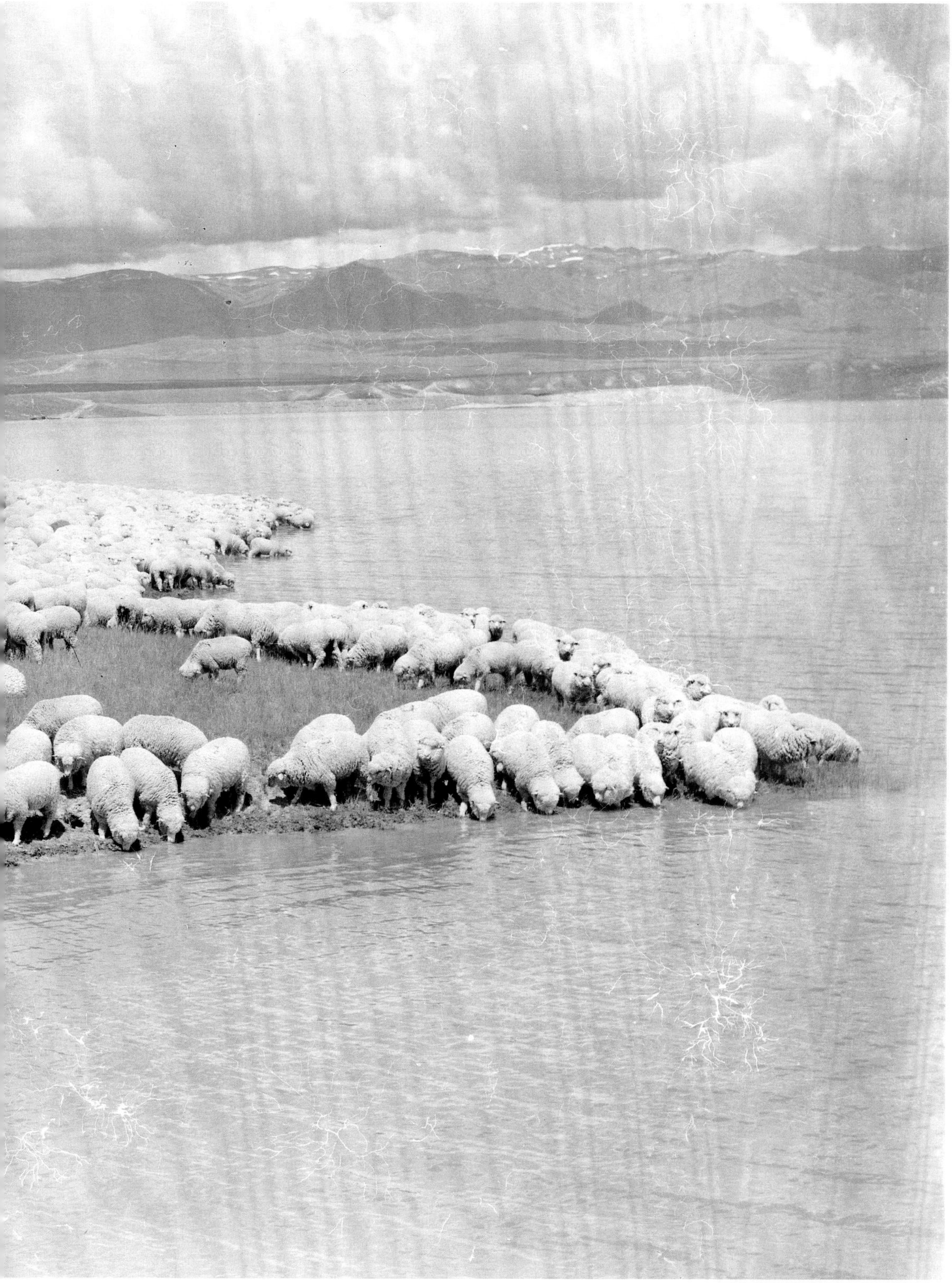

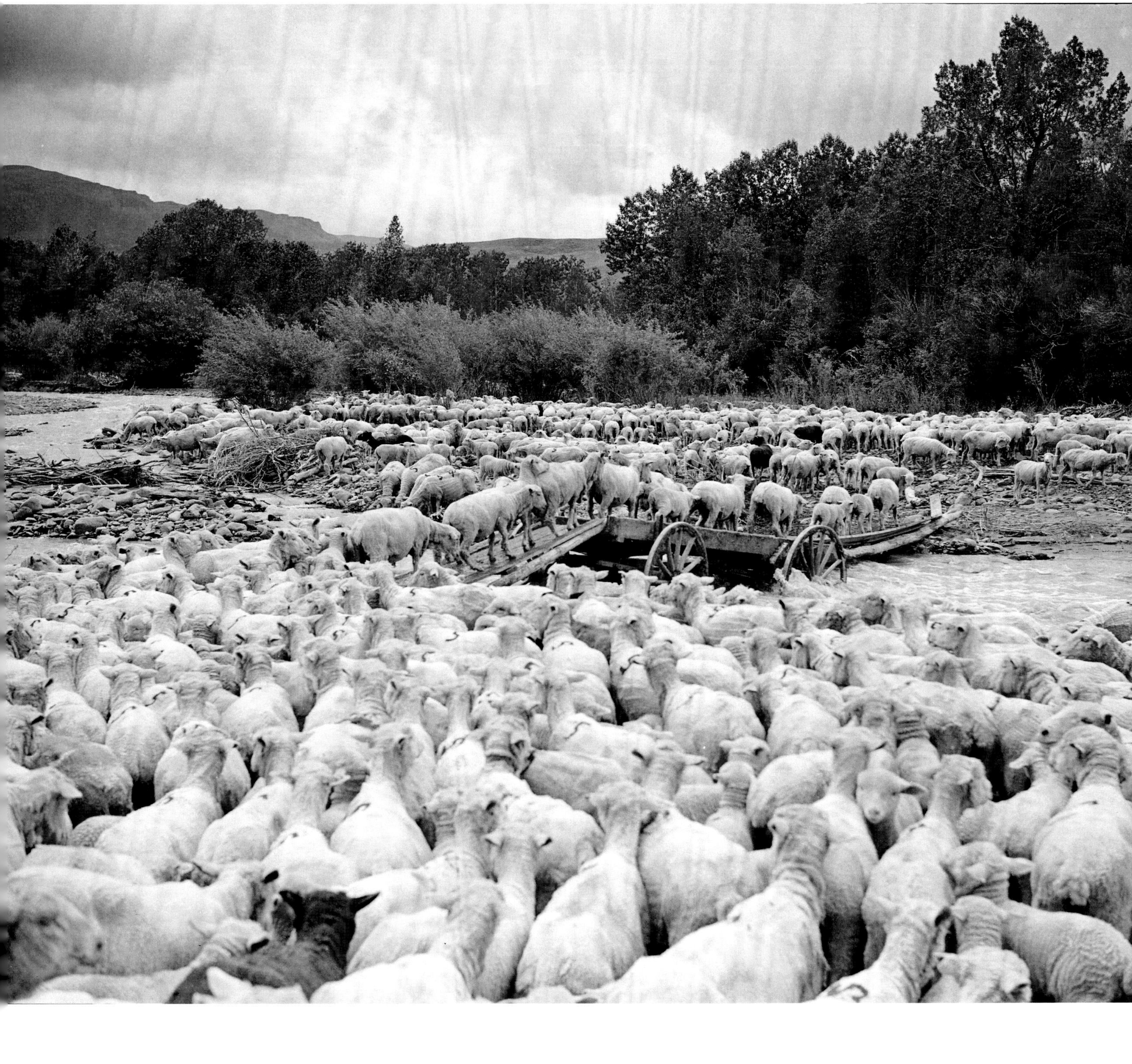

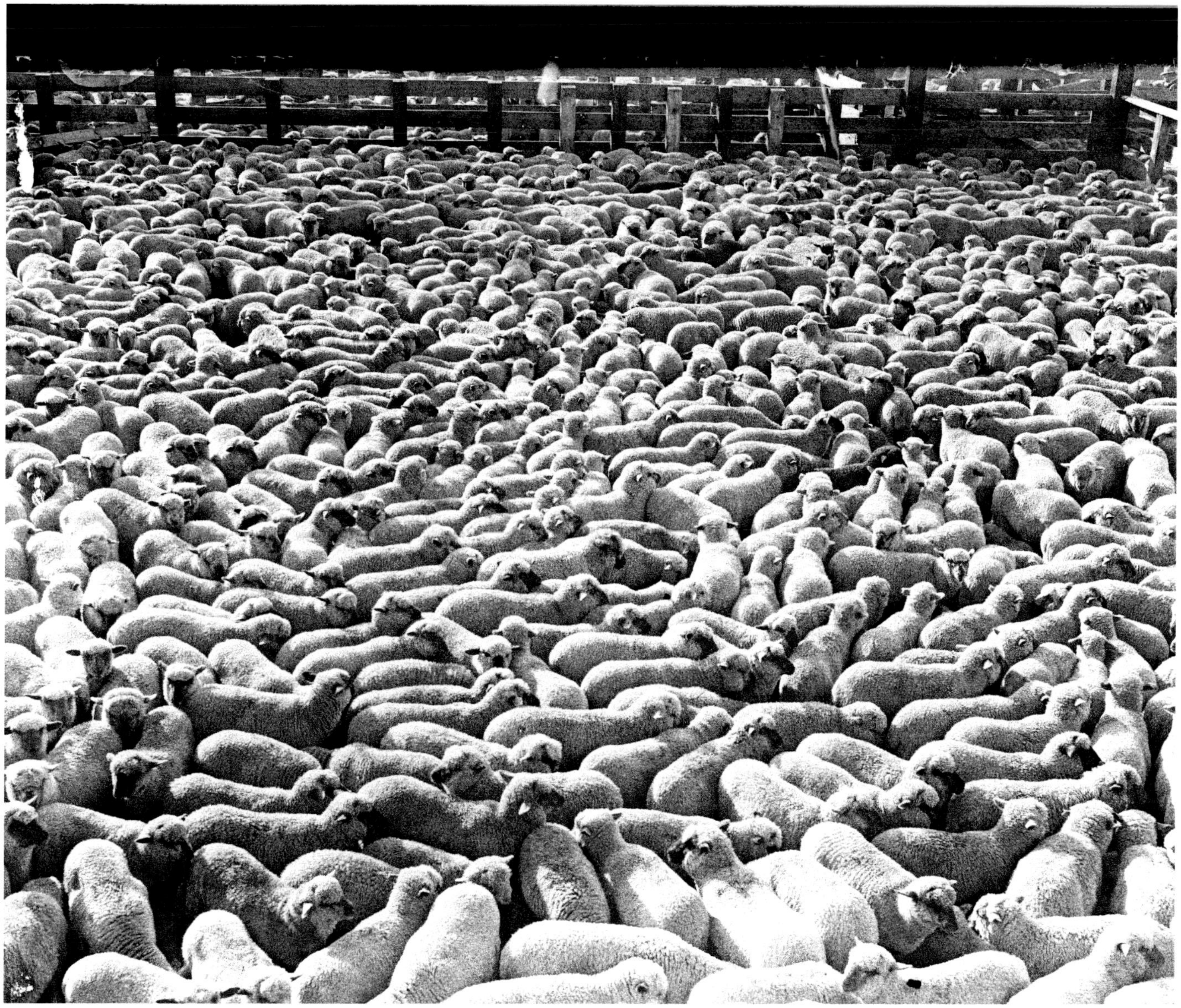

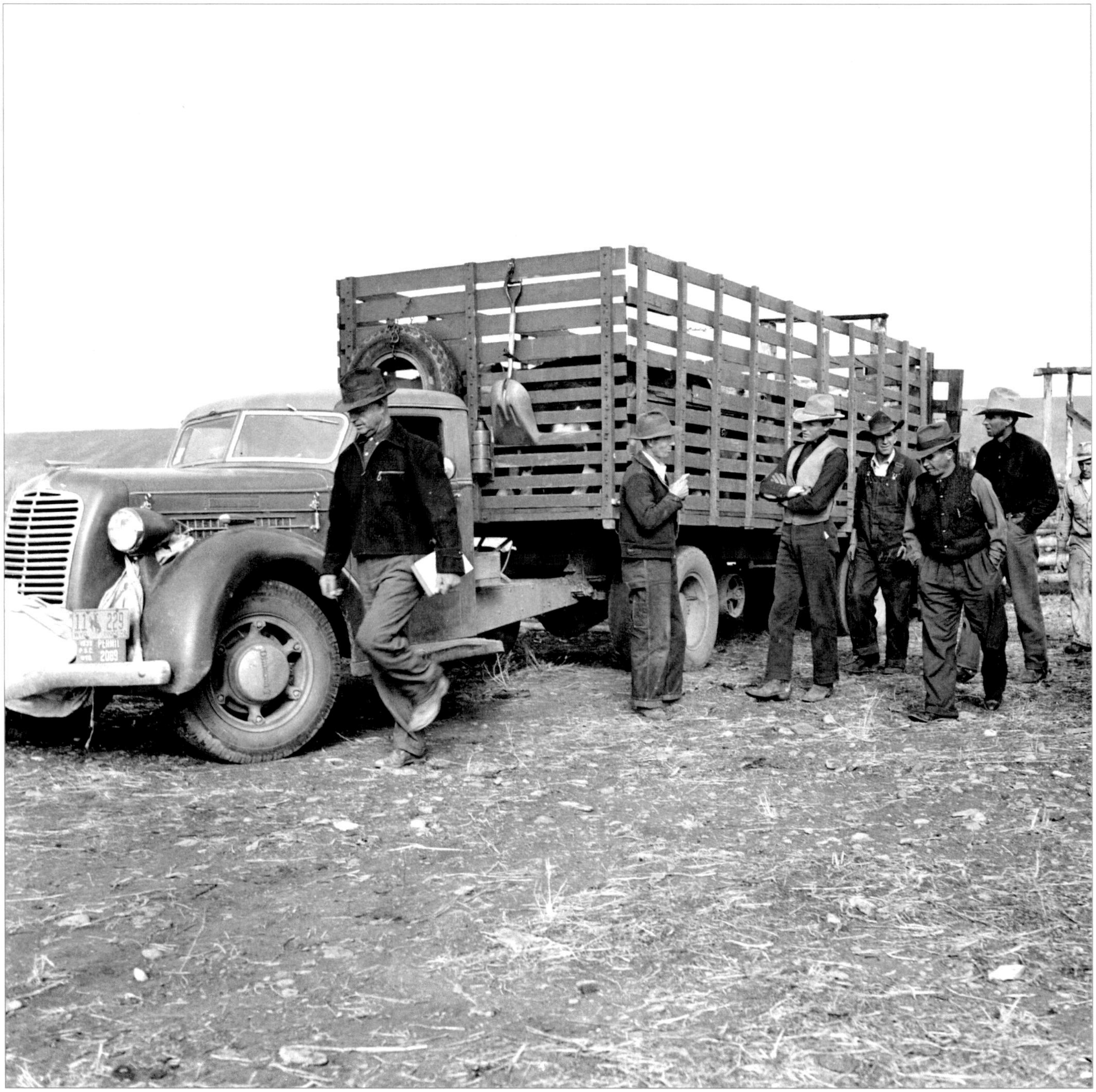

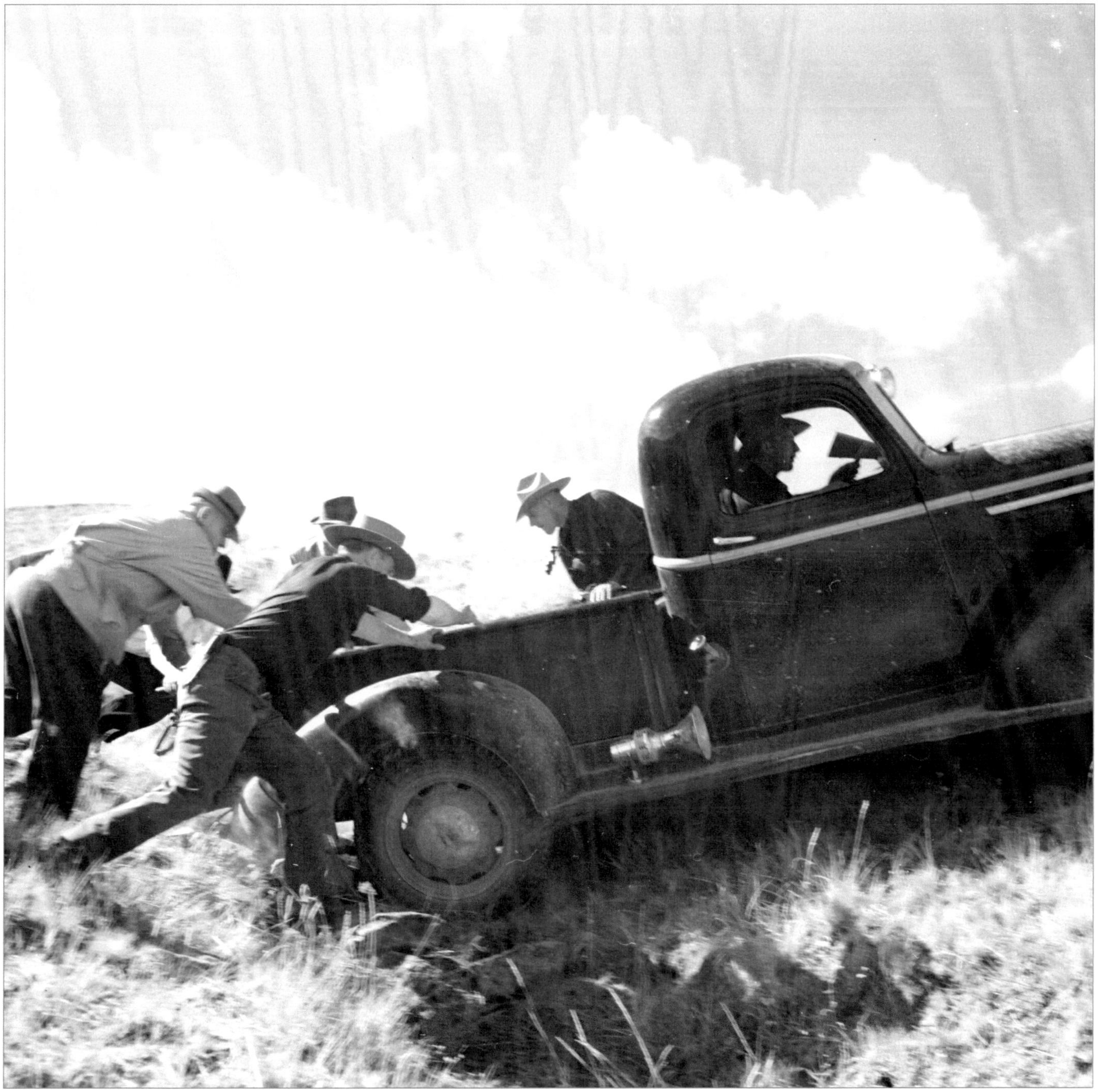

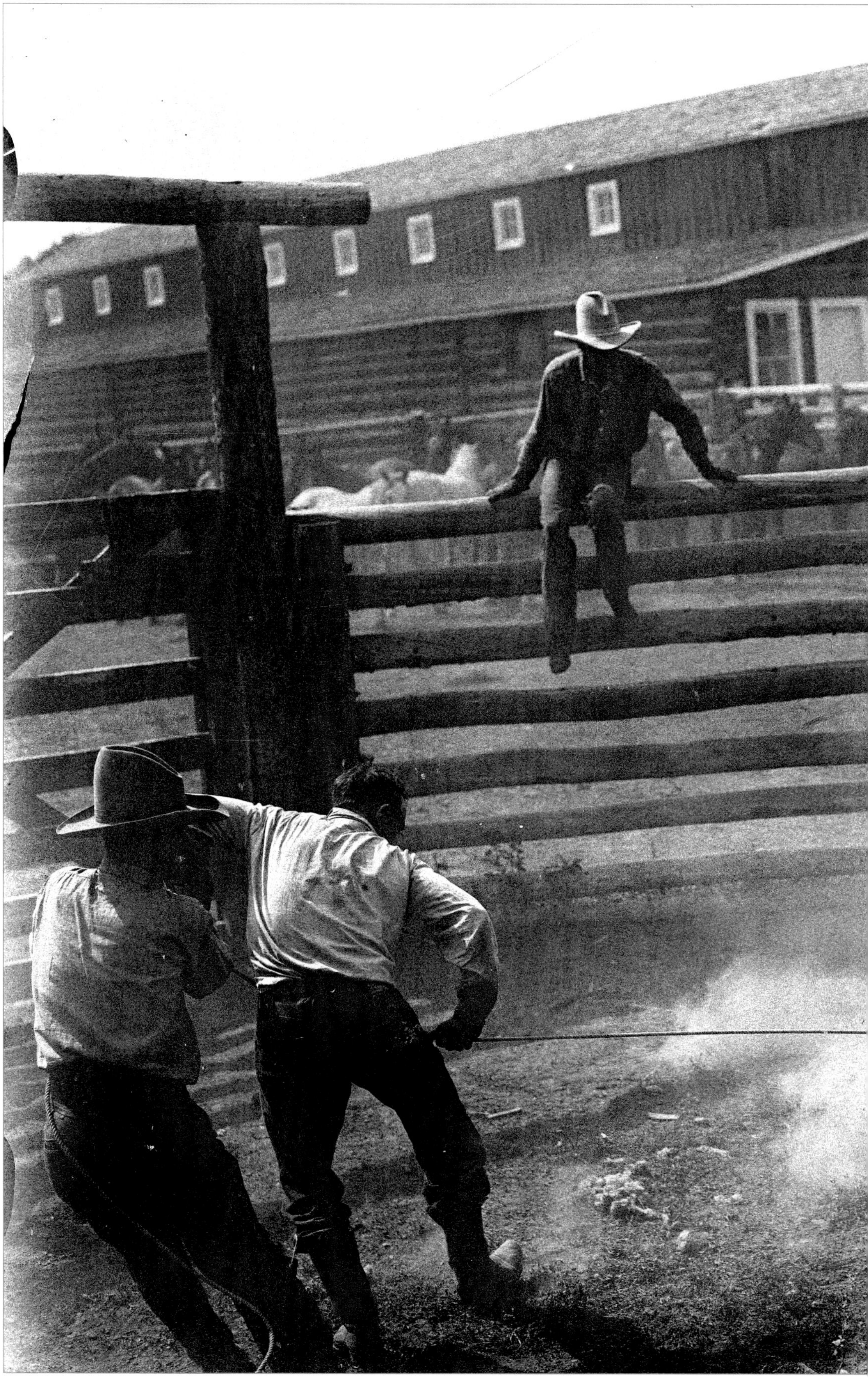

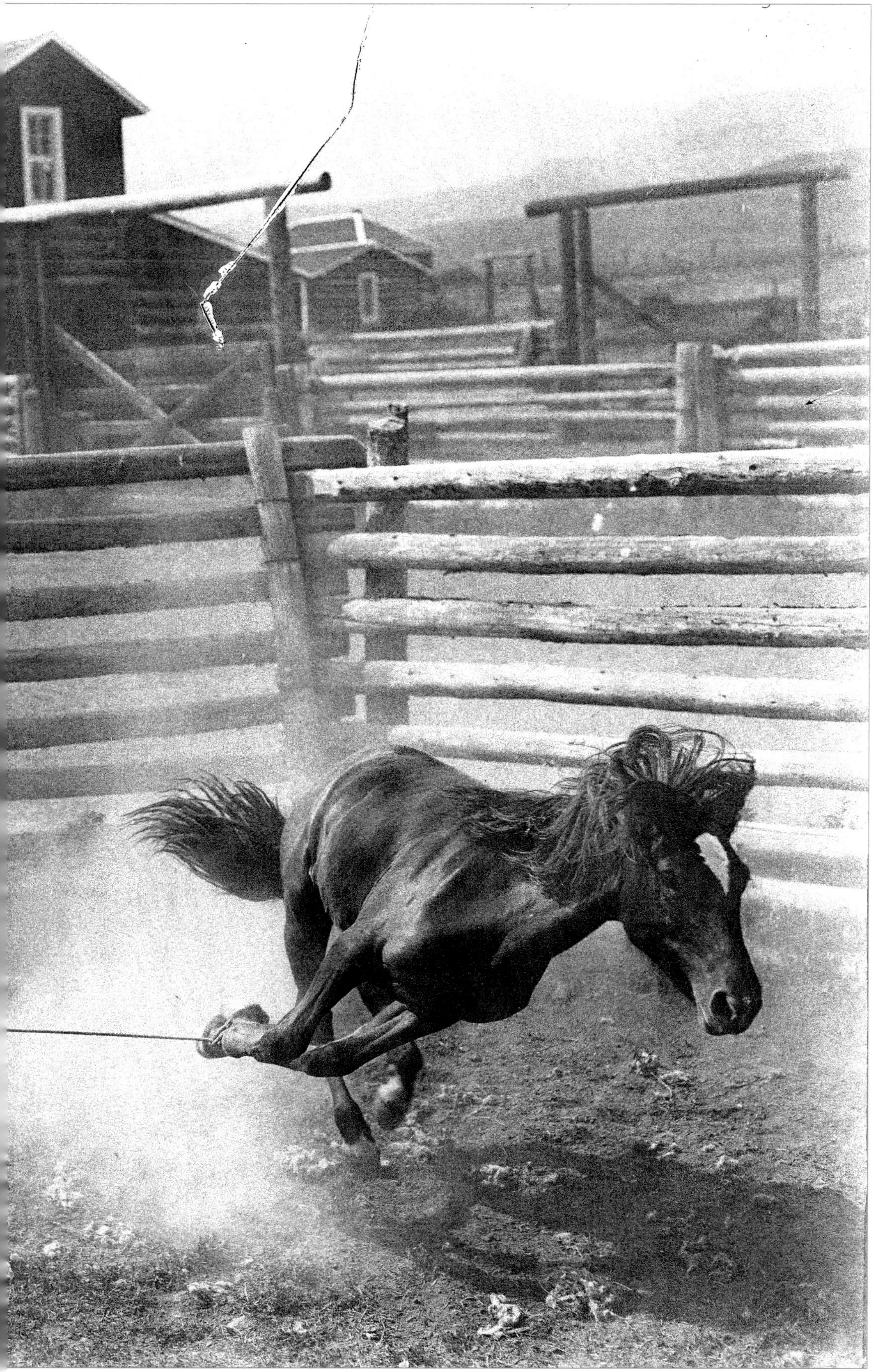

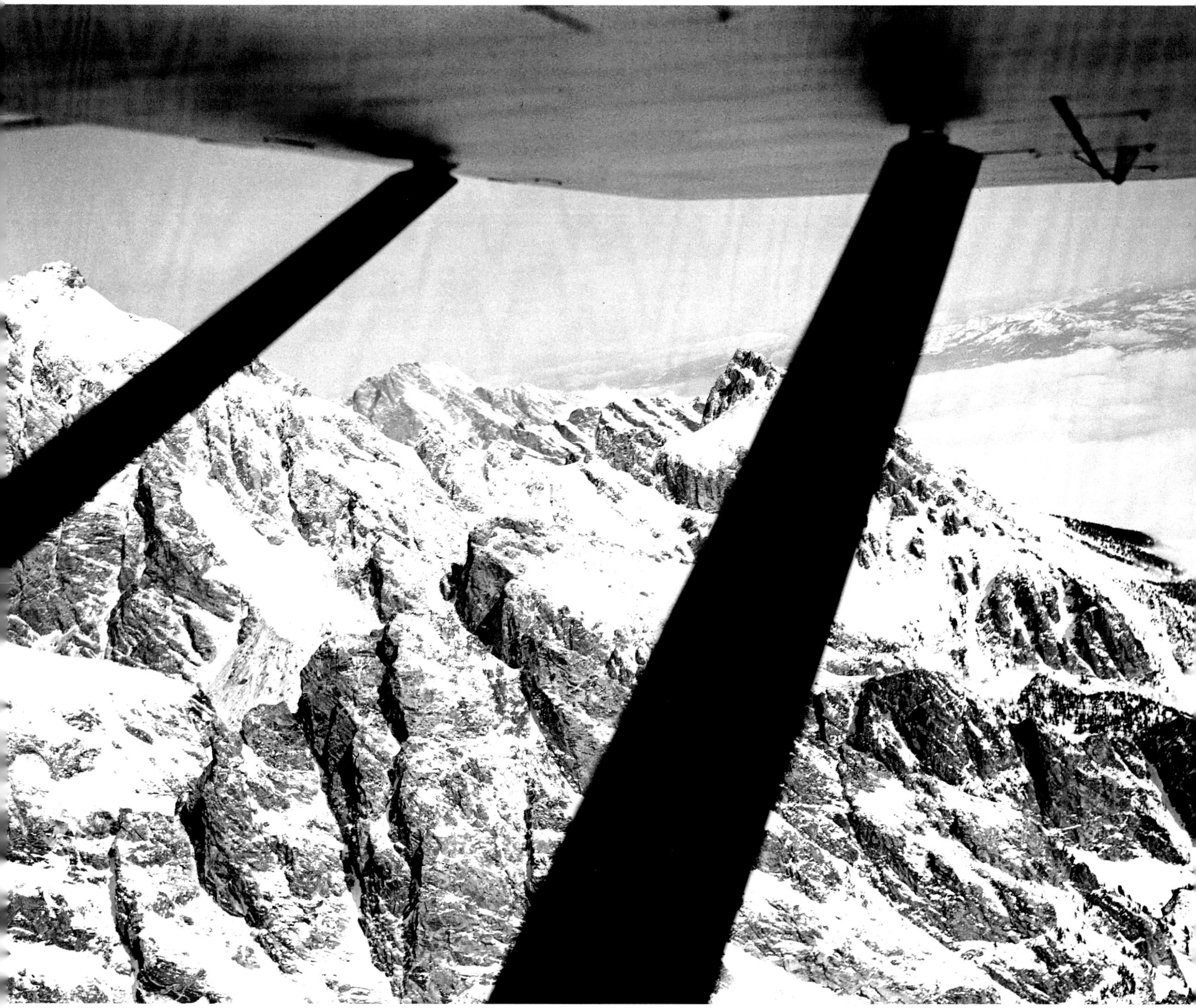

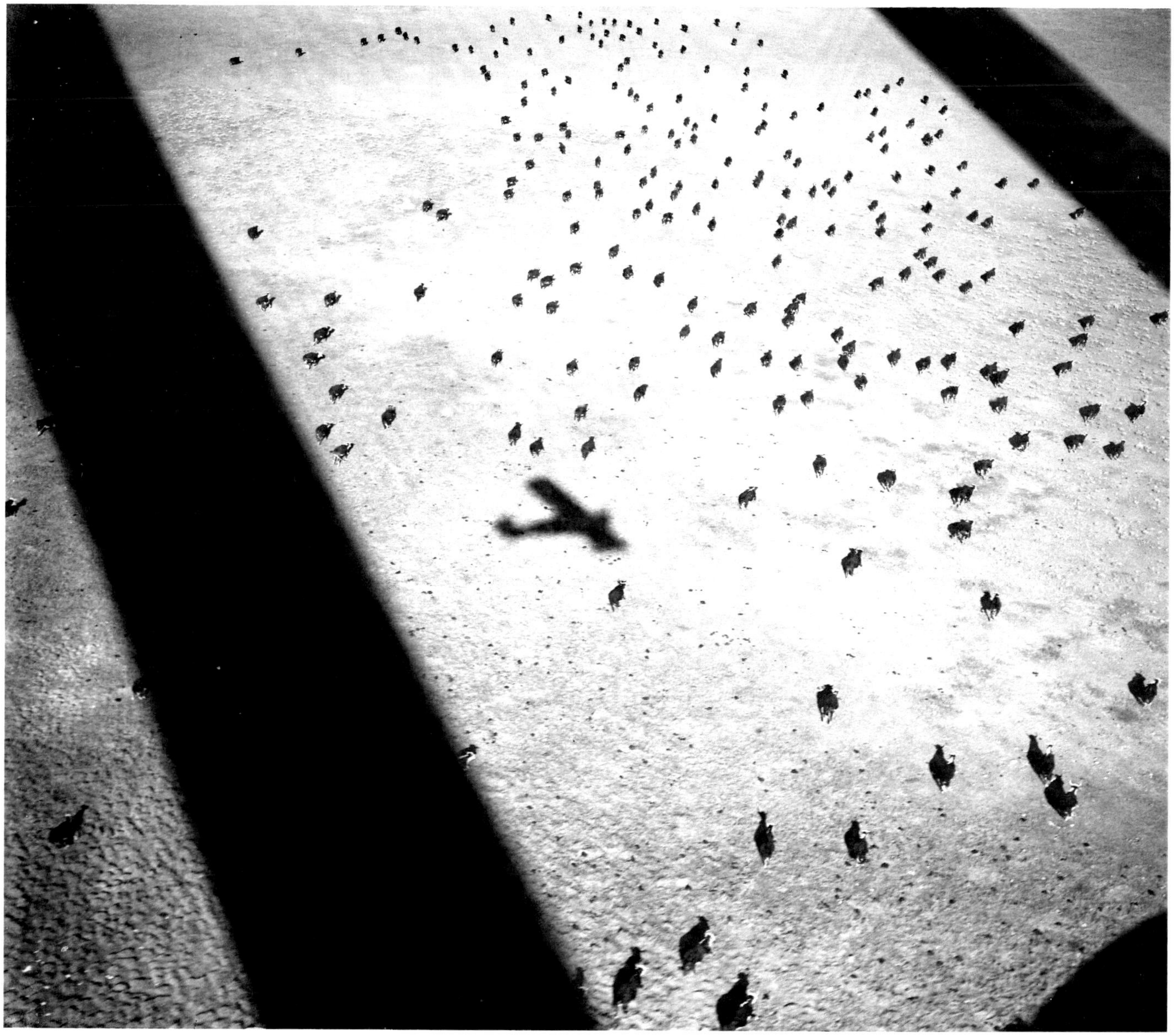

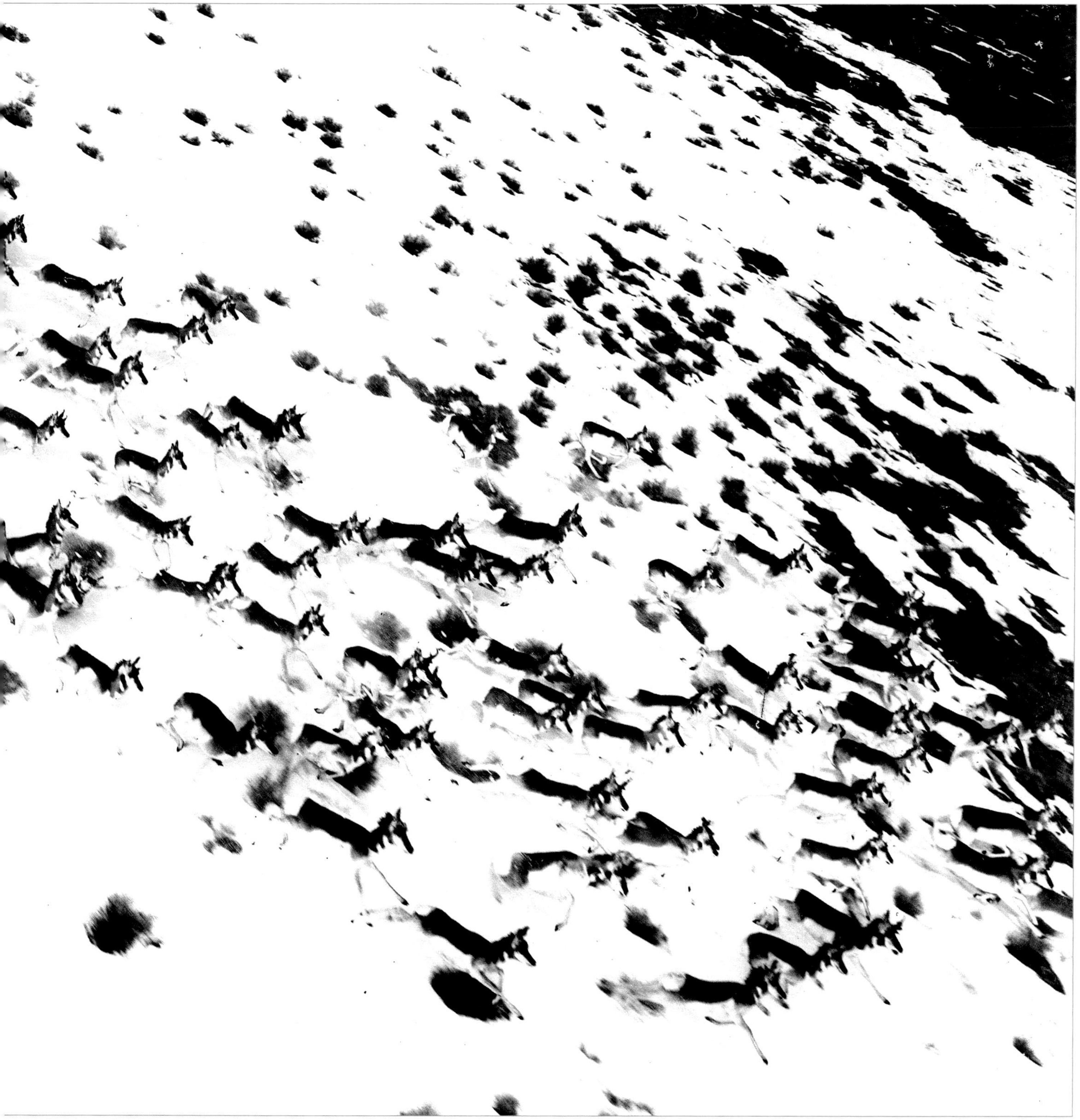

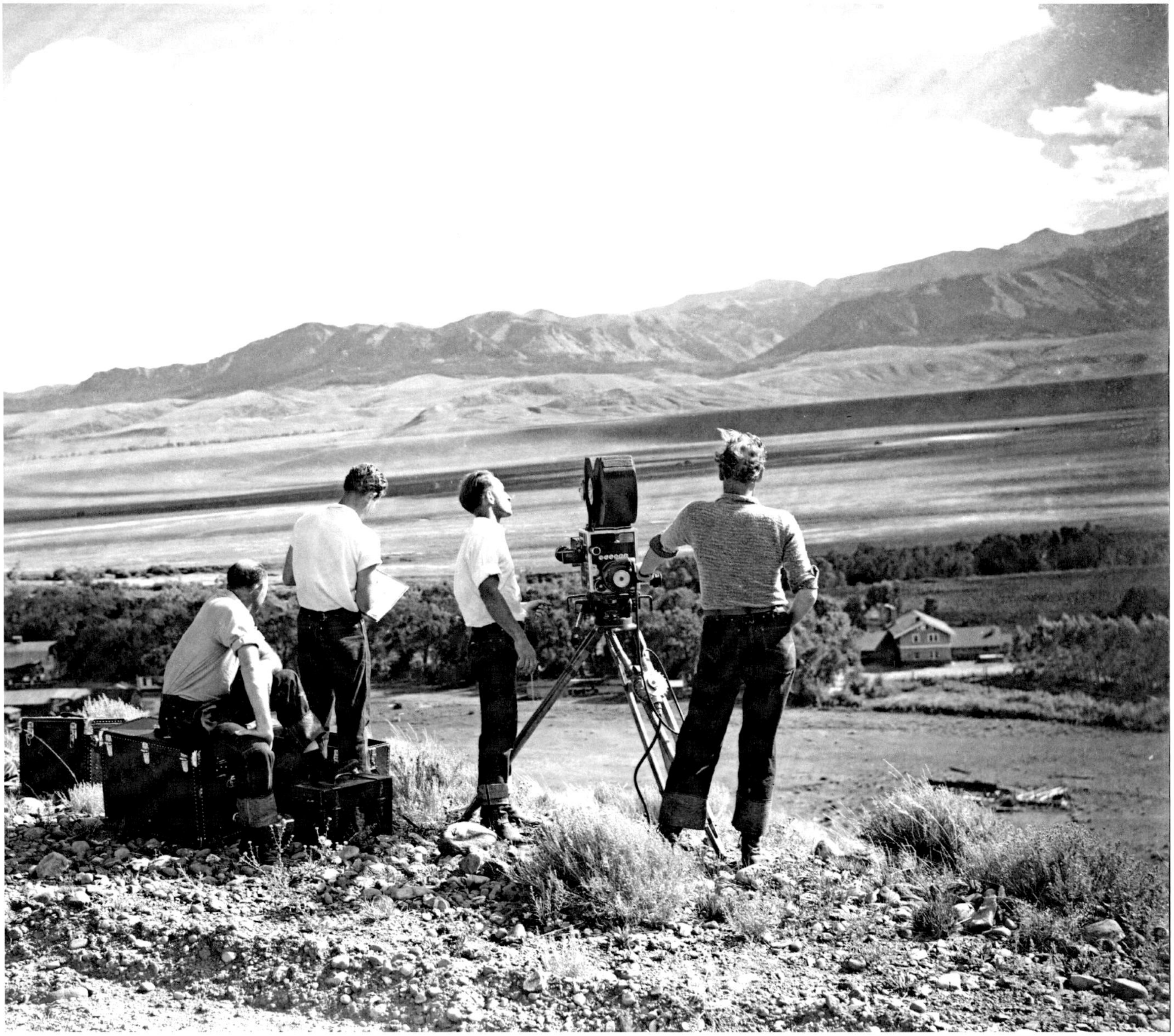

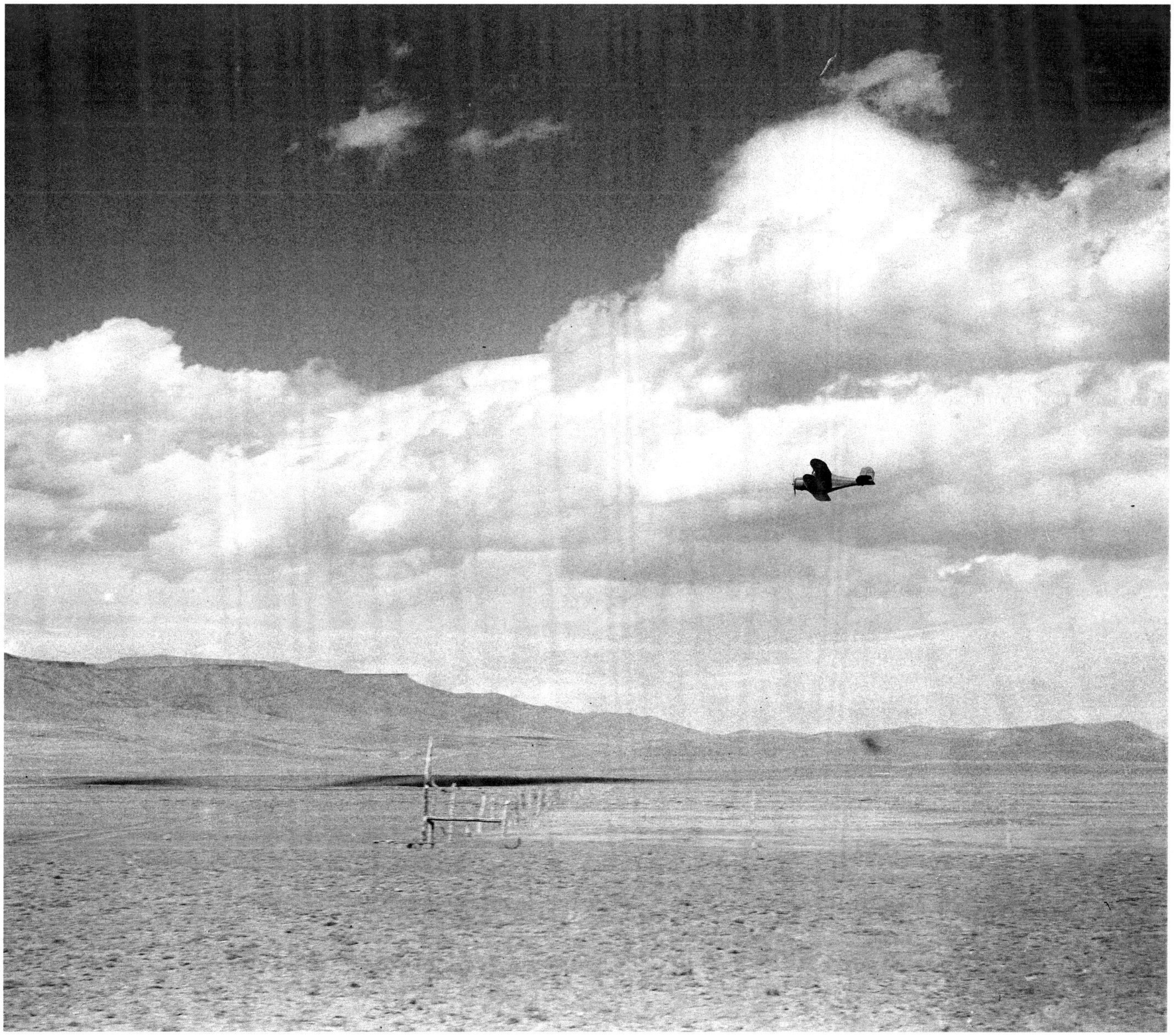

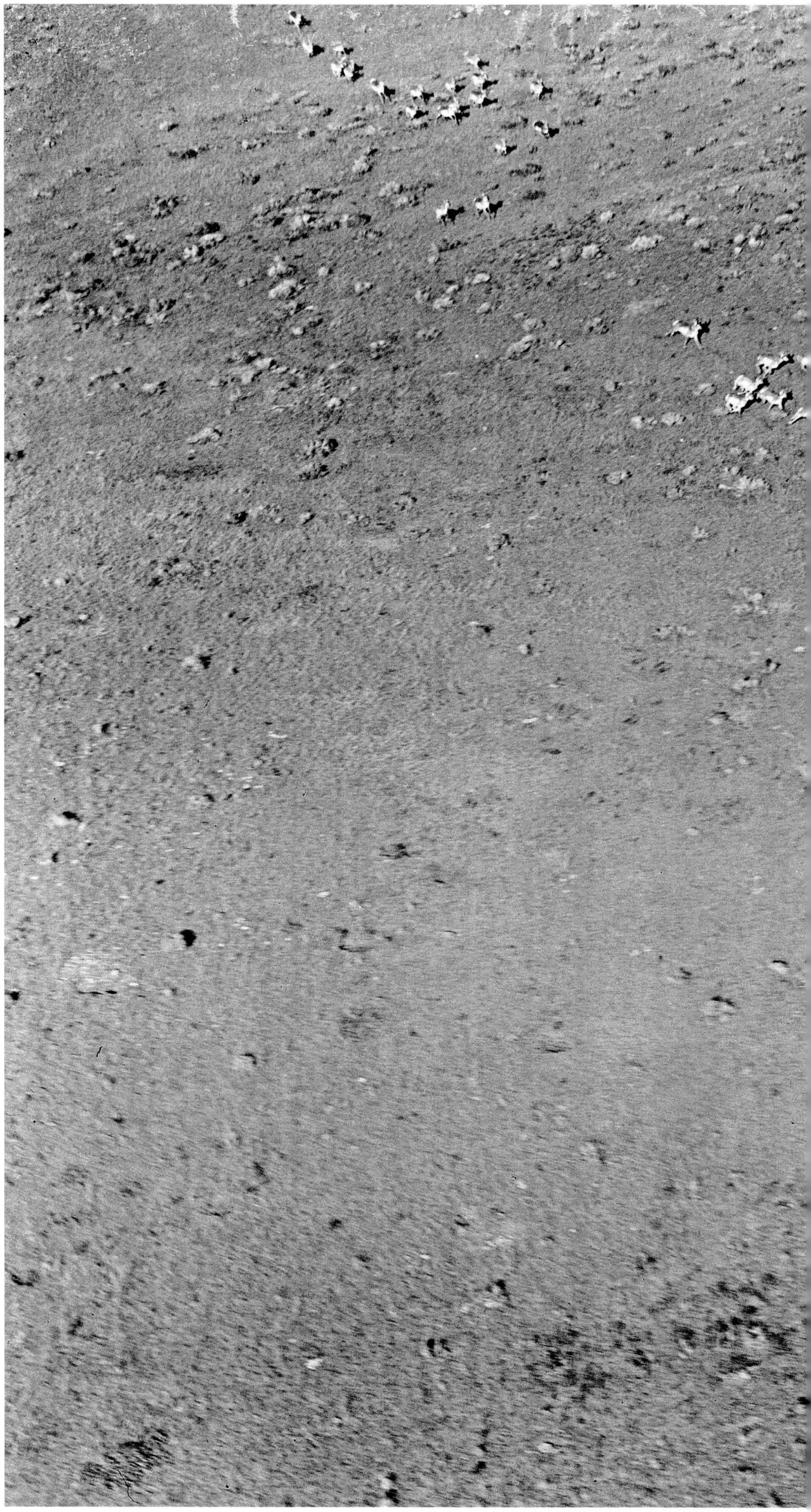

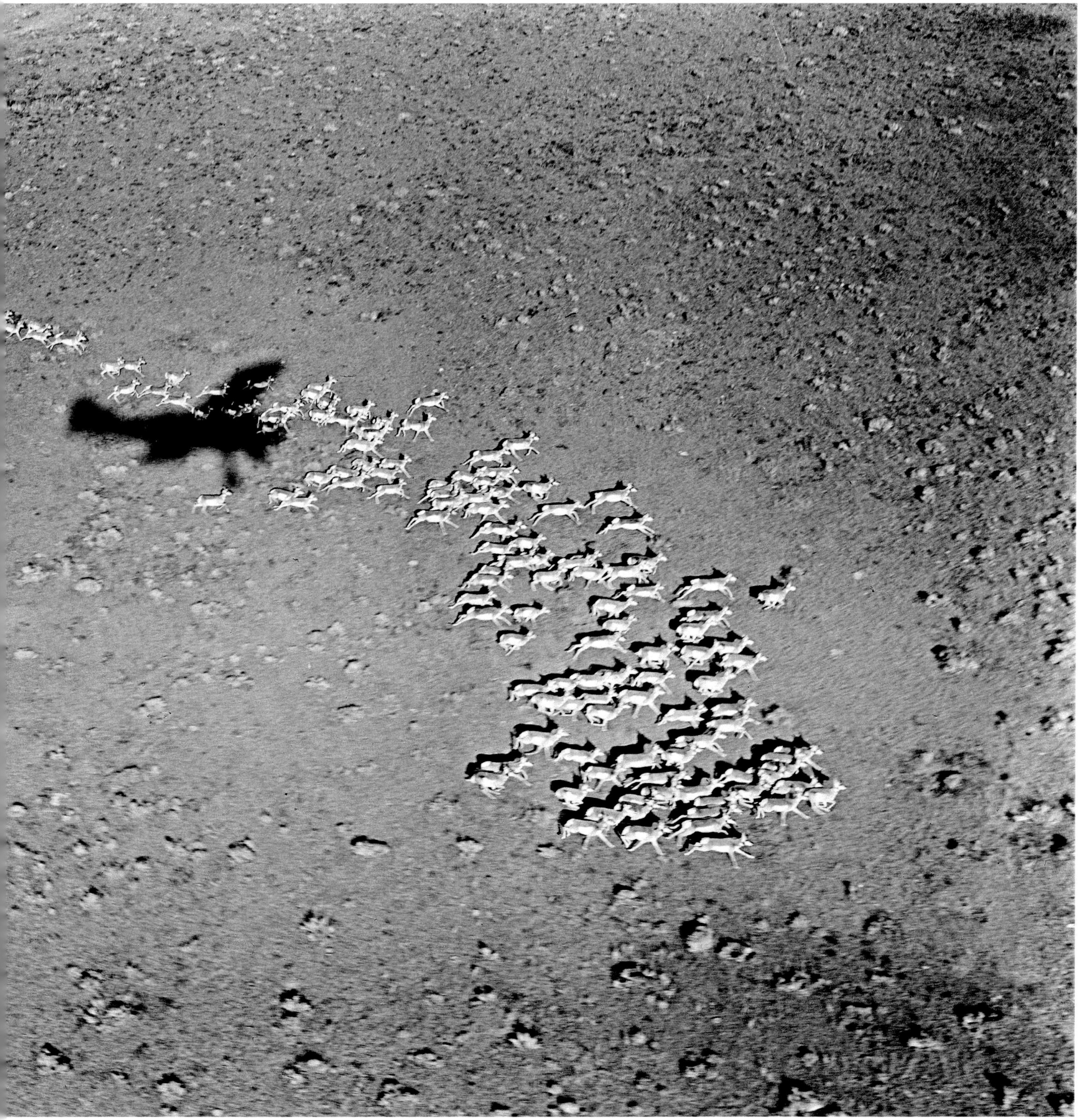

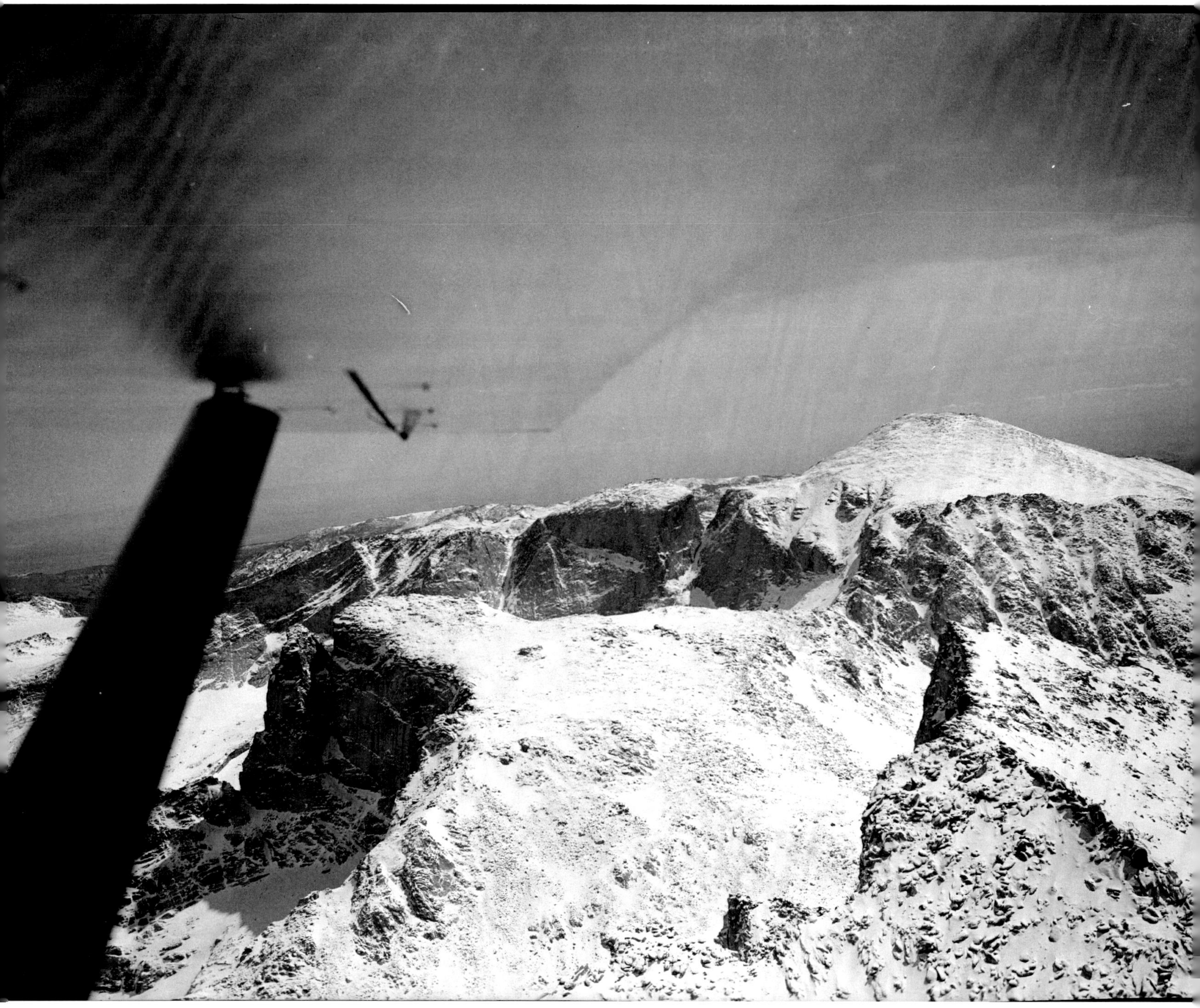

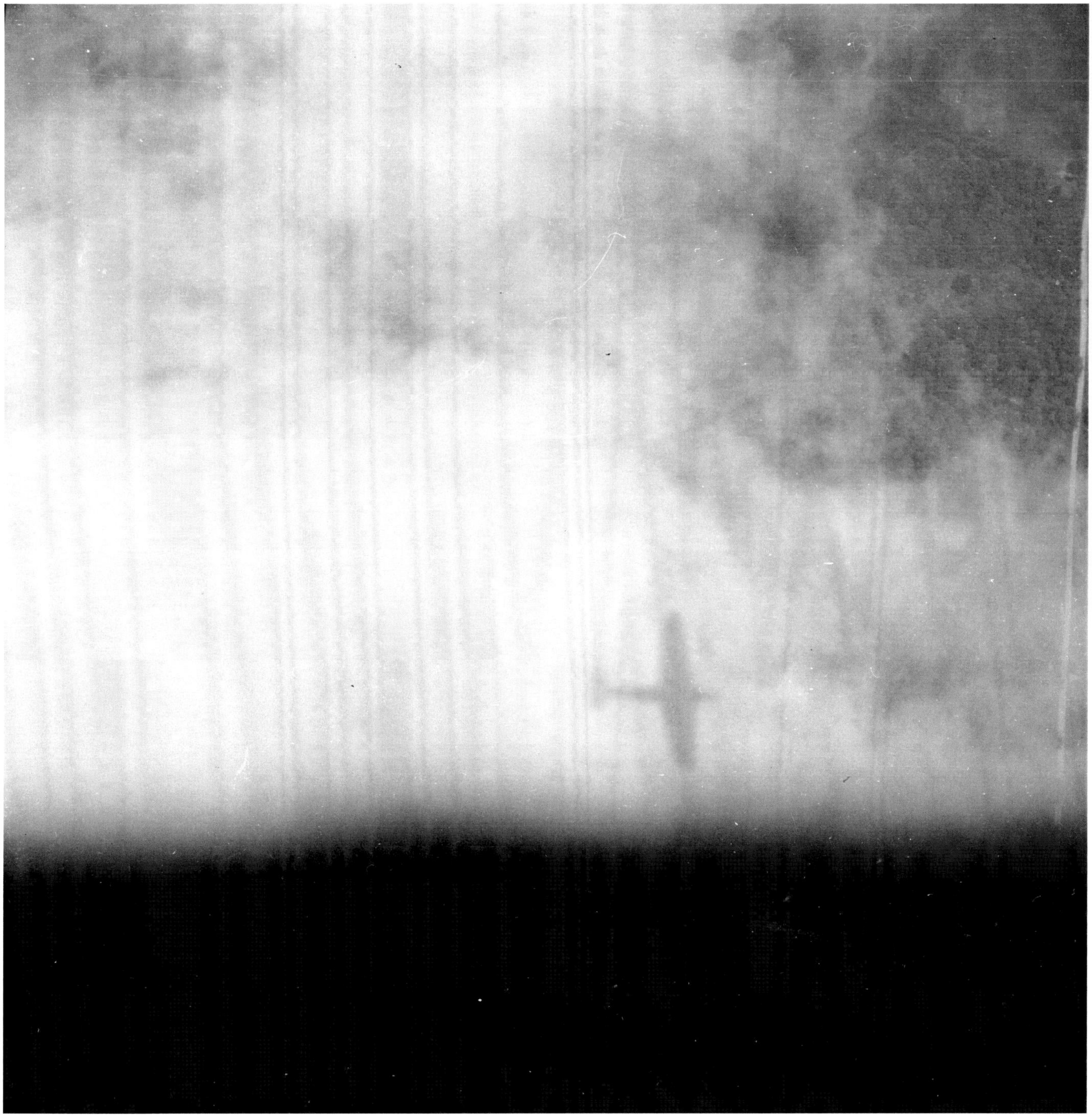

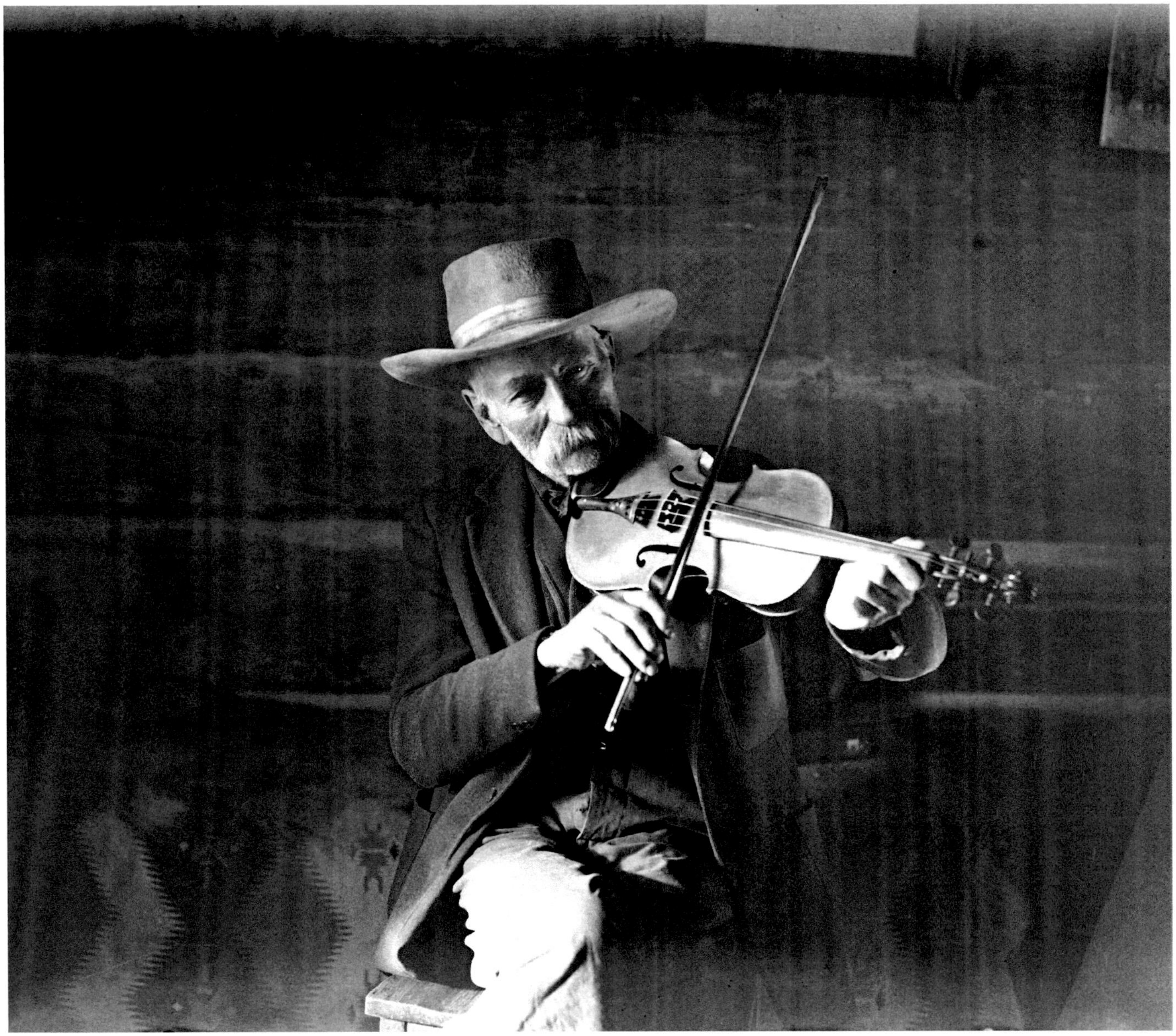

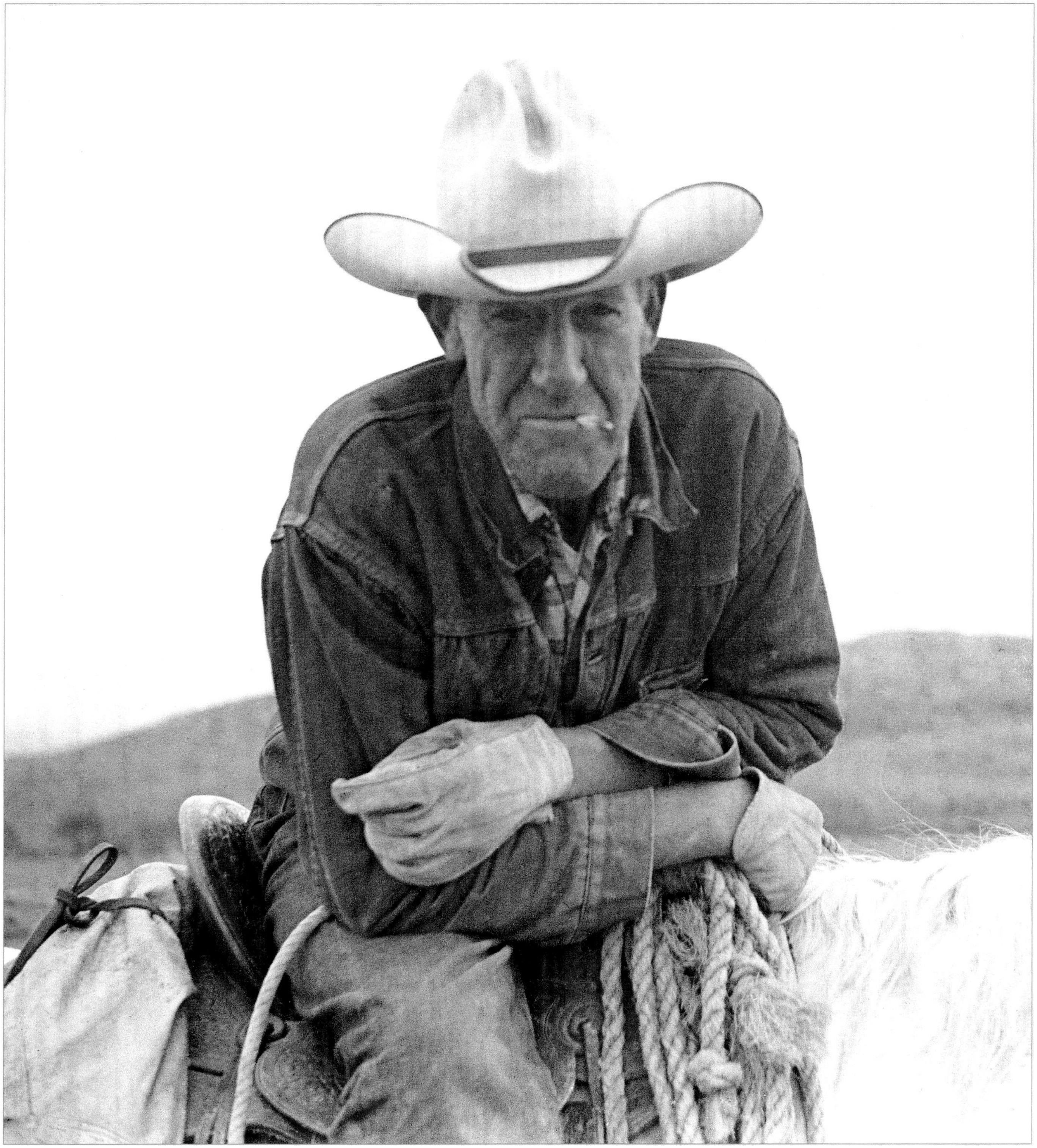

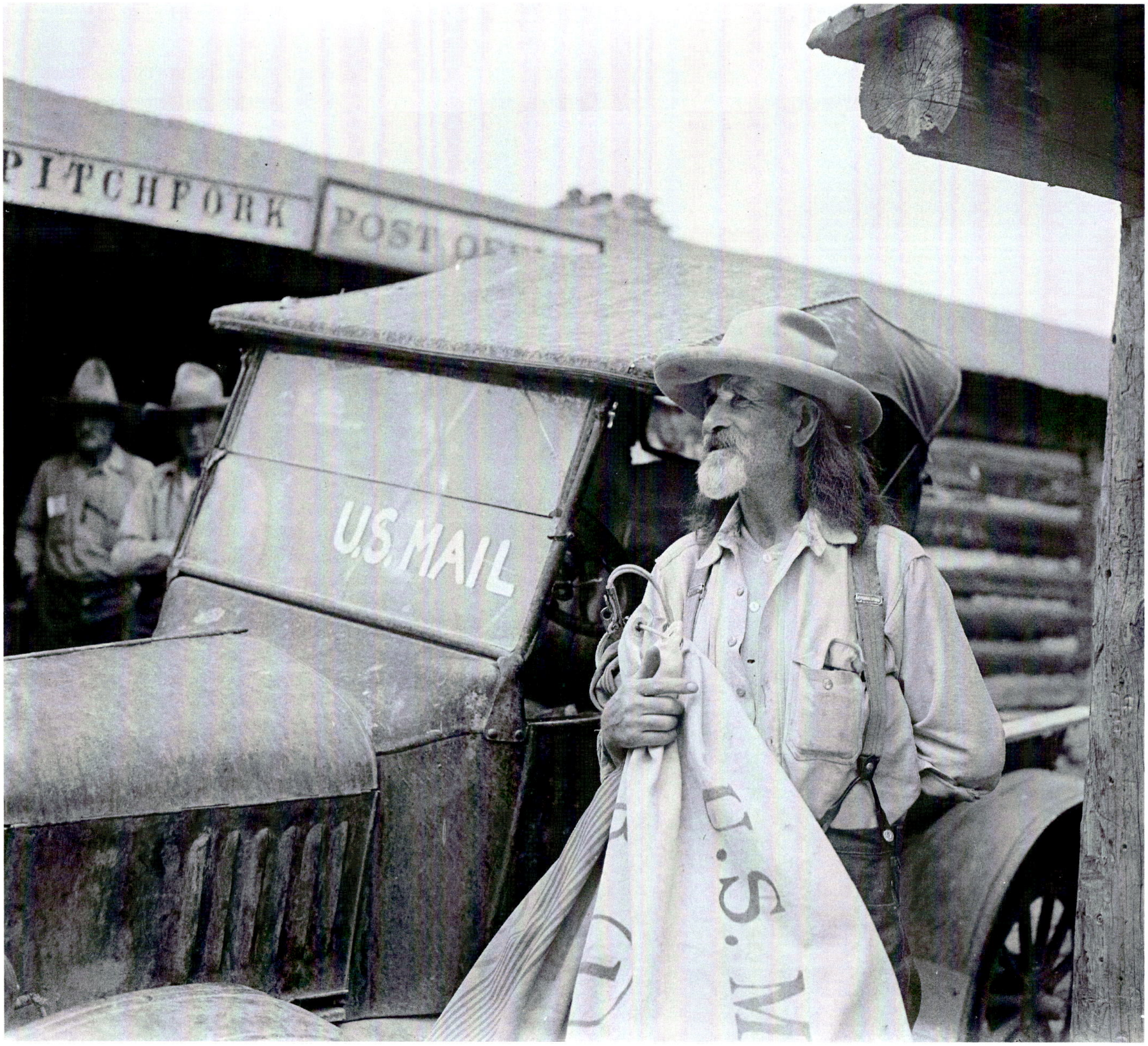
PITCHFORK
POST OFF
U.S. MAIL
U.S. M

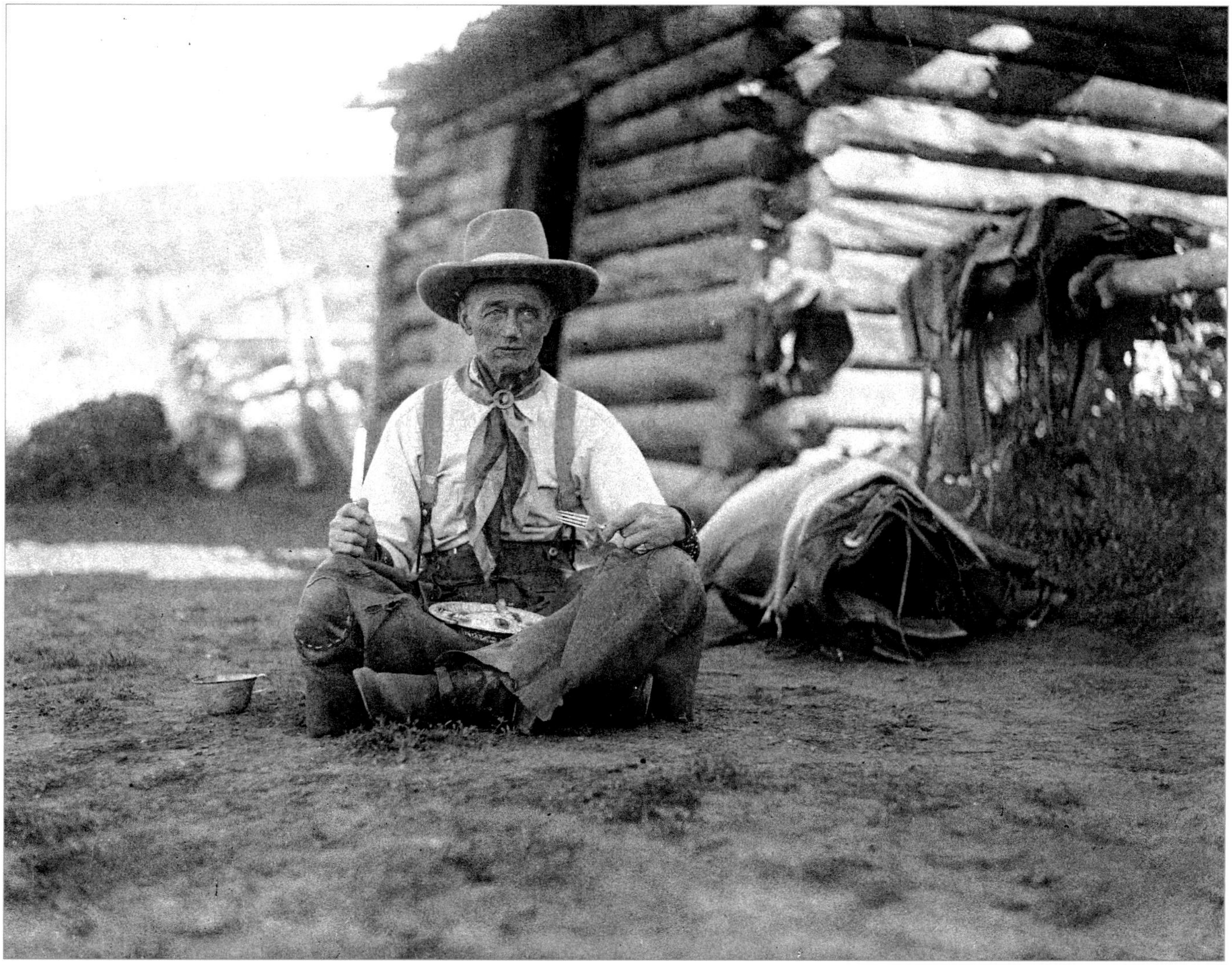

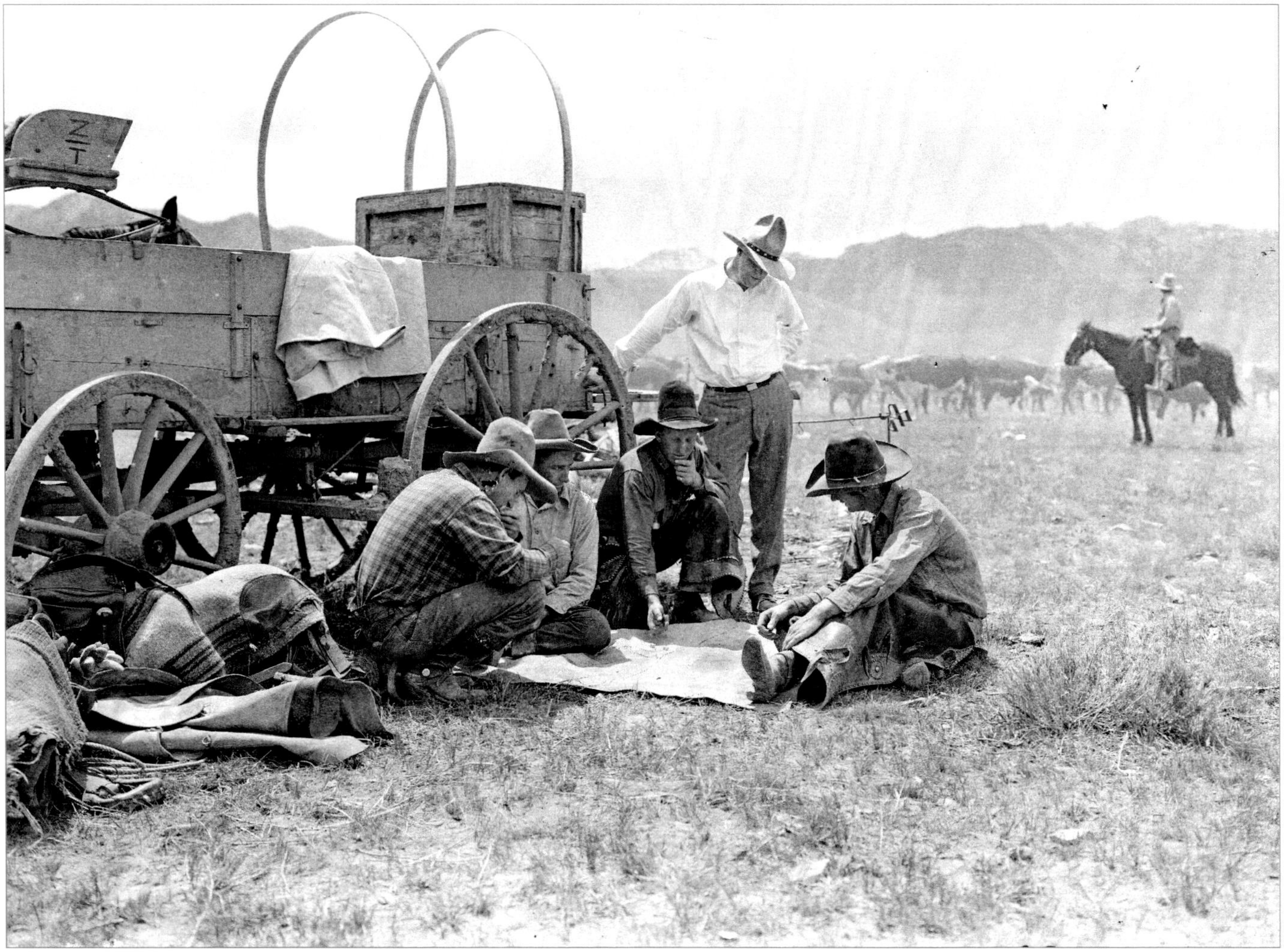

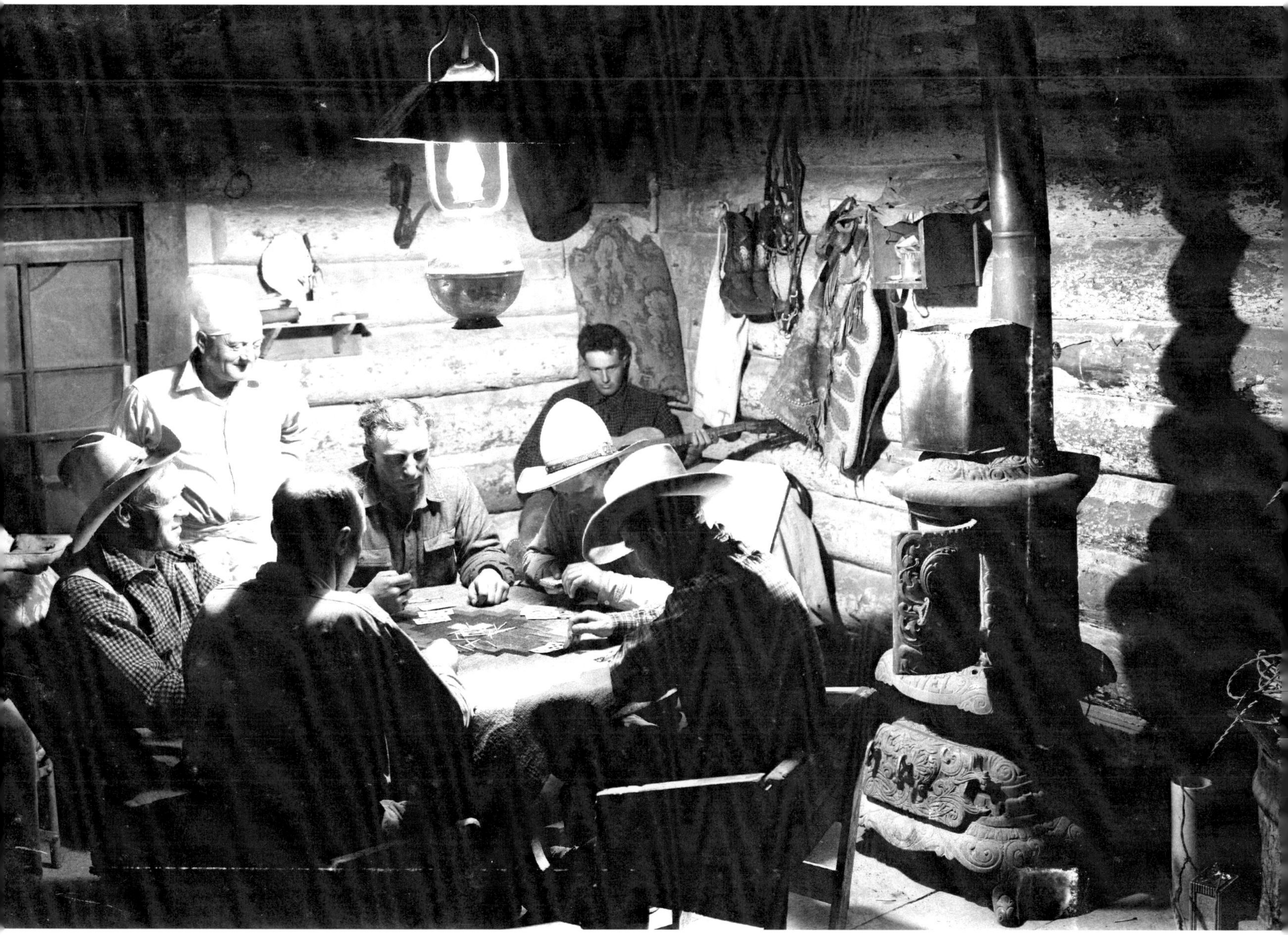

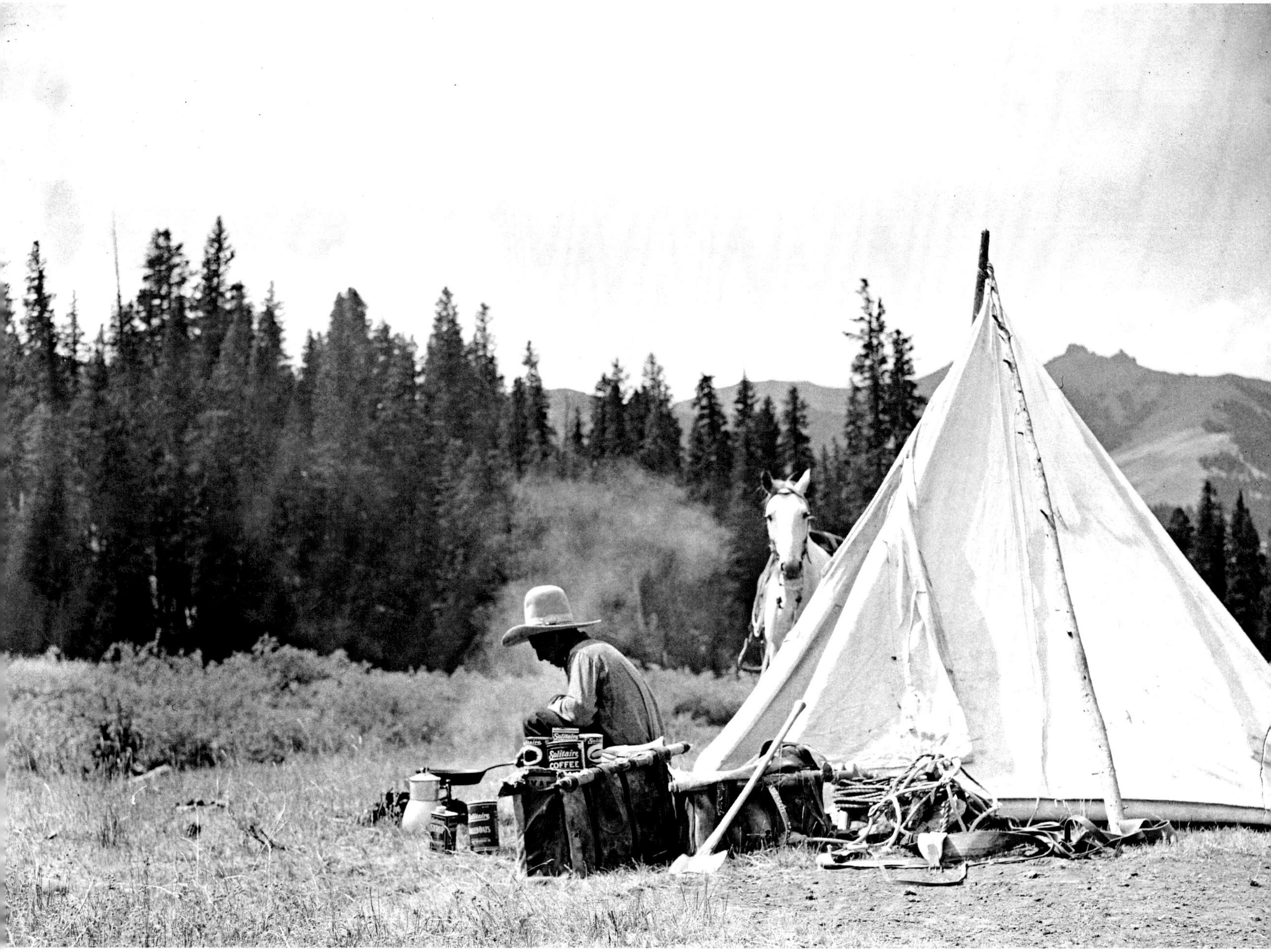
Solitaire
COFFEE

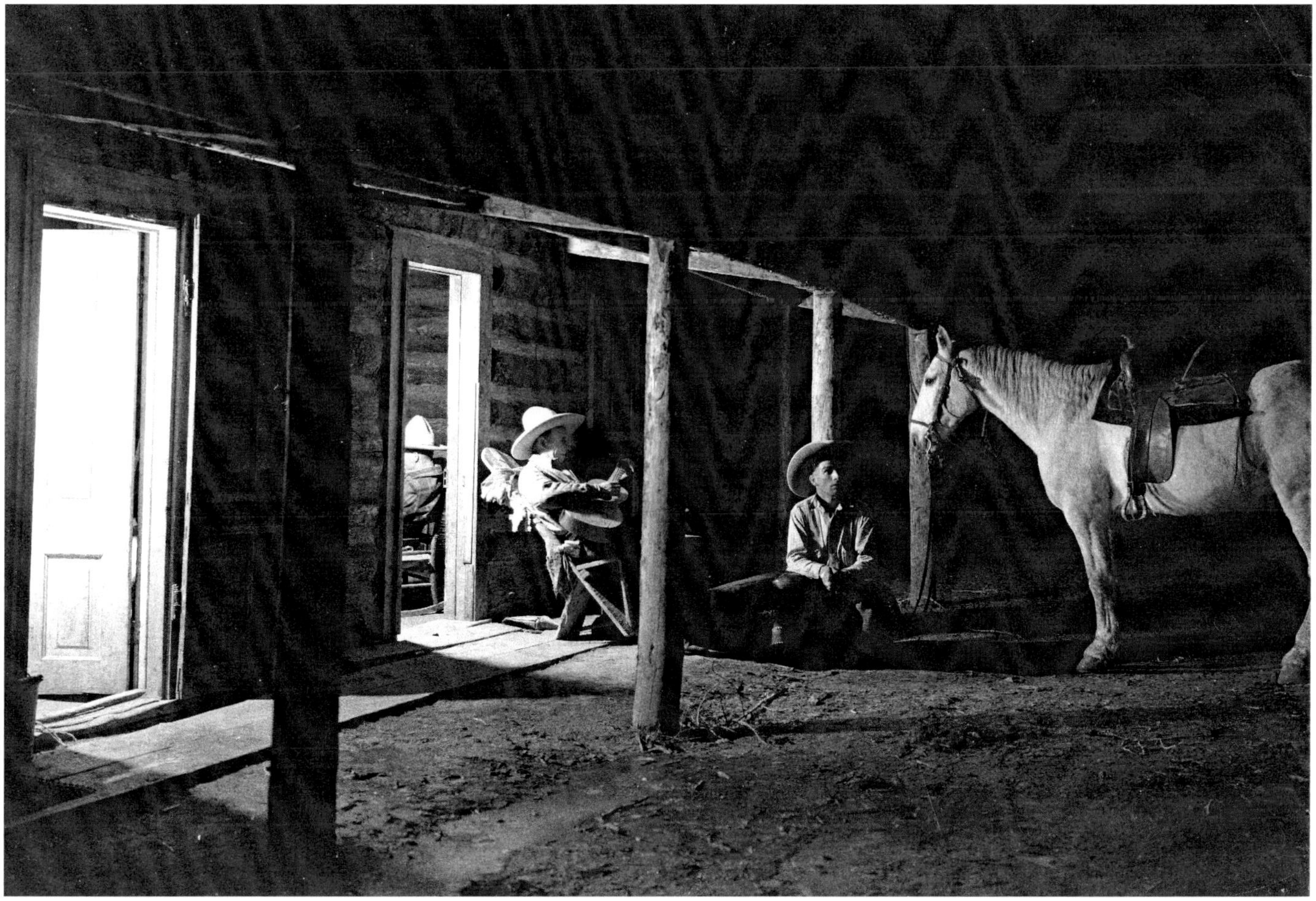

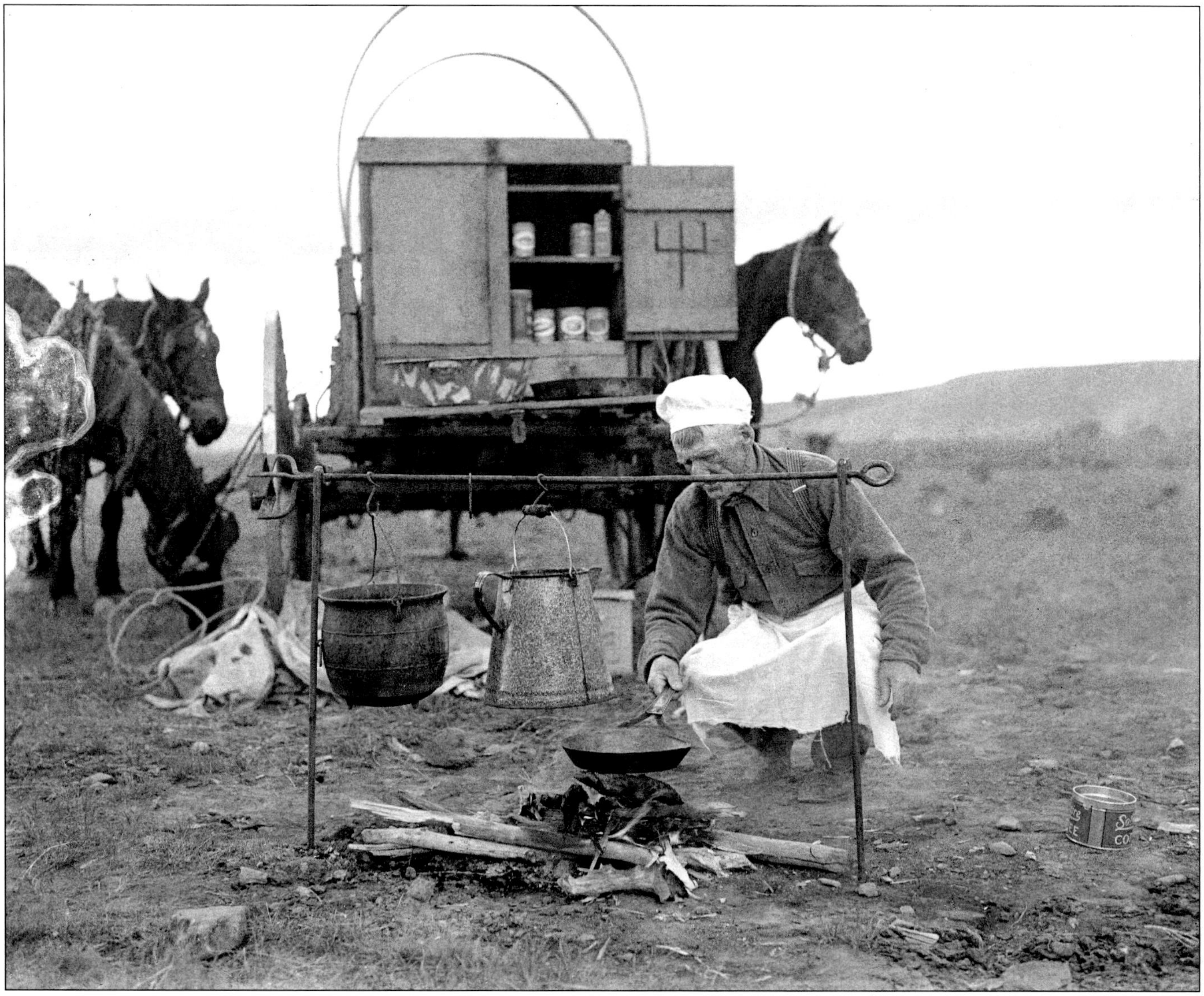

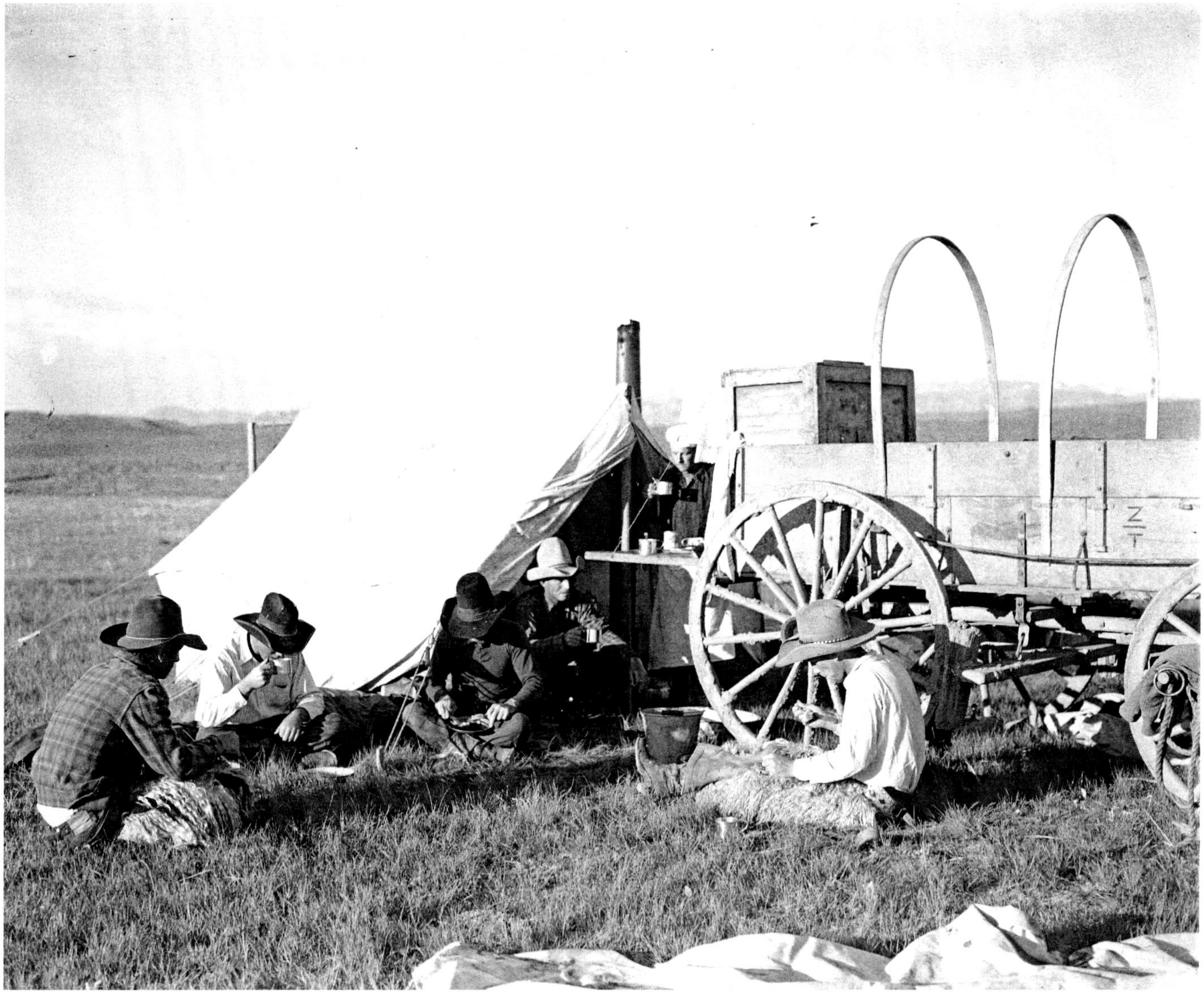

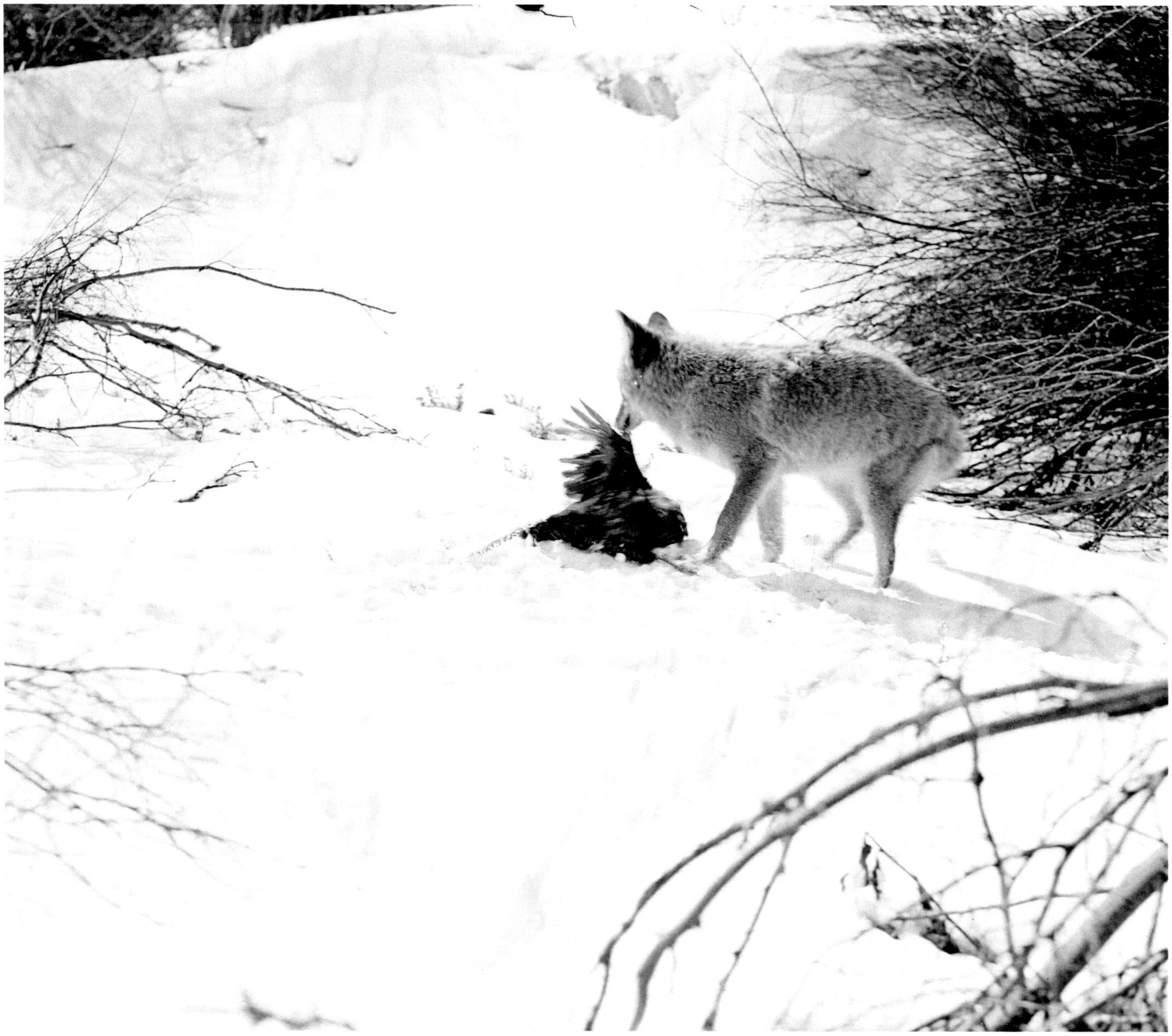

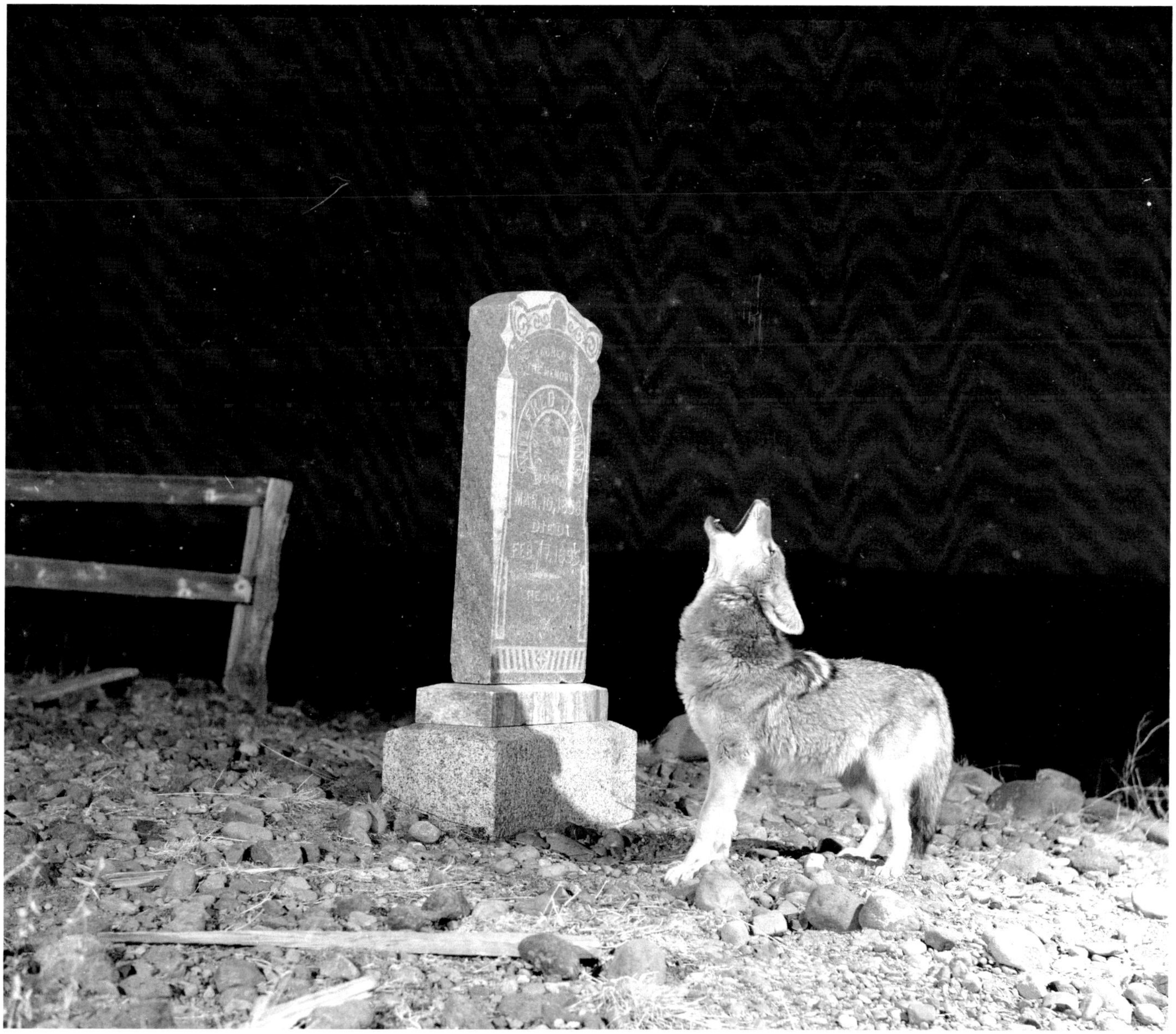

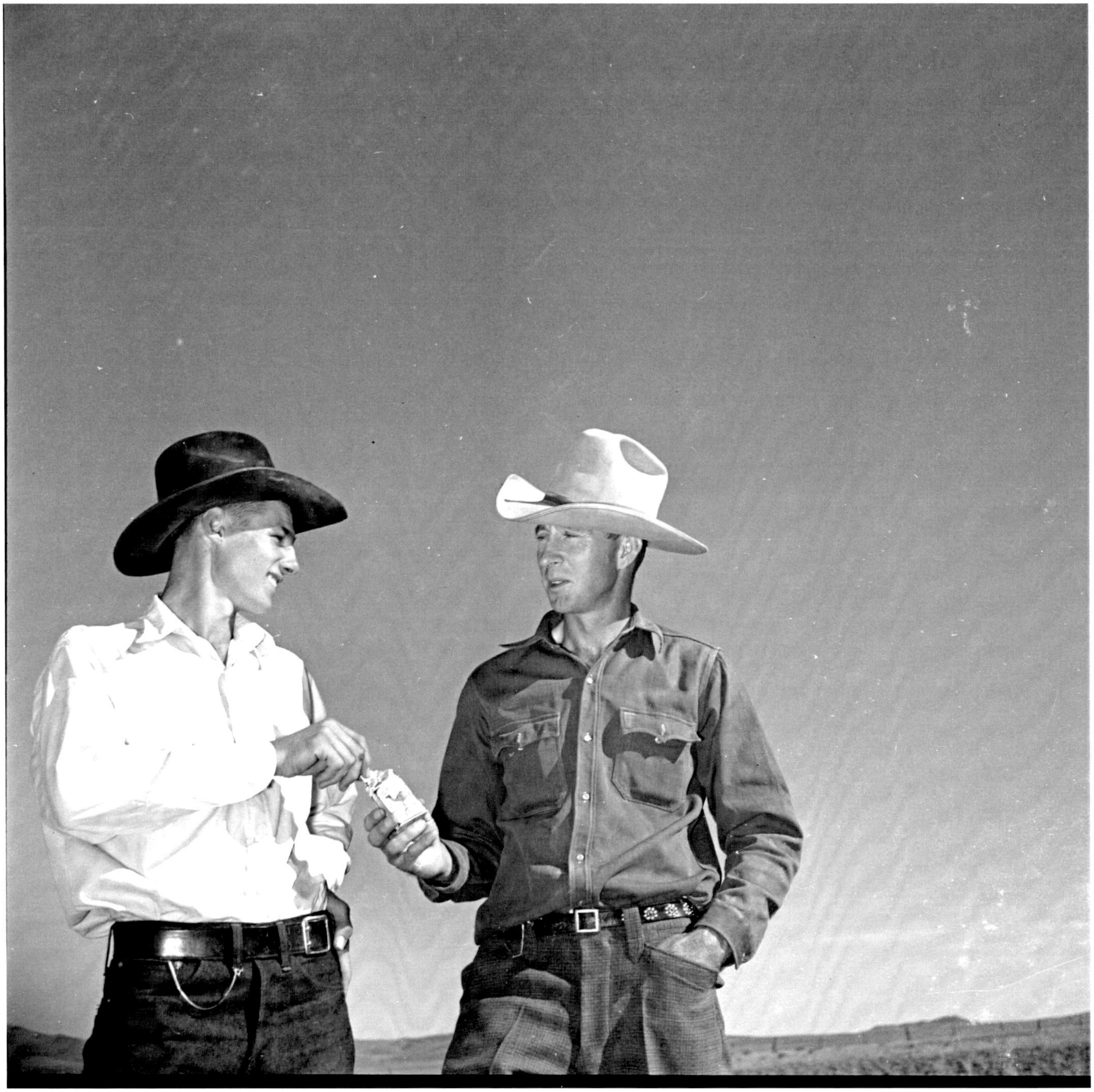

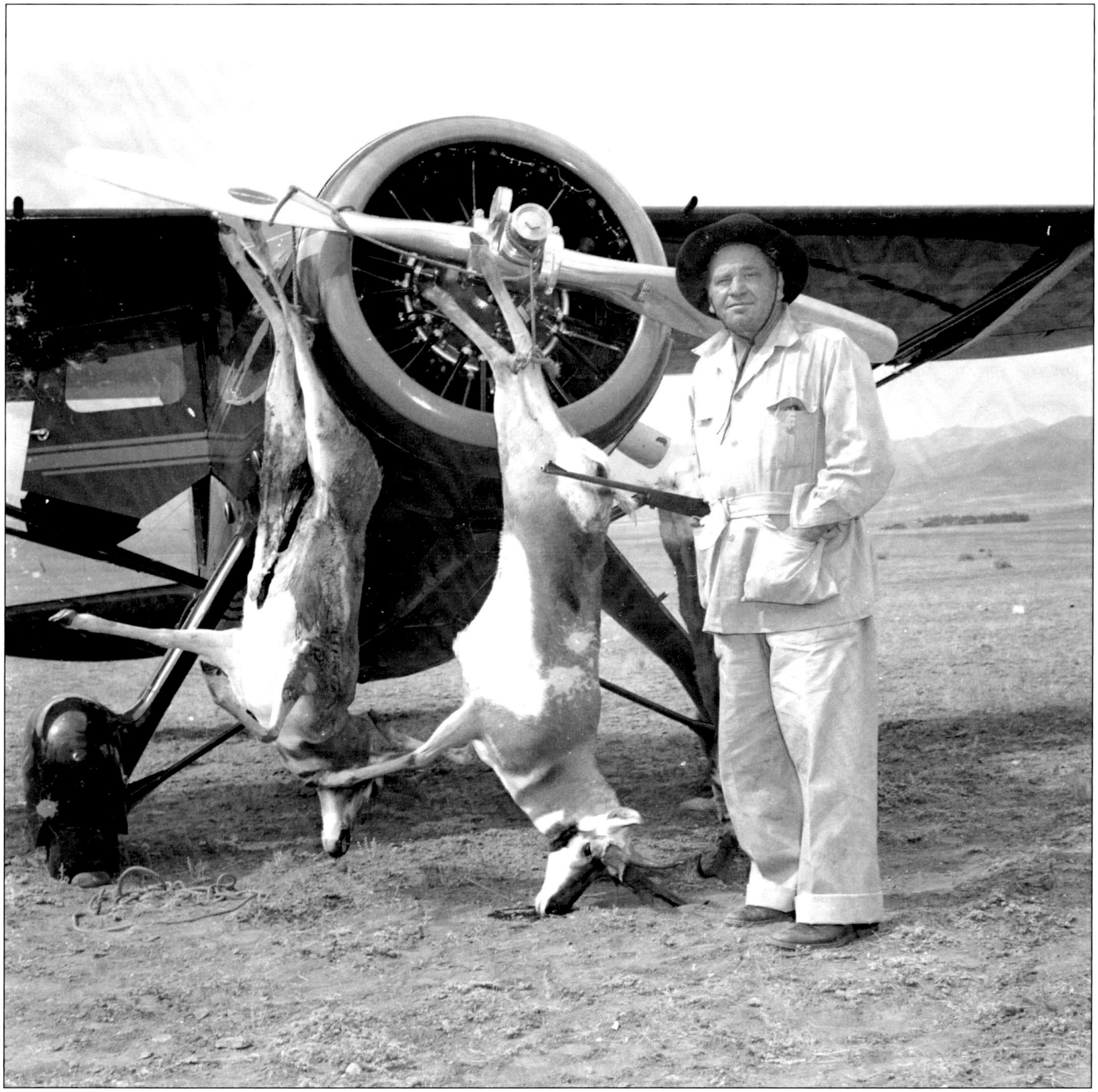

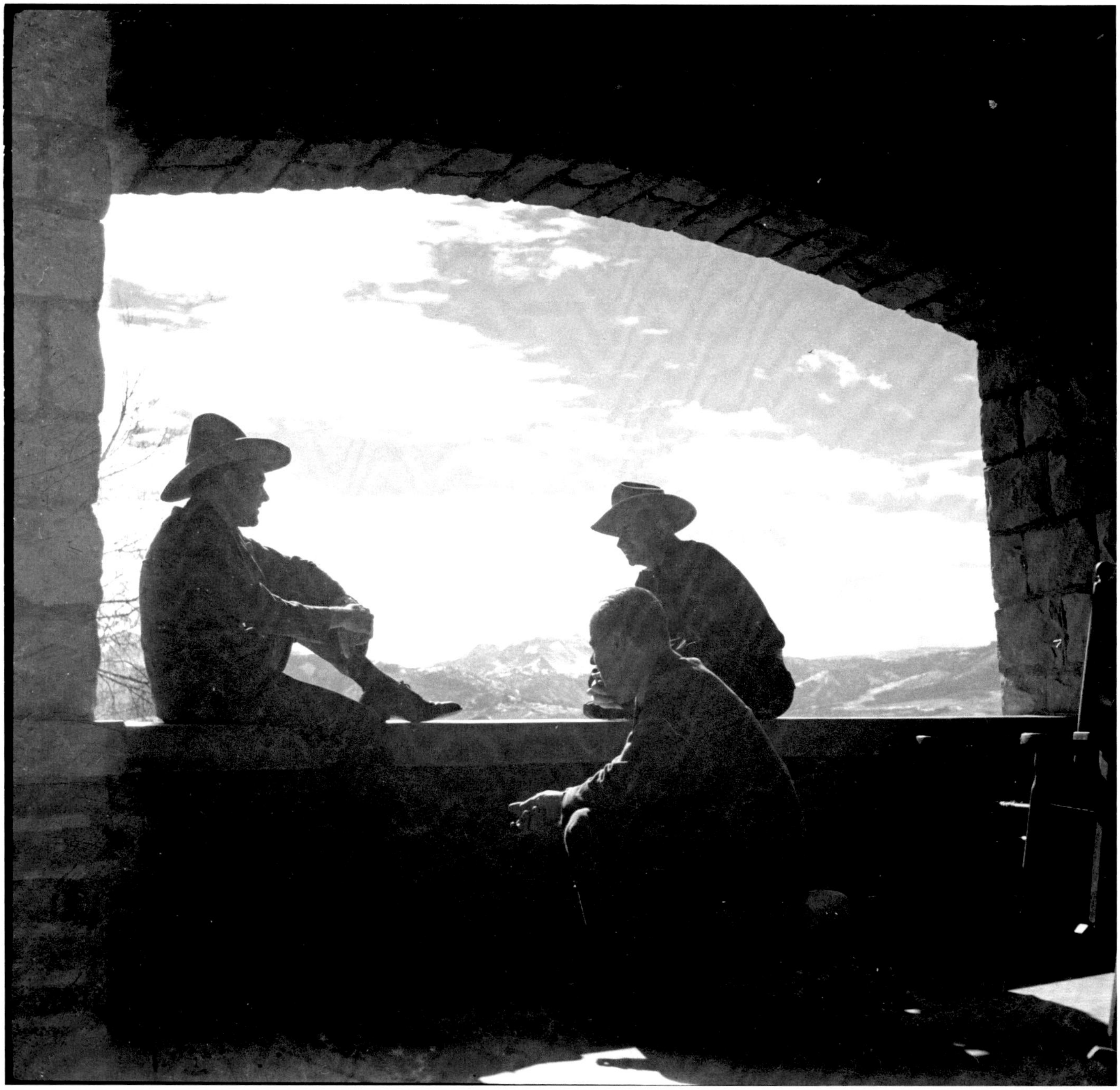

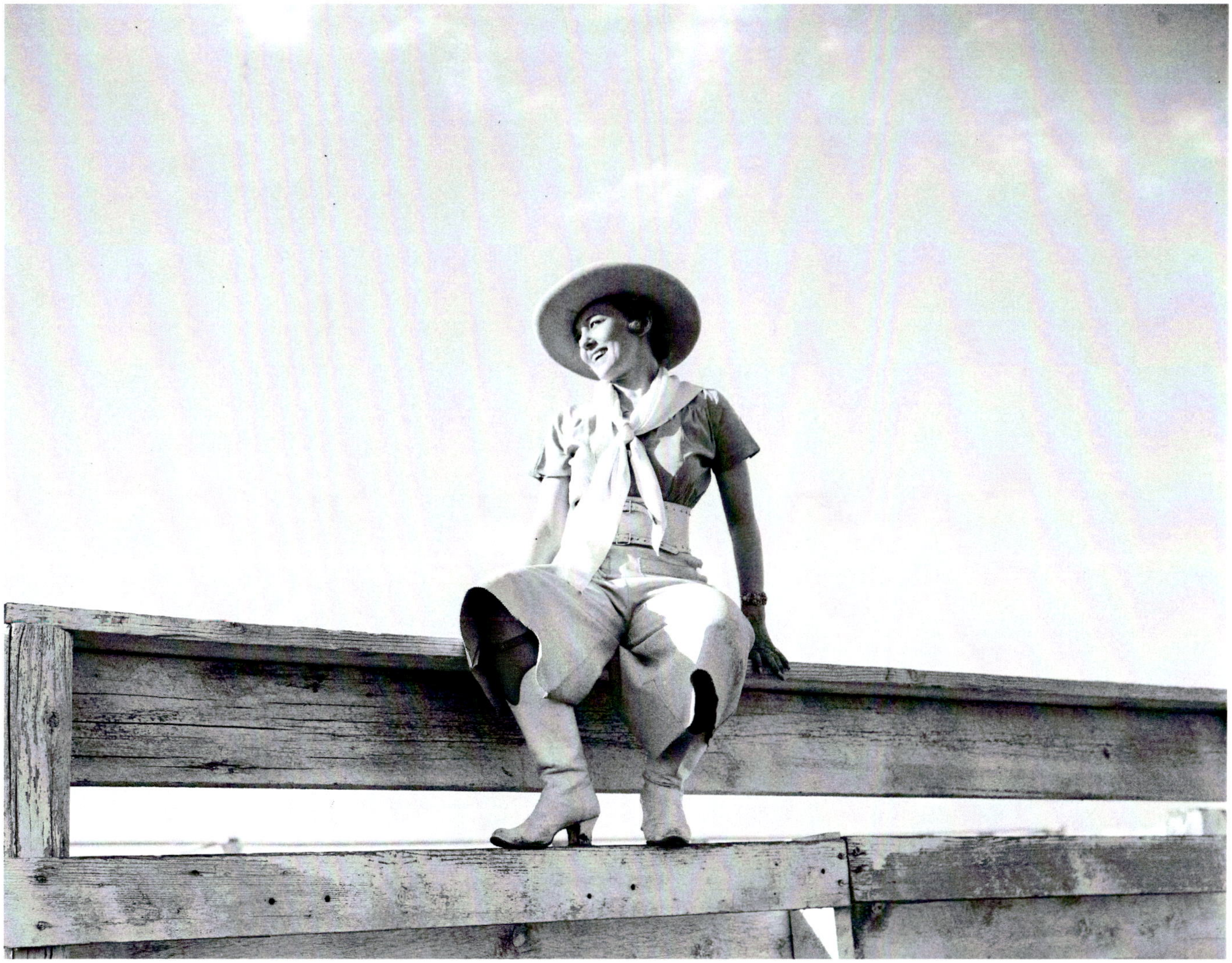

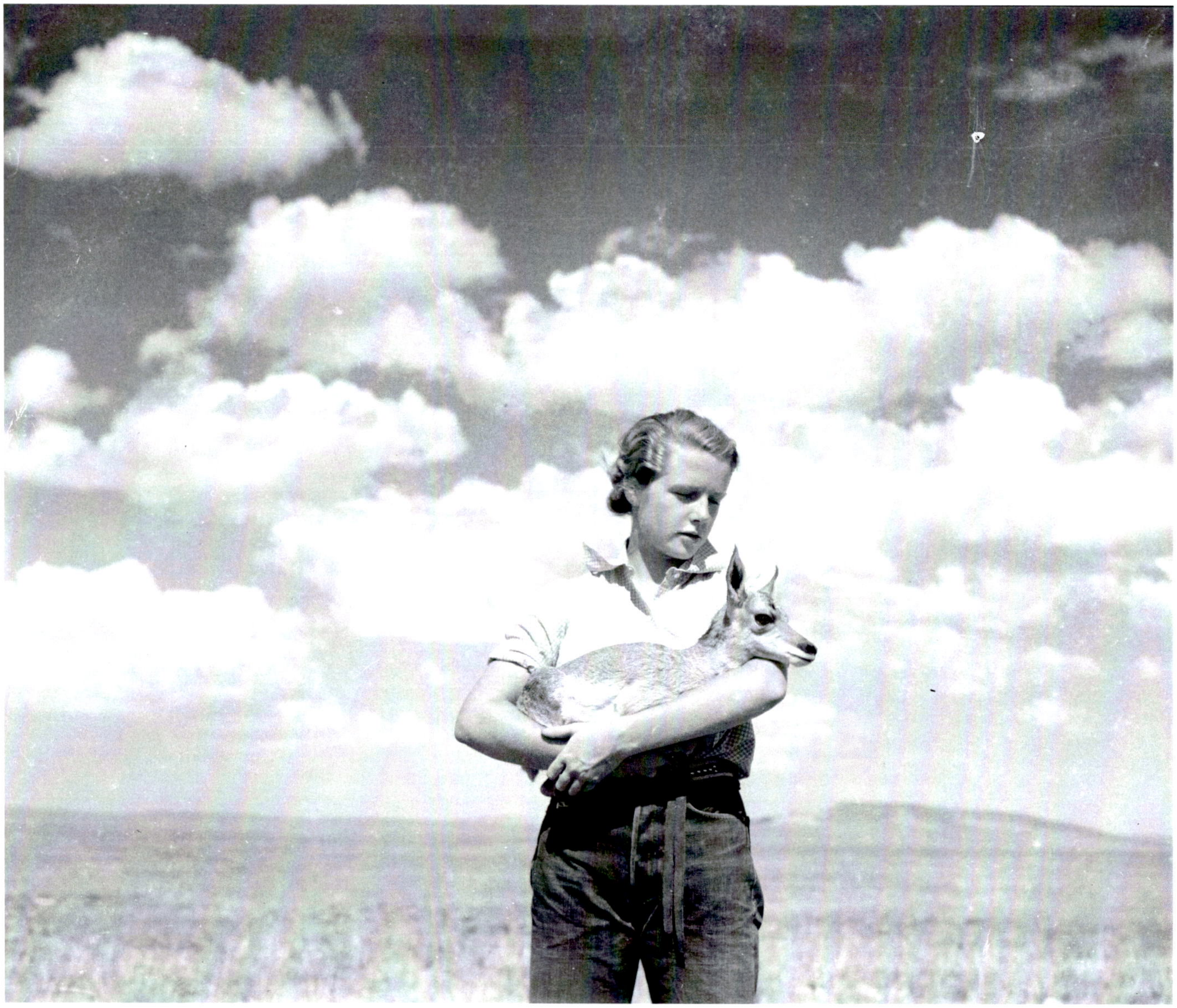

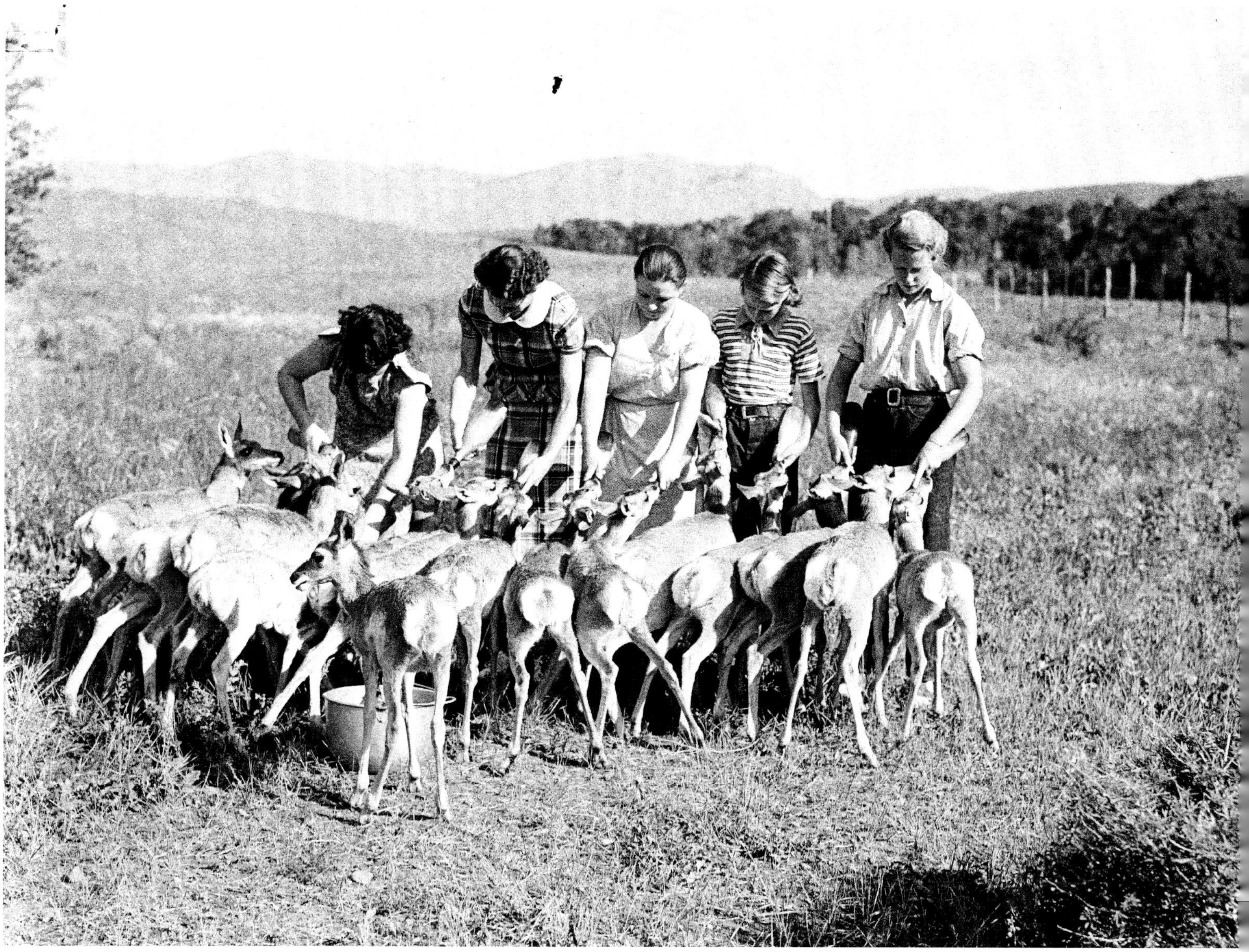

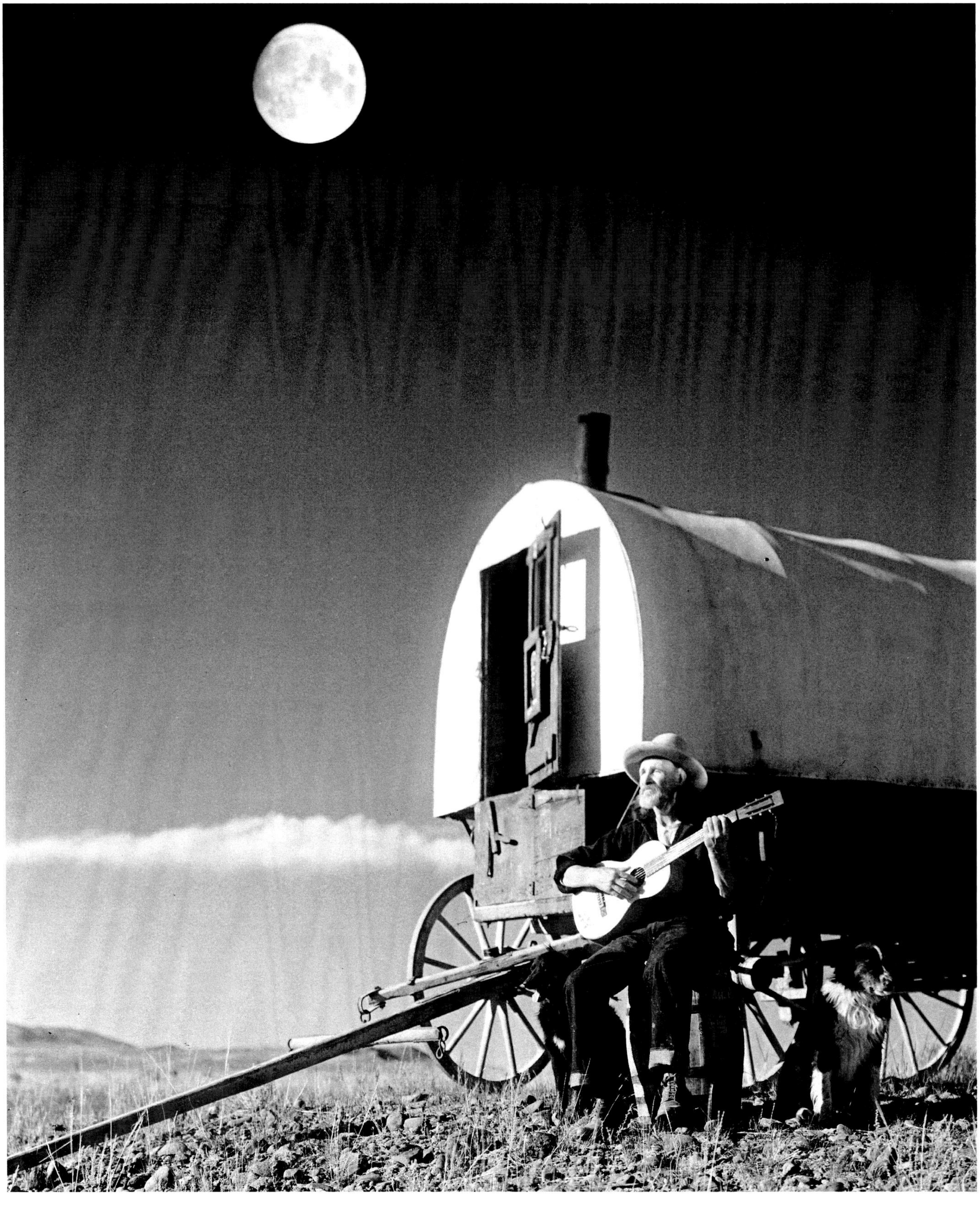

Timeline Charles J. Belden
(1888– 1966)

1888

Charles J. Belden born, November 16 in San Francisco, CA.

Eastman Kodak Company founded by George Eastman, Rochester, NY.

1889

The Eiffel Tower opens, Paris, France.

Brook trout introduced in the upper Firehole River, Yellowstone National Park.

1890

Wyoming becomes the 44th state to join the union. Vincent Van Gogh dies in Arles, France.

1891

Carnegie Hall opens, New York City, with Peter Tchaikovsky as guest conductor.

James Naismith invents the sport of basketball in Springfield, Massachusetts, and Serbian inventor Nikola becomes a naturalized American citizen.

1892

John Muir establishes The Sierra Club in San Francisco, campaigning for 'conservation.'

The Johnson County War breaks out in Wyoming.

1893

The iconic Salt Lake City Temple of the Church of Latter-Day Saints is dedicated after 40 years of construction.

Thomas Edison finishes building his first motion picture studio.

1894

Coca-Cola is sold in bottles for the first time.

1895

Alfred Nobel, the inventor of dynamite, arranges in his will to fund the Nobel Prize.

Frederick Douglass, writer, dies in Washington, D.C., at the age of 77.

1896

The US Supreme Court rules in Plessy v. Ferguson that the 'separate but equal' principle of Jim Crow laws in the segregated American south is legal.

Civil War photographer Mathew Brady dies in New York City.

1897

The Klondike Gold Rush begins in Alaska.

1898

The American battleship U.S.S. Maine explodes in the harbor at Havana, Cuba, an event that leads to the United States going to war with Spain.

1899

Writer Horatio Alger dies in Massachusetts, at age 67.

1900

Kodak introduces Brownie cameras. The cameras sell for $1, film costs 15 cents.

Sigmund Freud publishes his landmark book, *The Interpretation of Dreams.*

1901

U.S. President William McKinley is assassinated and, at the age of 42, his VP Theodore Roosevelt is inaugurated as the youngest U.S. president ever.

In Newfoundland, Guglielmo Marconi receives a radio signal from Cornwall, England, the first trans-atlantic radio transmission.

1902

The US renews the 1882 Chinese Exclusion Act, making Chinese immigration permanently illegal and extending the rule to include Hawaii and the Philippines.

1903

The first World Series is played in Major League Baseball between the Boston Americans and the Pittsburgh Pirates.

The Wright Brothers succeed in making a powered flight at Kitty Hawk, North Carolina.

1904

Panama sells the Panama Canal Zone to the U.S. for $10 million. Construction begins by the end of the year.

The first rapid transit subway line on the New York Subway makes its debut, running from City Hall to 145th Street.

1905

Albert Einstein proposes his 'Theory of Relativity,' explaining the behaviors of objects in space and time.

The first movie theatre opens in the U.S., the Nickelodeon in Pittsburgh, showing "The Baffled Burglar."

1906

The San Francisco earthquake devastates the city. Estimated at a 7.9 magnitude, the quakes kills up to 3,000, destroying as much as 80% of the city.

W.K. Kellogg opens a factory in Battle Creek, Michigan, hiring 44 employees to produce the initial batch of 'Kellogg's Corn Flakes.'

1907

Charles Belden of San Francisco is accepted at Massachusetts Institute of Technology (M.I.T.) and begins his freshman year of studies.

Pablo Picasso, Cubist, turns heads in the art world with his painting, "Les Demoiselles d'Avignon."

1908

The first production Model-T automobile is released by Henry Ford's factory in Detroit, Michigan.

1909

Charles Belden and his college roommate Eugene Phelps travel through Europe in a new Packard Touring Auto, the first Americans to enter Russia by car.

The NAACP is founded by a group that includes W.E.B. DuBois.

1910

The Boy Scout association is formed.

Halley's Comet arrives, April.

1911

John D. Rockefeller loses an anti-trust battle in the Supreme Court; Standard Oil is broken up into 34 separate companies.

Norwegian explorer Roald Amundsen reaches South Pole on December 14.

1912

Nabisco makes its first Oreo cookie.

The Steamship R.M.S. Titanic strikes an iceberg and sinks, killing over 1500 passengers and crew.

1913

Charles Belden marries Frances Phelps and the newlyweds take up residence in San Francisco. Charles is employed by the City, injured when a loose barrel crashes into him on the job; Belden walks with a limp the rest of his life.

16th Amendment to the U.S. Constitution ratified, allowing the federal government to collect personal income taxes.

1914

World War I begins in August, initiated by the assassination of Archduke Ferdinand and his wife in Sarajevo, June 28.

The first modern red-green traffic lights are installed on the streets of Cleveland, Ohio.

1915

German forces use 150 tons of chlorine gas against French troops at the Second Battle of Ypres, the first use of modern chemical warfare.

San Francisco hosts the 'Panama-Pacific International Exposition', a world's fair. Several early Belden photos in color are exhibited.

1916

Jeannette Rankin, a Republican from Montana, becomes the first American woman ever elected to Congress.

Margaret Sanger establishes the first birth control clinic in the U.S. in the Brownsville neighborhood of Brooklyn on October 16, after which she is promptly arrested.

Charles and Frances Belden move to Meeteetse, Wyoming, making their home on the Pitchfork Ranch.

1917

The Russian Revolution begins in February with the toppling of the Russian monarchy.

Congress declares war on Germany, and the U.S. officially joins allies Britain, France and Russia, fighting in World War I.

1918

Germany and Austria begin 'saving daylight' in 1916 to conserve fuel needed to produce electric power; the U.S. formally adopts this standard in March 1918.

1919

The nationalistic German Worker's Party is founded, and Adolf Hitler attends his first party meeting.

The Treaty of Versailles is signed, and registered by the Secretariat of the League of Nations in October.

1920

Women in the U.S. win the right to vote with the adoption of the 19th Amendment. Prohibition begins.

1921

Bessie Coleman becomes the first female African-American pilot.

The lie detector is invented.

Charles Belden begins selling feature photographs of the American West to *The Saturday Evening Post, National Geographic, The New York Times* and other publications.

1922

The *Readers Digest,* a monthly magazine, is founded.

Tomb of King Tut discovered.

1923

The Teapot Dome (in Wyoming) scandal dominates front-page news in the United States.

Adolf Hitler jailed in Germany after a failed coup.

1924

The first Olympic Winter Games takes place in the French Alpes.

J. Edgar Hoover appointed Director of the F.B.I.

1925

The Scopes 'Monkey' Trail convenes.

1926

Henry Ford announces the 40-hour work week.

Route 66, the 'Mother Road,' is established across the U.S.A.

Milne publishes *Winnie-The-Pooh.*

1927

Babe Ruth hits 60 home runs, a record that stands for 70 years.

Charles Lindbergh flies solo across the Atlantic Ocean.

Nicola Sacco and Bartolomo Vanzetti, anarchists, are executed for murder.

1928

Sliced bread, penicillin, and bubble gum are invented. First 'Mickey Mouse' cartoon plays in theatres nationwide.

The Kellogg-Briand Treaty outlaws war.

1929

First Academy Awards, held at the Ambassador Hotel, Los Angeles.

U.S. stock market crashes in October, marking the beginning of the 'Great Depression.'

1930

Pluto discovered.

Josef Stalin begins collectivizing agriculture in the Soviet Union, a massive failure.

Cartoon character *Betty Boop* makes her screen debut.

1931

Al Capone imprisoned for income tax evasion.

Nine black teens the 'Scottsboro Boys' are falsely accused for raping two white women in a landmark civil rights case.

The Empire State Building is completed in New York City.

1932

Charles Lindbergh's baby is kidnapped.

Amelia Earhart becomes the first woman to fly solo across the Atlantic.

Air conditioning is invented.

1933

President Franklin D. Roosevelt launches the New Deal.

Adolf Hitler is appointed Chancellor of Germany.

Prohibition against alcohol ends in the U.S.

1934

The 'Dust Bowl' in the Great Plains of the U.S. makes the Great Depression worse, as families lose their livlihoods. The cheeseburger is invented.

1935

Social Security enacted in the U.S.

Alcoholics Anonymous is founded.

Parker Brothers introduces the board game, Monopoly.

1936

In Germany, all German boys are required to join Hitler Youth.

The Spanish Civil War begins.

Hoover Dam is completed.

1937

The Hindenburg airship bursts into flames in New Jersey, killing 36 of the 97 people on board.

The Golden Gate Bridge opens in San Francisco.

Amelia Earhart vanishes along with her co-pilot over the Pacific Ocean.

1938

British Prime Minister Chamberlain announces 'Peace in Our Time', signing a pact with Germany.

Hitler immediately annexes Austria.

The first Volkswagen 'Beetle' comes off the assembly line in Berlin.

The House Un-American Activities Committee is

established, chaired by US Senator Joseph McCarthy.

1939

World War II begins as Hitler invades Poland on September 1.

Albert Einstein writes a letter to President Roosevelt regarding the building of the atomic bomb.

The helicopter is invented.

1940

Charles Belden leaves the Pitchfork Ranch in Wyoming for Clearwater, Florida .

Warner Brothers cartoon rabbit 'Bugs Bunny' debuts in "A Wild Hare", co-starring Elmer Fudd.

Germans open the Auschwitz concentration camp; at least six million Jews would be killed.

1941

Japanese attack Pearl Harbor, December 7.

Joe DiMaggio begins his 56-game hitting streak, still a Major League Baseball record.

Mount Rushmore, a sculpture featuring the 60-foot-high faces of four U.S. presidents, is completed in South Dakota.

1942

In Amsterdam, Anne Frank and her family go into hiding from the Nazi's.

The Manhattan Project, a U.S. federally funded effort to develop and produce nuclear weapons, begins.

1943

The Pentagon, the world's largest office complex, is dedicated in Arlington, Virginia.

FDR becomes the first President of the US to travel by airplane while in office, meeting Winston Churchill in Morocco at the *Casablanca Conference.*

1944

Batman and Robin comic strip premieres in US newspapers.

In India, pacifist leader Mahatma Gandhi is released from prison.

In Florida, photographer Charles Belden continues his career, taking pictures mostly of apartment buildings, restaurants, and Chamber-of-Commerce events.

1945

The United Nations is founded in San Francisco, California by representatives of 50 countries.

FDR dies at his Warm Spring, Georgia estate—his Vice President Harry S. Truman takes office.

1946

Nuclear testing begins in the Marshall Islands, the first of 23 detonations by the US between 1946 and 1958.

Bikini swimsuits made their 'debut' on a beach in France, quickly spreading to beaches everywhere.

1947

Polaroid cameras are introduced.
Jackie Robinson joins the Brooklyn Dodgers, becoming the first African-American baseball player in the Major Leagues.

1948

Despite headlines saying "Dewey Defeats Truman", Harry Truman is elected President of the US.

Jewish politician and diplomat David Ben-Gurion announces the establishment of the State of Israel.

1949

George Orwell's landmark book *Nineteen Eighty-Four* (also titled *1984*) is published.

Party chairman Mao Zedong proclaims the creation of the People's Republic of China.

Charles Belden writes an article for *Florida Speaks Magazine,* which also features Belden photos of snakes taken while on assignment in the Everglades.

1950

Diners Club introduces the first modern credit card.

Wisconsin Senator Joe McCarthy claims in a speech in West Virginia that there are over 200 Communists in the US State Department, leading to the 'blacklisting' of many Americans.

1951

The first regularly scheduled color TV program is introduced by CBS.

Truman signs the Treaty of San Francisco, a treaty with Japan officially ending World War II.

Charles Belden and his second wife Vera travel to Europe, his first visit there since the auto trip he made in 1909 with Eugene Phelps.

1952

Londoners suffer through "The Great Smog," a severe air pollution event that causes thousands of deaths from breathing issues.

Jonas Salk and colleagues begin testing for a successful polio vaccine at a lab in Pittsburgh, Pennsylvania.

1953

After the death of her father King George VI, Britain's Princess Elizabeth is crowned Queen of England.

Playboy Magazine, created by Hugh Hefner, is published, featuring actress Marilyn Monroe on its cover.

1954

US Supreme Court rules segregation is 'illegal' in the Brown vs. Board of Education decision.

Jonas Salk's polio vaccine given to 1.8 million children in a massive 'field trial'.

The *Marlboro Man* character, first conceived as a way of popularizing cigarettes, is introduced—the Pitchfork Ranch in Wyoming is chosen as one of the sites as the location for a national print and broadcast ad campaign.

1955

Disneyland Park opens in Anaheim, California. Civil Rights Movement begins in the US.

1956

Singer Elvis Presley appears on national television, "The Ed Sullivan Show."

The TV 'remote' is invented by Robert Adler who called

the ultrasonic device, the *Zenith Space Command.*

1957

Launch of Soviet satellite *Sputnik*.

The author Theodor Geisel, otherwise known as Dr. Seuss, publishes the children's classic 'The Cat in the Hat', selling over one million copies.

1958

American Bobby Fisher becomes the world's youngest chess Grandmaster at the age of 15.

US President Dwight Eisenhower signs the act establishing The National Aeronautics and Space Administration (NASA).

1959

Fidel Castro becomes dictator of Cuba.

The legendary musical "The Sound of Music" opens on Broadway in New York City, closing June, 1961 after 1,443 performances.

Charles Belden's Florida photographs are featured on postcards, advertising restaurants, apartment buildings, and a motel in St. Petersburg, Florida.

1960

'The Pill', a contraceptive, is made available to women for the first time.

1961

TV called a 'vast wasteland' by FCC commissioner Newton Minnow.

Bob Dylan makes his first public appearance, at Gerde's Folk City, New York.

1962

'Cuban Missile Crisis' as JFK orders a naval blockade of Cuba to prevent delivery of Russian missiles.

Author Ken Kesey publishes *One Flew Over the Cuckoo's Nest.*

1963

First artificial heart implanted by Dr. Michael DeBakey at a hospital in Houston, Texas. The patient lives 4 days.

JFK assassinated.

1964

President Lyndon Johnson signs Medicare Bill, and US Congress passes the Voting Rights Act.

The Beatles appear on The Ed Sullivan Show—over 40 million people watch.

1965

First Anti-Vietnam War Teach In: 3,000 protest US involvement.

Unsafe at Any Speed, Ralph Nader's best-selling expose questions motives of the auto industry.

1966

First Super Bowl. 40 million viewers watch the Green Bay Packers beat the Kansas City Chiefs.

NOW (the National Organization of Women) is born.

Charles Belden, 78, dies, North Redington, Florida.

Appendix

A Note About this Edition

In preparation for printing, the Buffalo Bill Center for the West provided digital images which were created from Charles Belden's original glass plate negatives. The negatives were scanned during 2005-2007, using a Kodak Creo flatbed scanner.

The photographic emulsion of the glass plate negatives is more delicate than modern sheet film negatives, and they tended to deteriorate over the years. Belden's negative filing system also was not proof against dust and scratches so most negatives had imperfections in them. No attempt was made to digitally correct any flaws that appear in the images using modern techniques to repair any visible flaws. However, a number of Belden's most popular photos were digitally corrected to a pristine condition for the production of prints for sale to the general public through the Center's Museum Store, matching Belden's own prints of the images, but do not appear in this edition.

Photo Captions

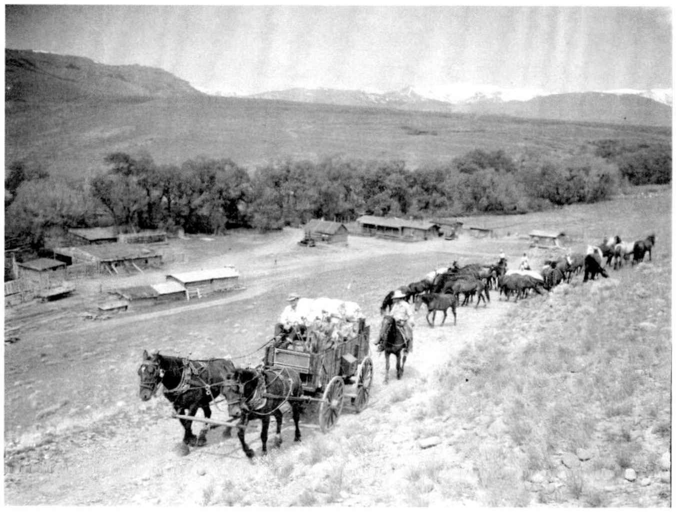

Title Page. Mounted cowboys and a horse drawn wagon lead a herd of horses up Z-T hill. Log buildings are at the bottom of the hill and snow covered mountains are along the horizon line.

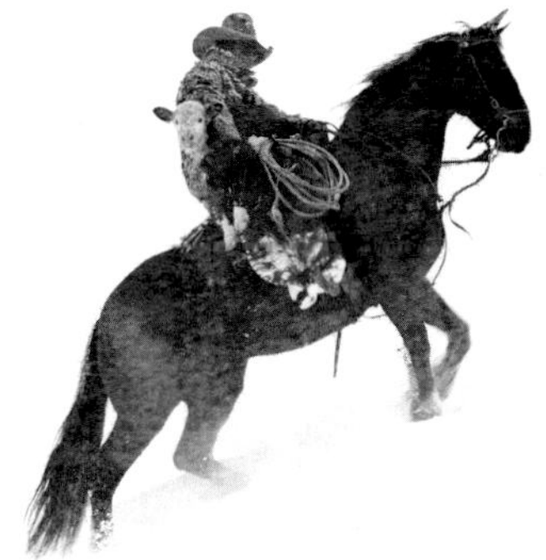

Page 10. The rescue. C. Jack Rhodes Sr. carries a Hereford calf in his saddle as he pushes his horse uphill through a winter storm on Pitchfork Ranch.

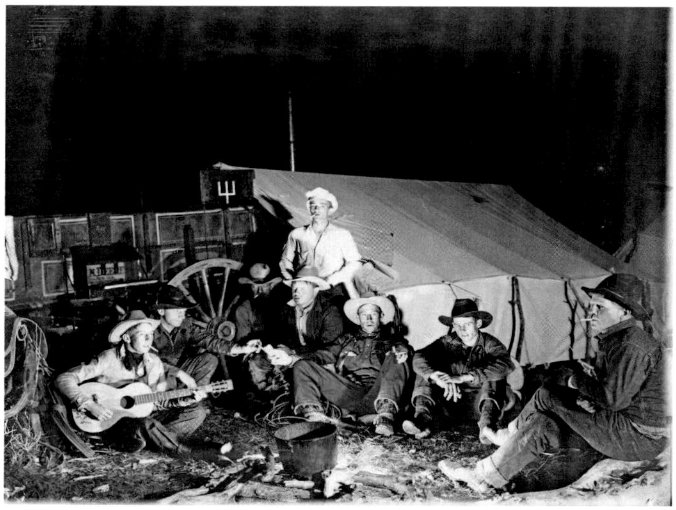

Page 8. Lee Wentworth, C. Jack Rhodes, Sr., Mark Windsor, and Shorty Graham (chore boy) gather near chuck wagon at night and sing on Pitchfork Ranch.

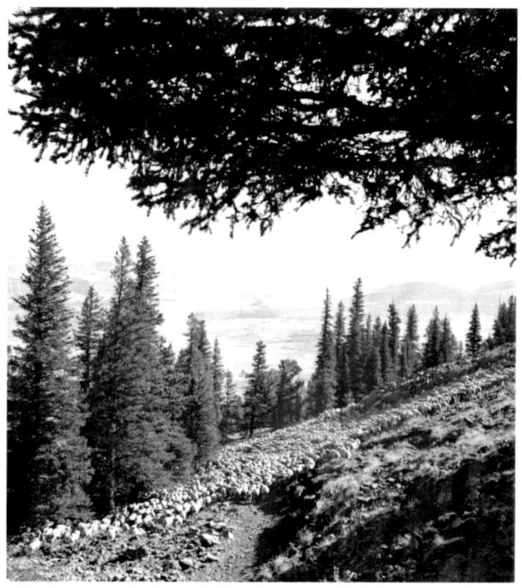

Page 12. Flock of sheep in mountains on Pitchfork Ranch.

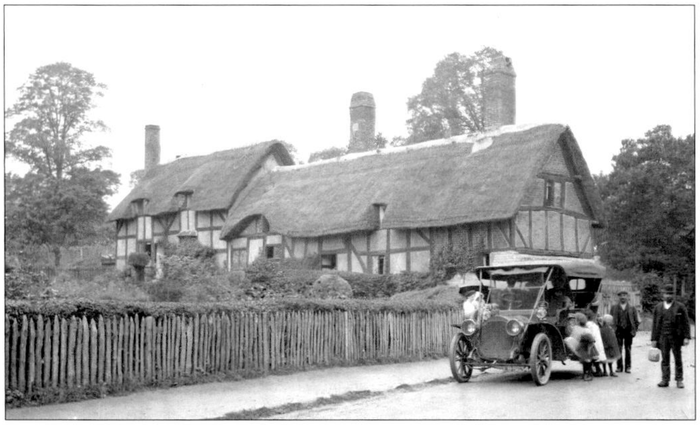

Page 14. The Packard at Anne Hathaway's cottage.

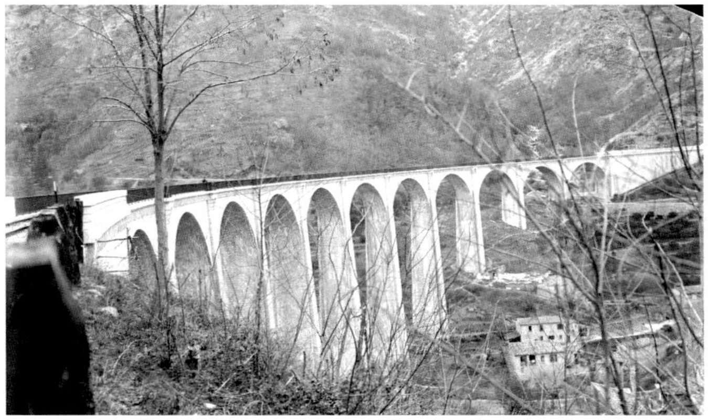

Page 18. Arched railroad bridge.

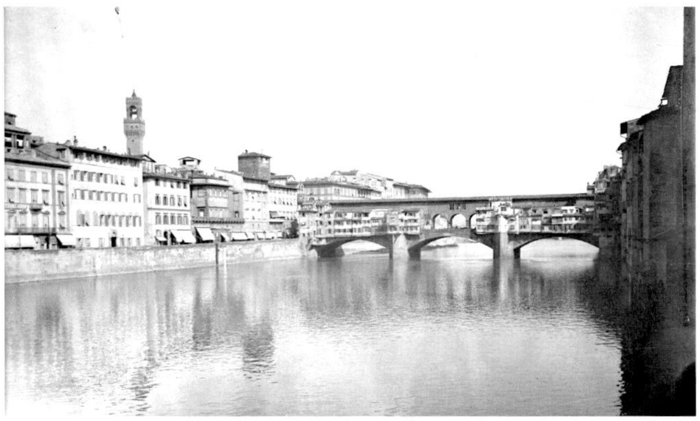

Page 15. Venice, Italy canals are bordered by residental buildings.

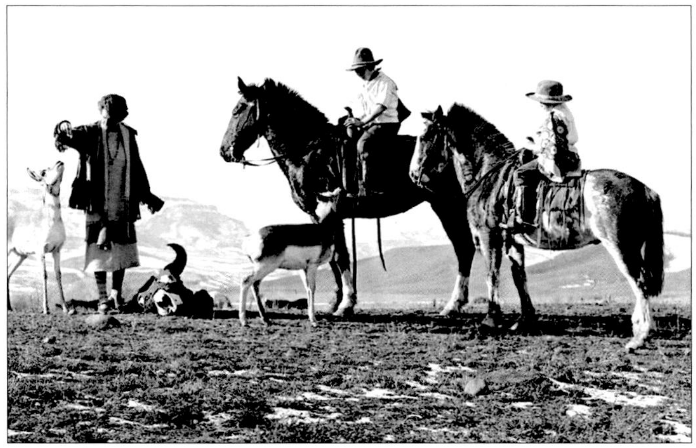

Page 22. Frances, Annice and Margot with antelope.

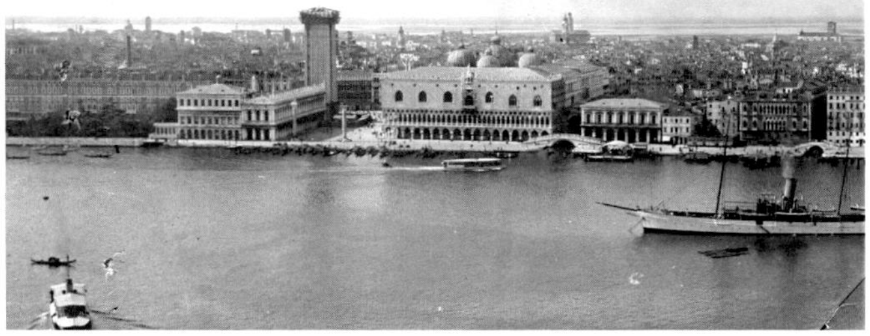

Page 16. Sea front senic of Venice, Italy.

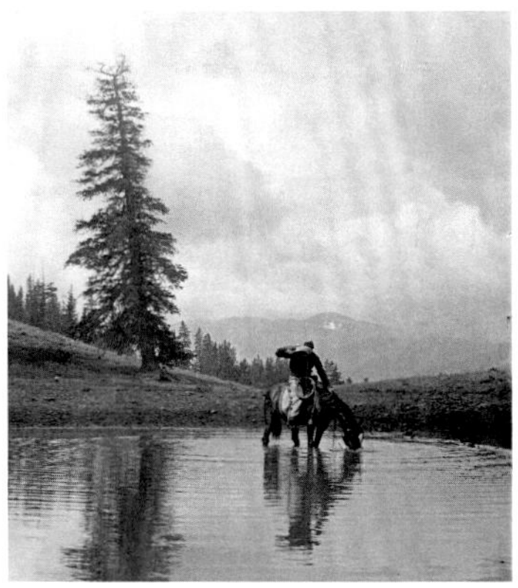

Page 27. Elmer Berkquist sits on a dark colored horse in a lake. He drinks water out of his hat while the horse drinks out of lake. Absaroka mountains are in the background.

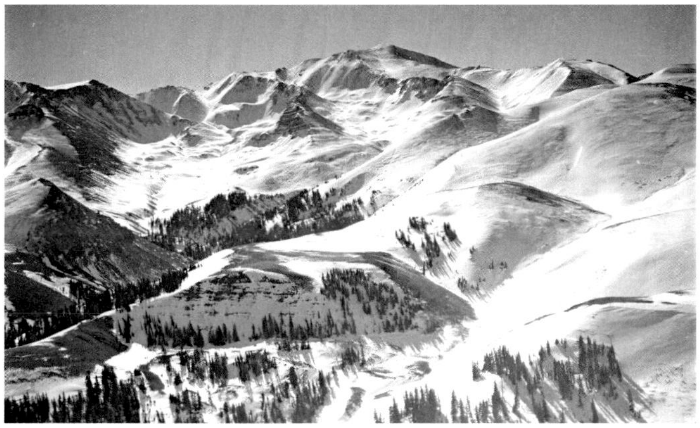

Page 28-29. Aerial view of snow-covered Francs Peak in Absaroka Mountains. Named after Otto Franc, first owner of Pitchfork Ranch.

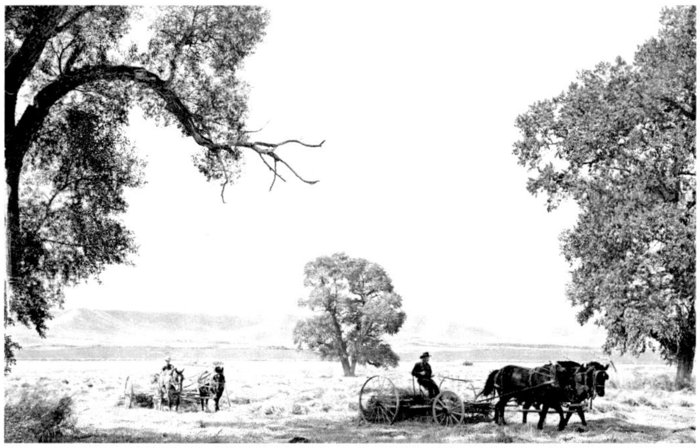

Page 30-31. Team of two, rake hay field with horse drawn rakes.

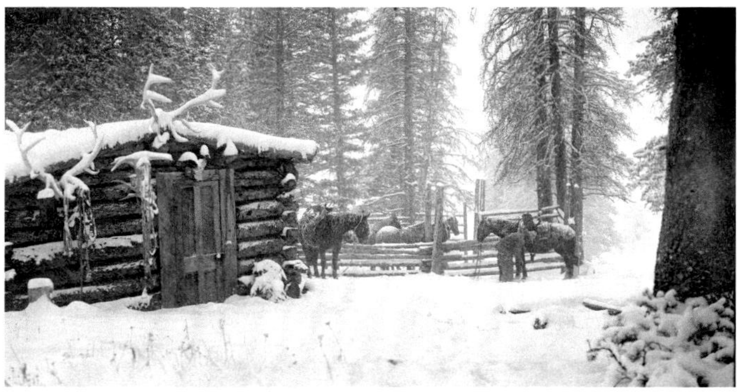

Page 32-33. Frank Owens checks a horse's leg at cow camp by a snow covered log cabin and corral at Jack Creek.

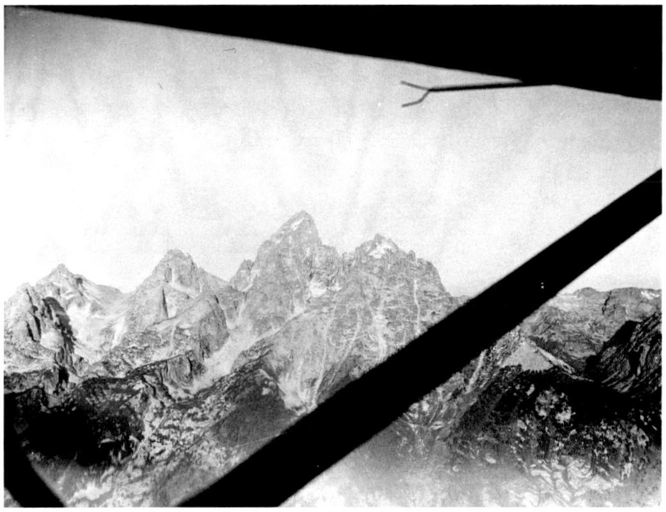

Page 34. Aerial view of top of Teton range. Airplane's struts and wing are visible in frame.

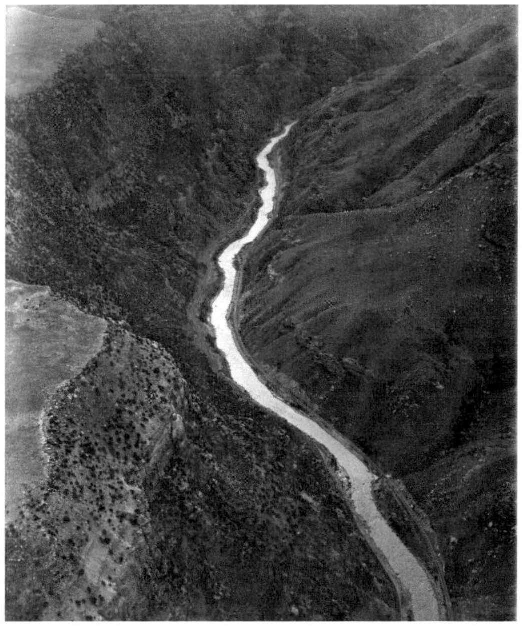

Page 35. Aerial view of Wind River flowing through Wind River Canyon, Wyoming.

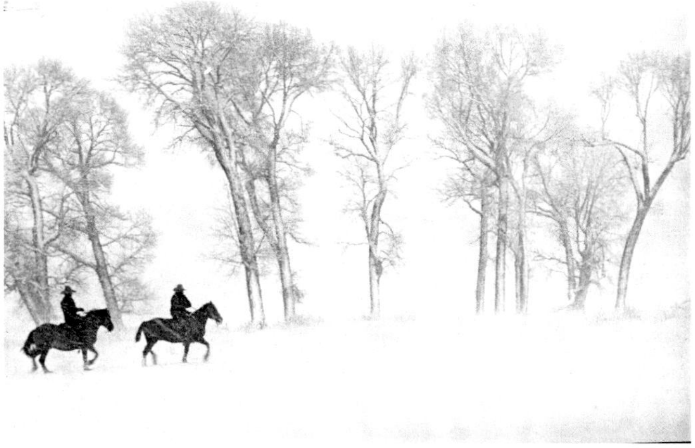

Page 36-37. C. Jack Rhodes Sr. and Charles J. Belden ride horses in front of tall cottonwoods on Timber Creek during a winter blizzard.

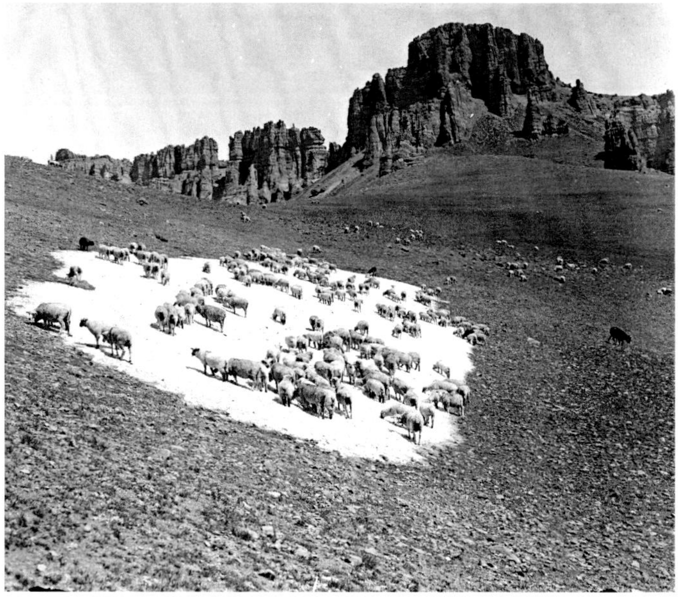

Page 40. Flock of sheep graze at Jack Creek with Irish Rock in background.

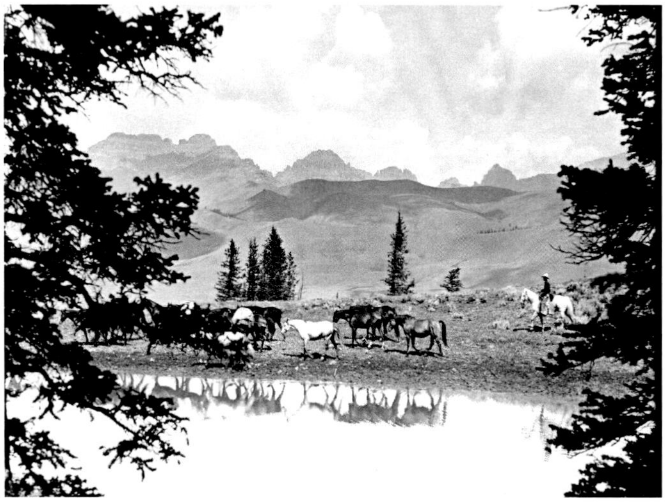

Page 38-39. Mounted cowboy trailing horses along mountain lake

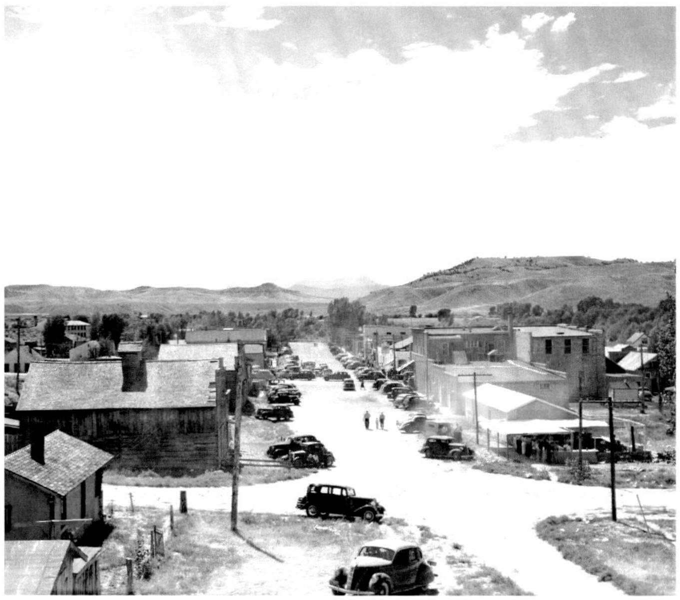

Page 41. Downtown Meeteetse with cars parked along main road and mountains in background.

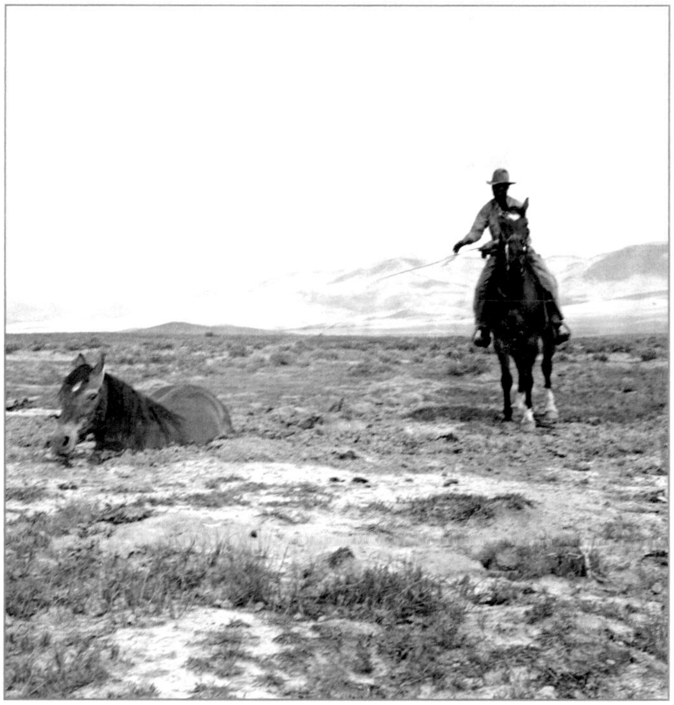

Page 42 Mounted cowboy roping horse stuck in mud on Pitchfork Ranch.

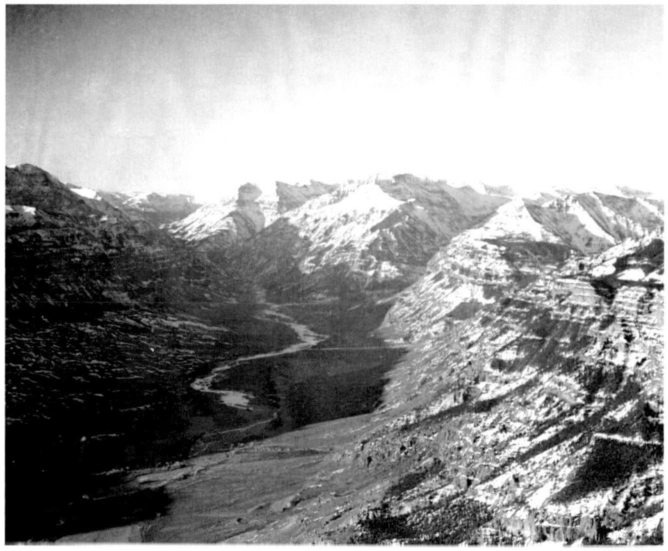

Page 44-45. Aerial view of the Upper Southfork of the Shoshone River. Ishawooa Mesa on the right

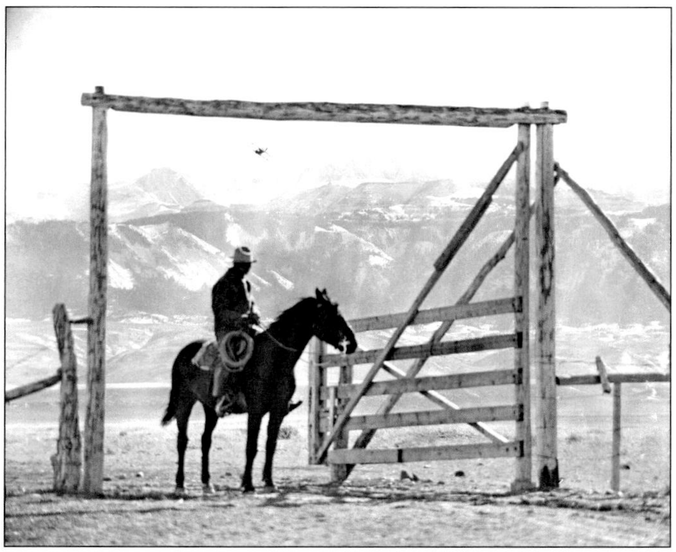

Page 43. Mounted cowboy at Pitchfork Ranch gate looking back at airplane with Absaroka Mountains in background.

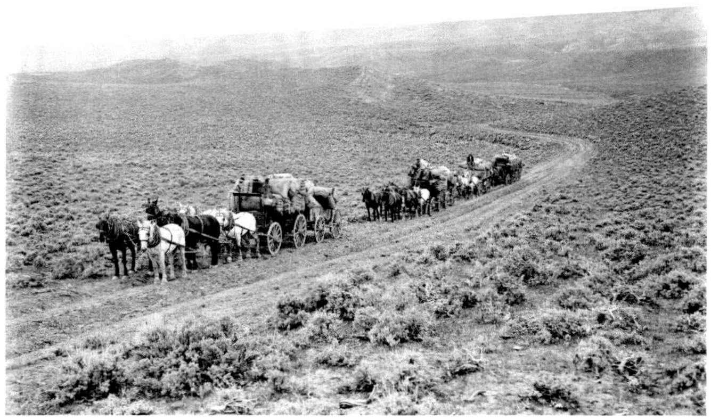

Page 46.47. Four wagons loaded with sheep's wool roll out of Cottonwood Creek, where the shearing pens were, and head to the Cody rail yard.

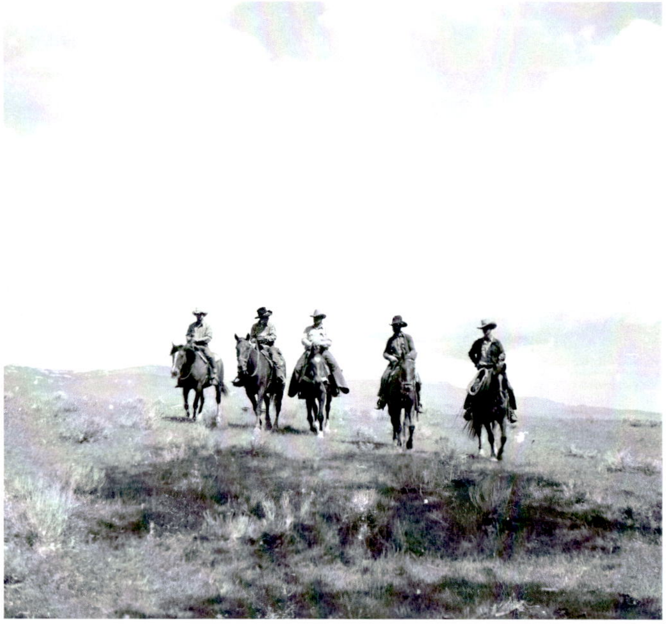

Page 48. Five cowboys riding horses on the range.

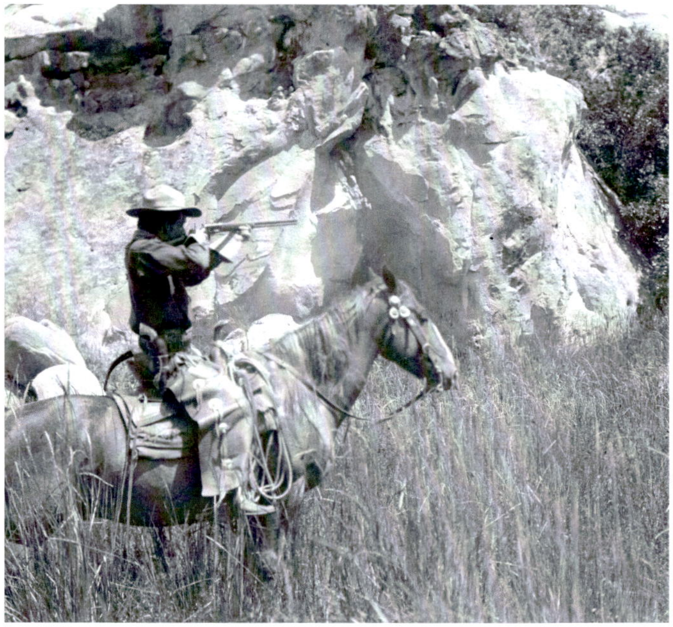

Page 50-51. Mounted hunter taking aim with his rifle.

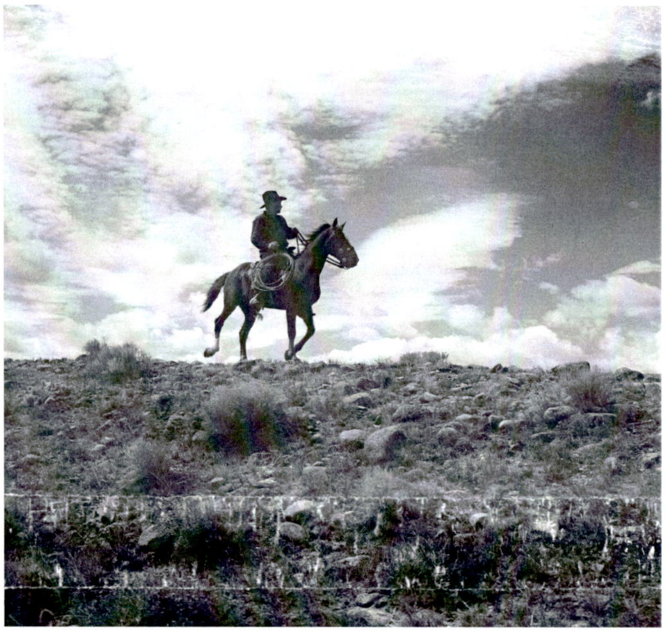

Page 49. Clarence (Dusty) Dustin rides a gamboling horse, silhouetted against a cloudy sky on Pitchfork Ranch.

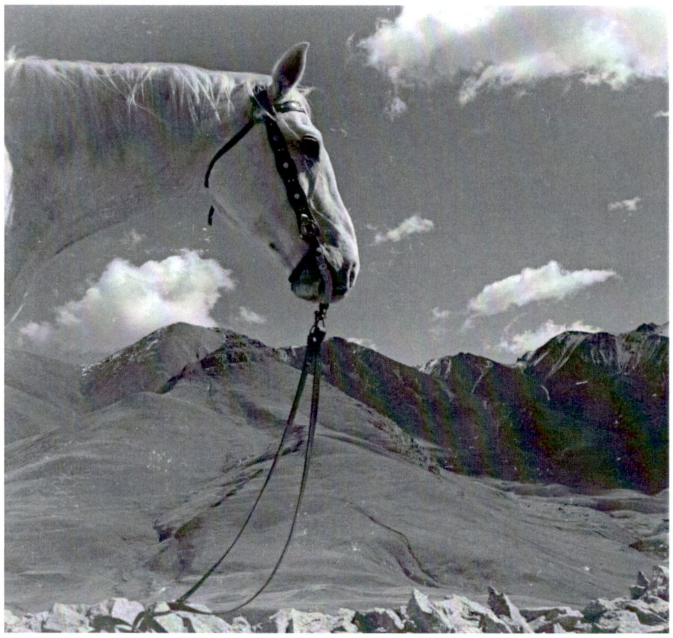

Page 52. Absaroka Range with bridled horse head on left on Pitchfork Ranch.

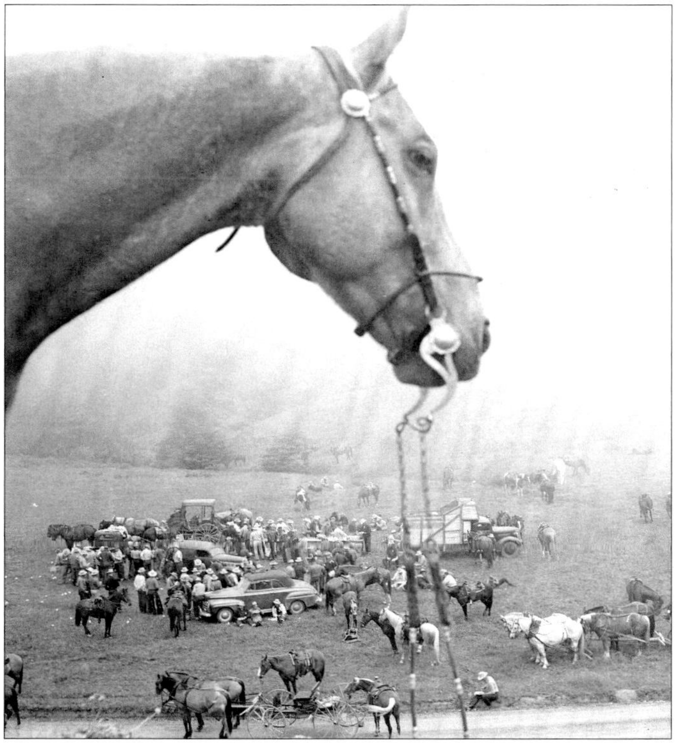

Page 53. People, horses, wagons, and automobiles gather together to meet, framed by horse head.

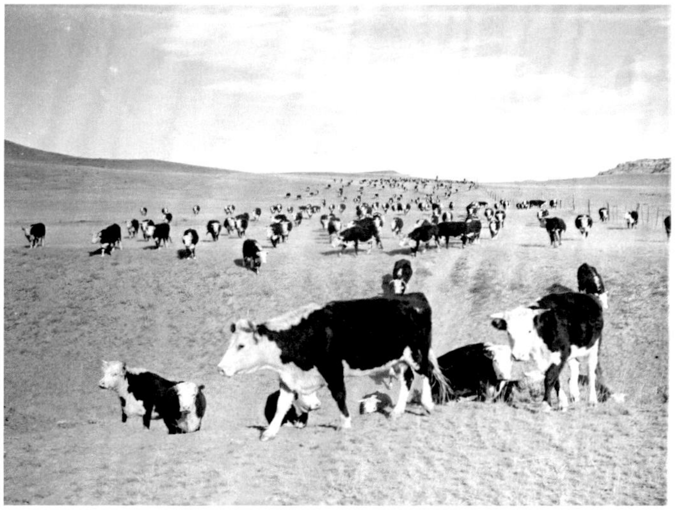

Page 54. Herd of Herefords on Pitchfork Ranch.

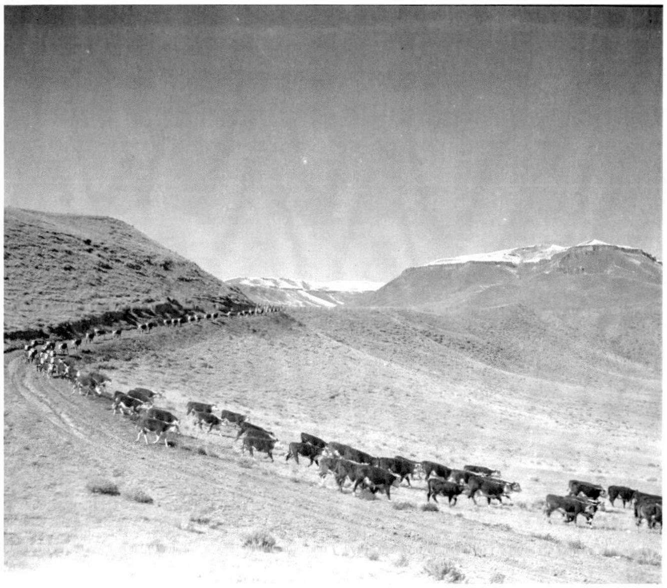

Page 55 . Hereford herd trailing down Pitchfork Ranch road. Carter Mountain in background.

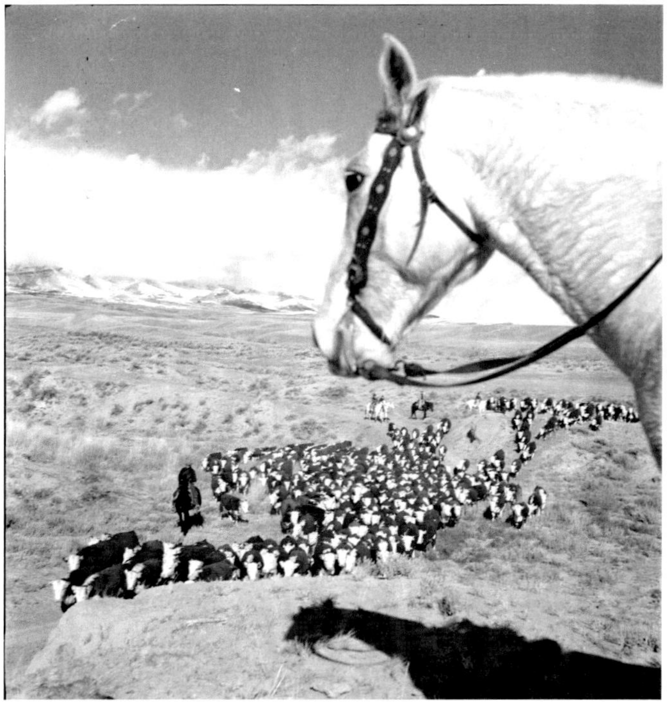

Page 56 Mounted cowboys trailing herd of Herefords across range on Pitchfork Ranch.

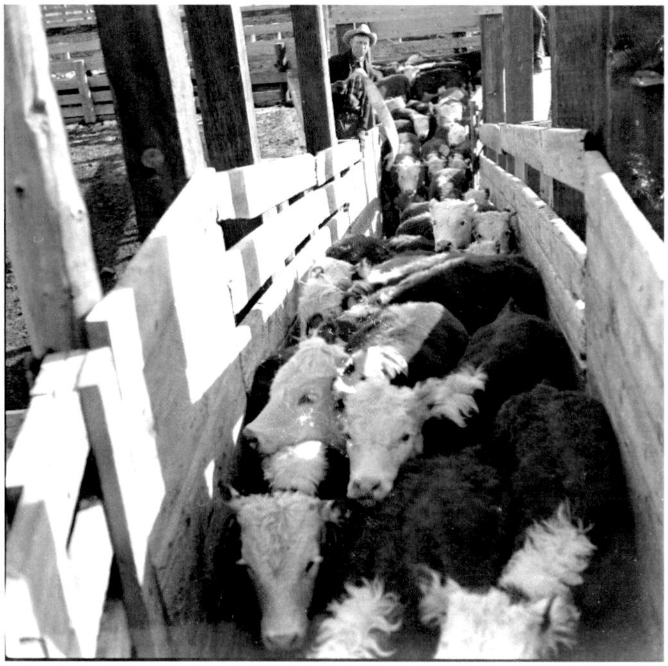

Page 57. Herefords going up corral chute to load onto rail cars at Cody Stockyards.

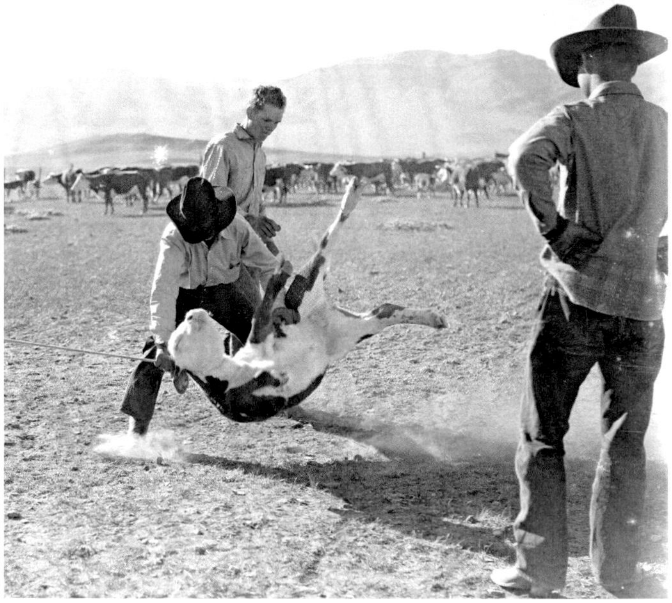

Page 60. Roped calf is thrown to the ground for branding by cowboys.

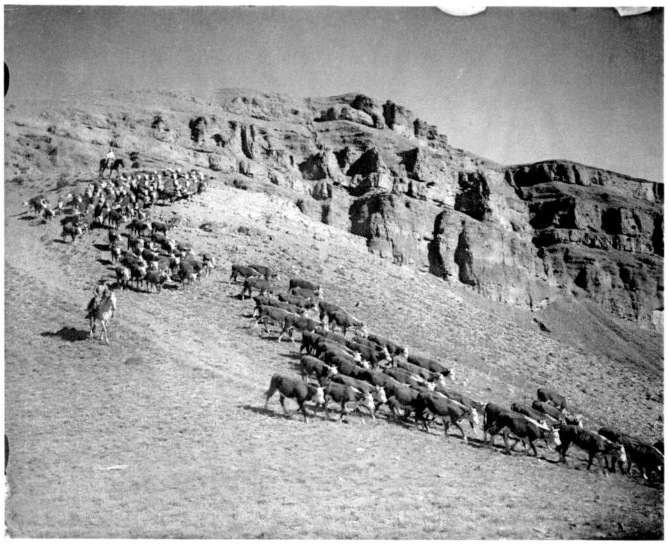

Page 58-59. Mounted cowboys trail a herd of Herefords down hillside, possibly Red Creek.

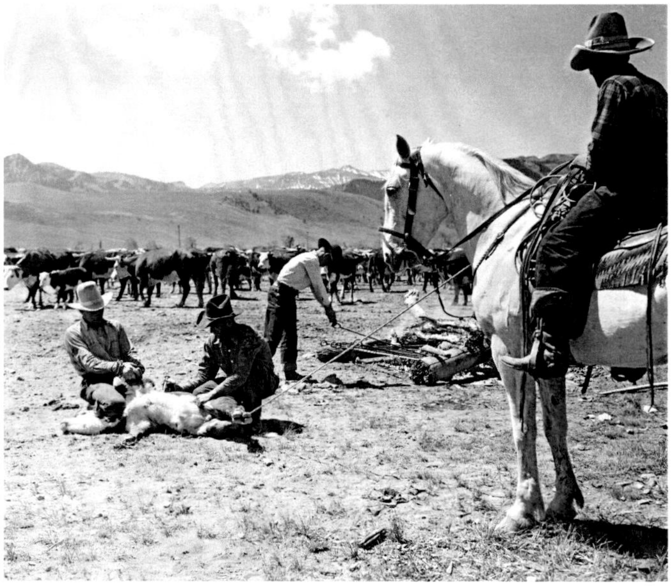

Page 61. Two cowboys hold a calf down and vaccinate him while another cowboy grabs the branding iron out of the fire on Timber Creek. C. Jack Rhodes, Sr. is on a pale horse holding the rope tight on the calves back. legs.

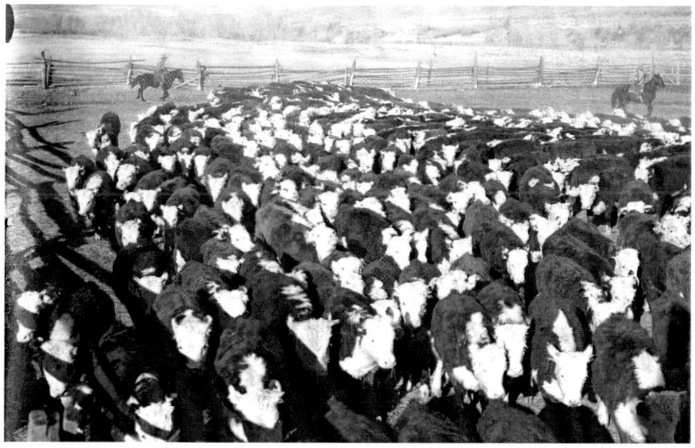

Page 62-63. Two cowboys herd yearling cattle toward a gate in a corral.

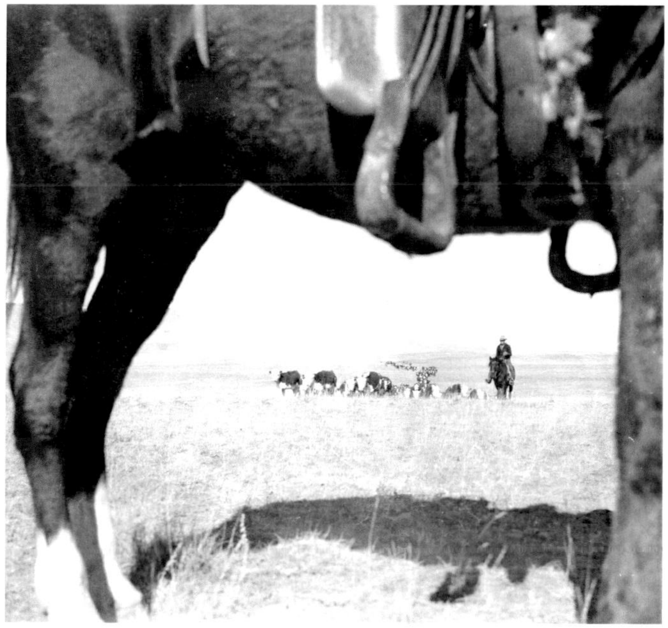

Page 65. Mounted cowboy trailing Hereford herd across Pitchfork Ranch; saddled horse in foreground.

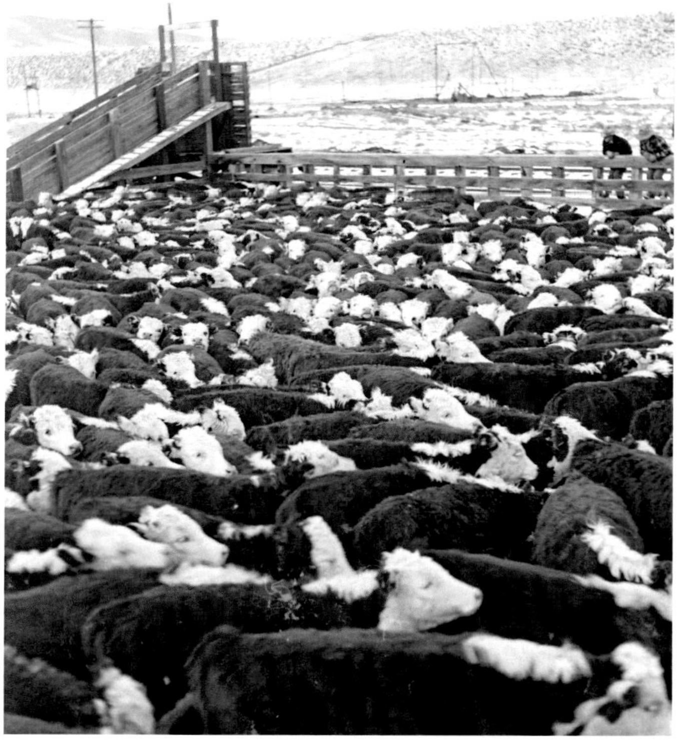

Page 64. Hereford cattle in corral at Cody Stockyards. Two men stand on edge of corral in background.

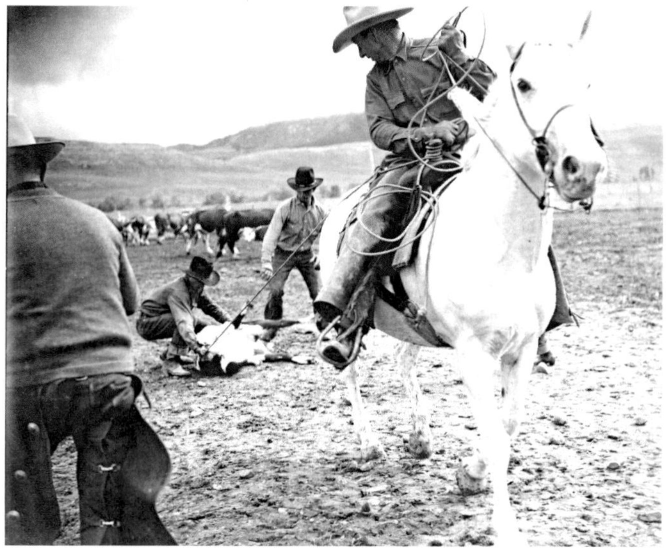

Page 66. Cowboy on a pale horse ropes a calf to brand while three other cowboys assist.

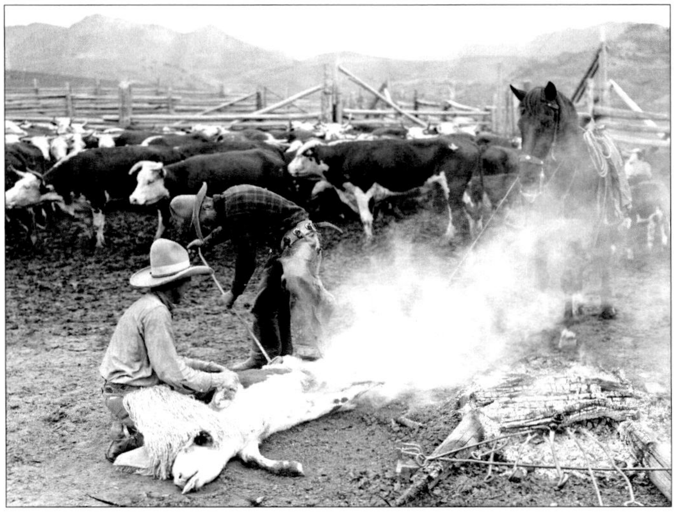

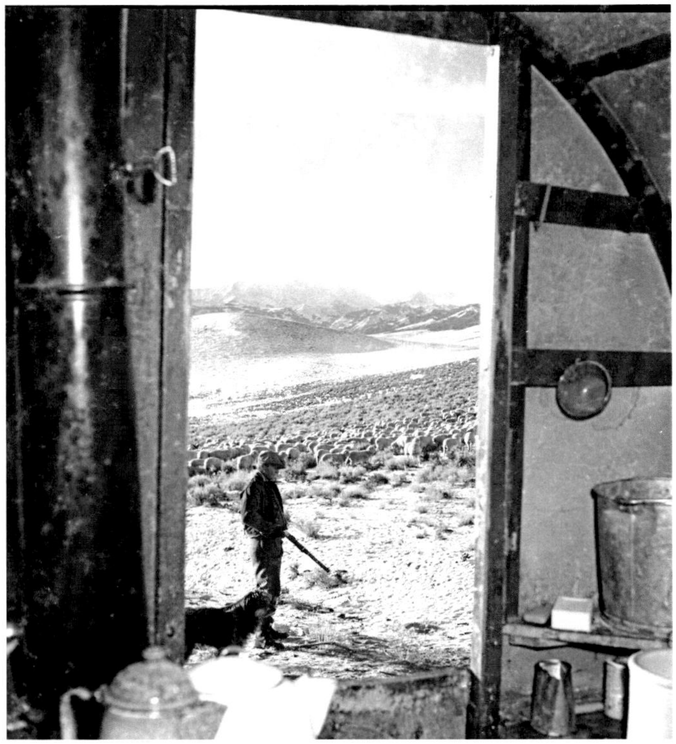

Page 67. C. Jack Rhodes, Sr. and another cowboy brand a calf while a horse pulls the rope tight on the calf's hind legs at Timber Creek corrals.

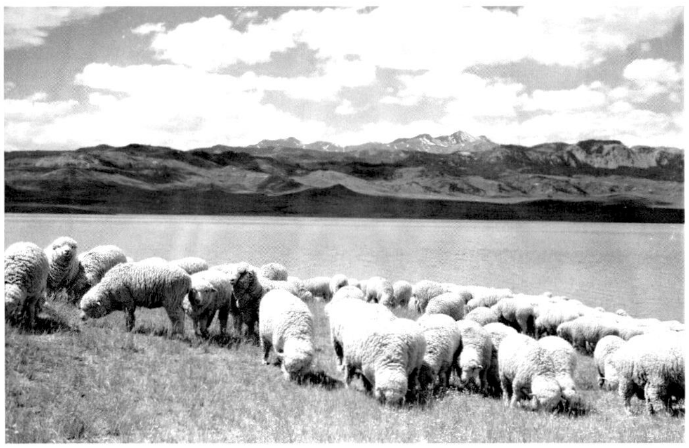

Page 68-69. Sheep graze near Upper Sunshine Reservoir with Jojo Mountain in background on Pitchfork Ranch.

Page 70 top right. The sheep wagon was 'home' in the summer, double occupancy for a shepherd and his dog. The basics—food, coffee, ammo—were brought in from the Pitchfork.

Page 71. A young man, recognized by a family member to be Bob McGee, shepherded up on Jack Creek many summers in the late 1930s, early '40s.

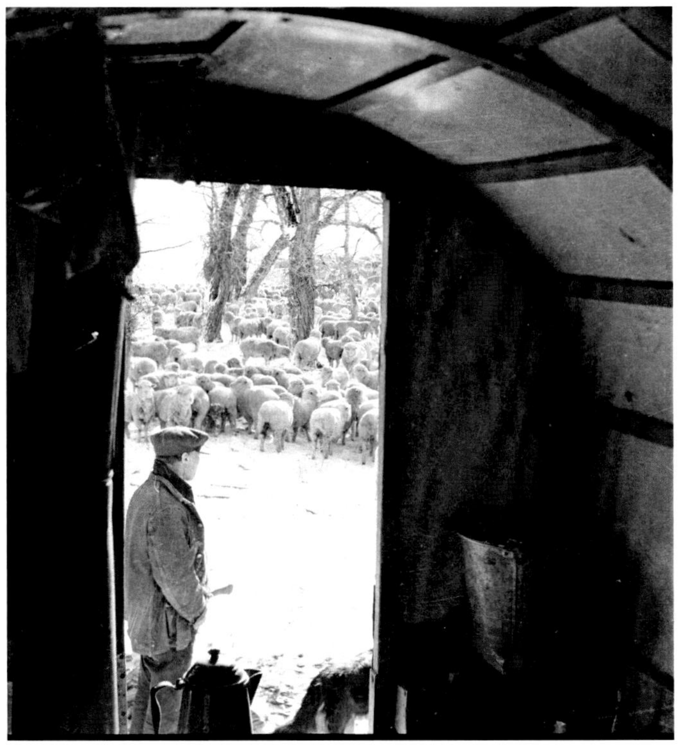

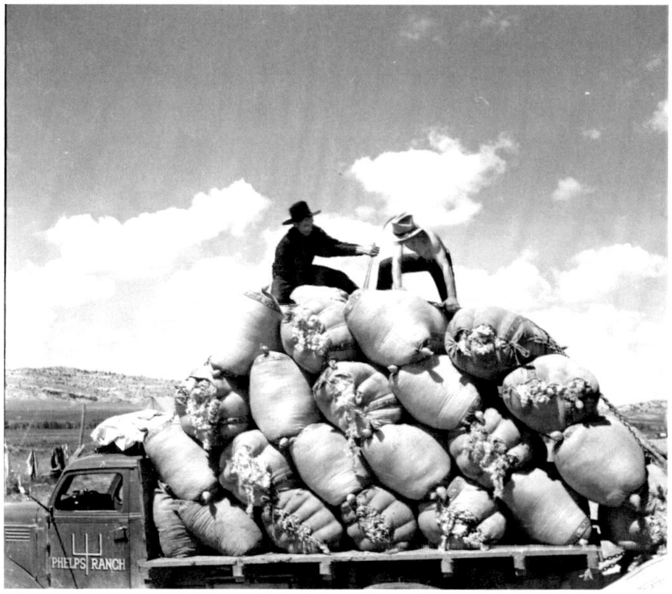

Page 72. Two men load bags of wool on truck on Pitchfork Ranch.

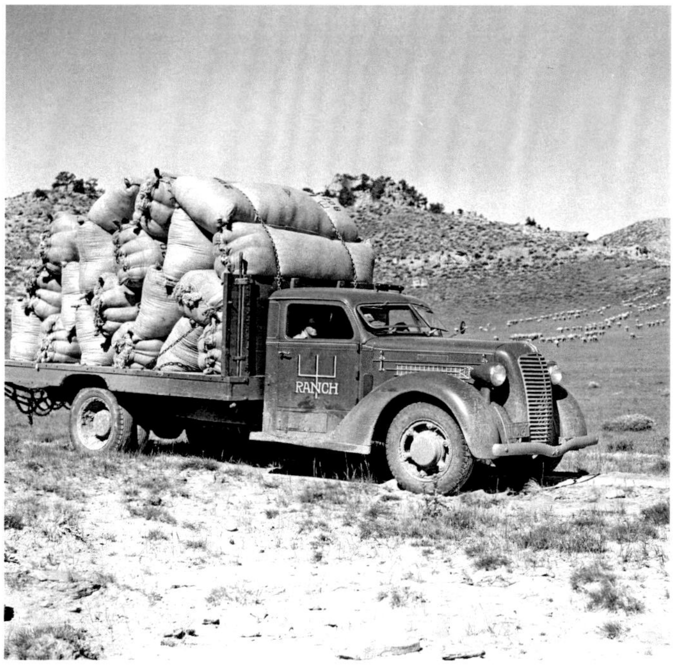

Page 73. Old Diamond T truck with Pitchfork brand on side door loaded with wool.

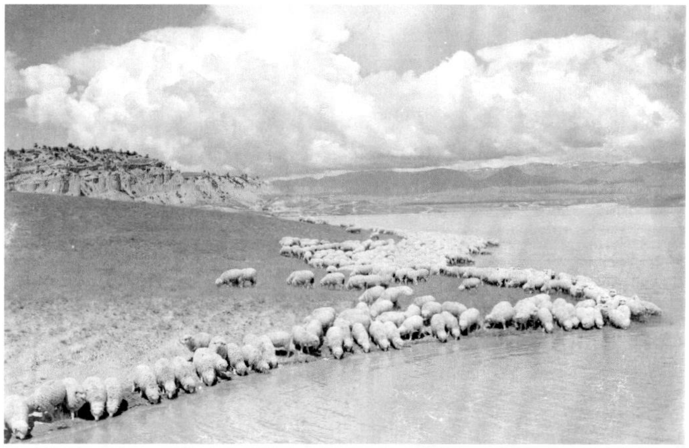

Page 74-75. Sheep drinking from Upper Sunshine Reservoir on Pitchfork Ranch.

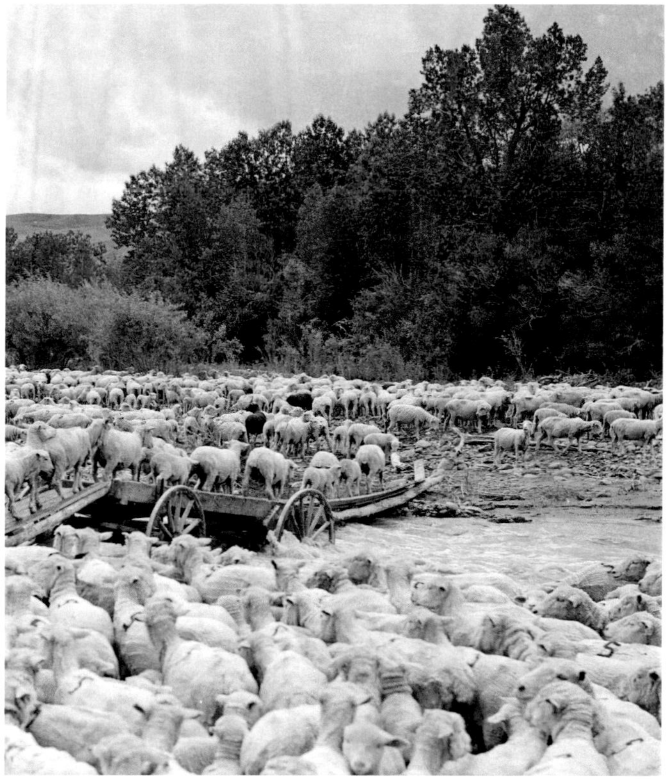

Page 76. Sheep cross Greybull River on bridge made from a wagon on Pitchfork Ranch.

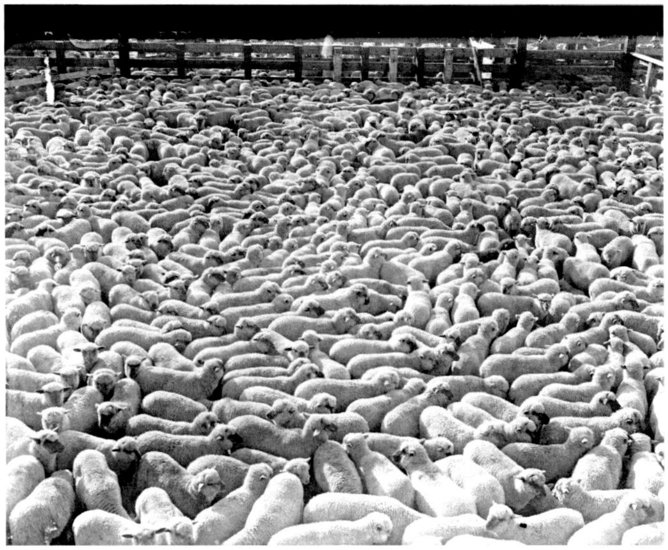

Page 77. Corral full of lambs on Pitchfork Ranch.

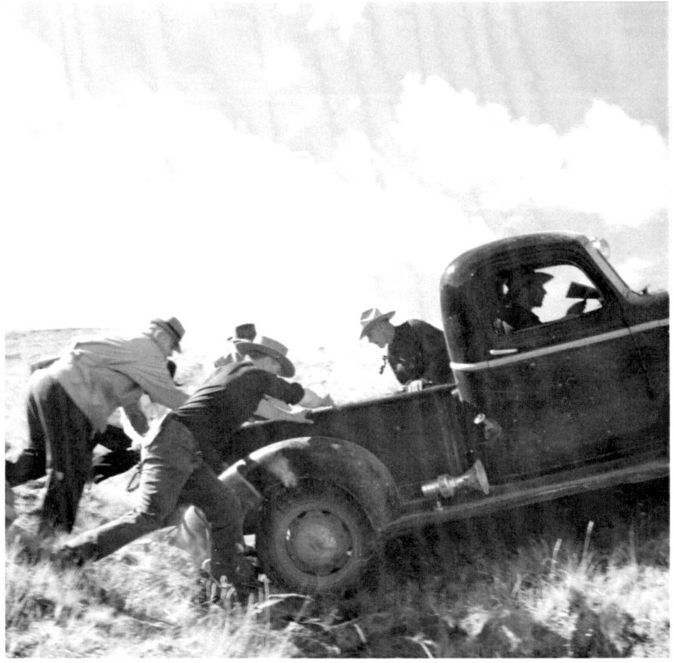

Page 79. Hunters help push a truck out of a ravine on Pitchfork Ranch.

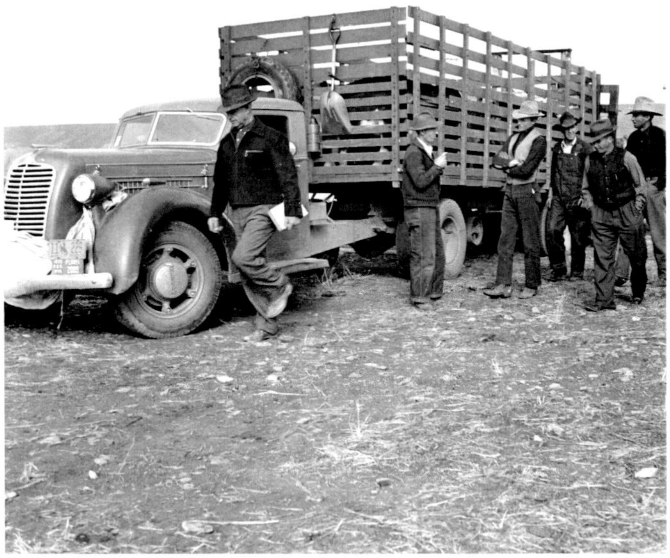

Page 78. Men visiting beside truck full of Hereford calves at Timber Creek.

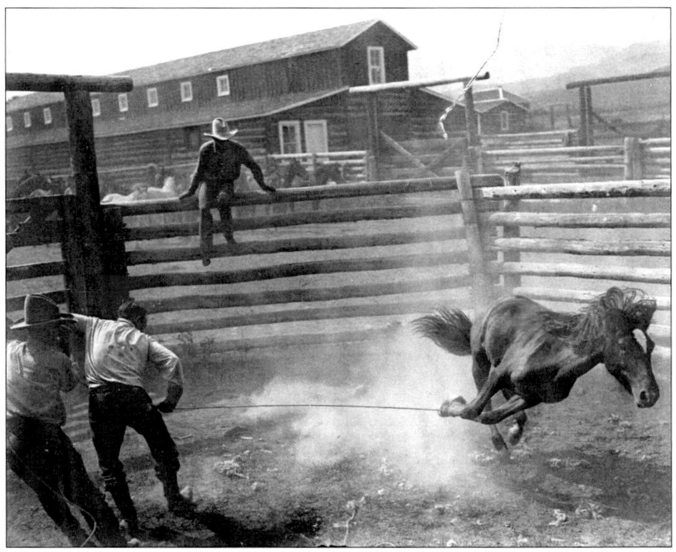

Page 80-81. Shorty Shaper and Sunny Owens rope a horse in the corral while Harry Nevins sits on the fence.

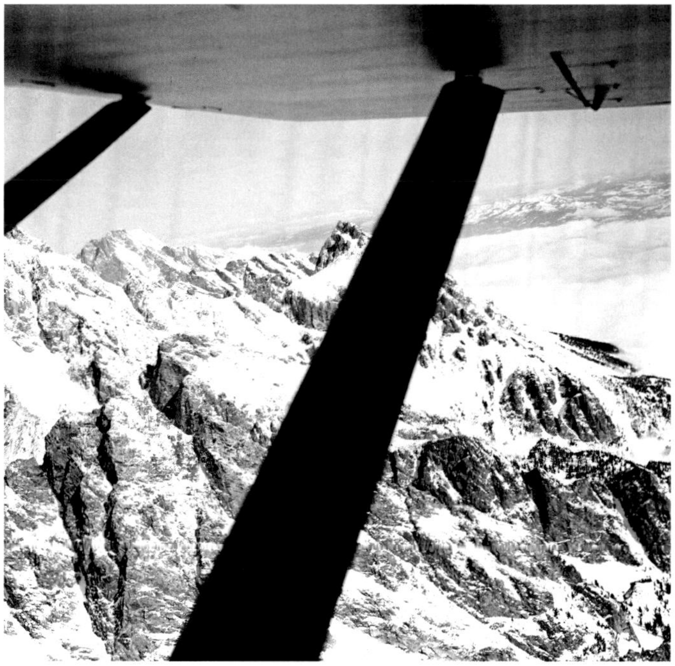

Page 82. *Aerial view of snow covered Teton range from south. Airplane's struts and wing tip are visible in frame.*

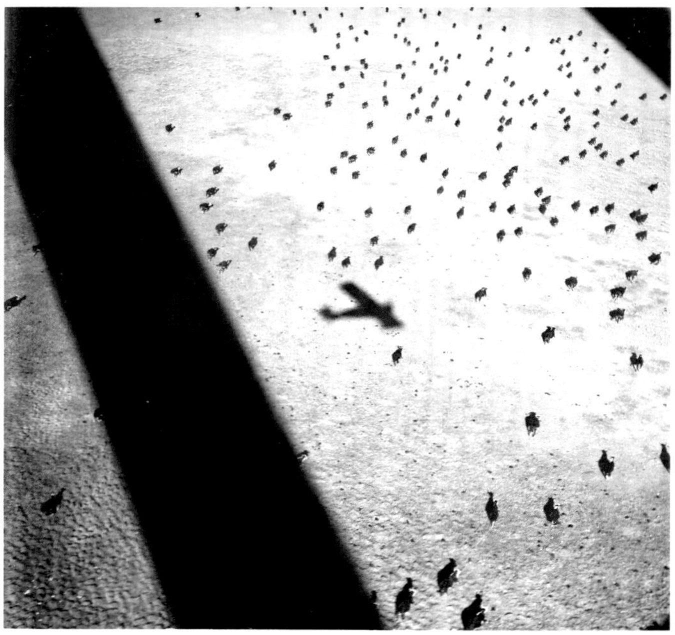

Page83. Aerial view of Herefords grazing on plains of Pitchfork Ranch.

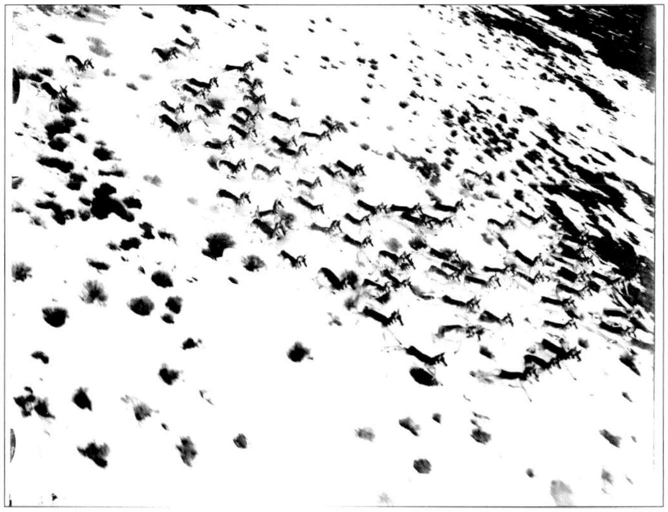

Page 84-85. Pronghorn antelope run swiftly across the snowy plains. Antelopes can run at a mile a minute over rough terrain.

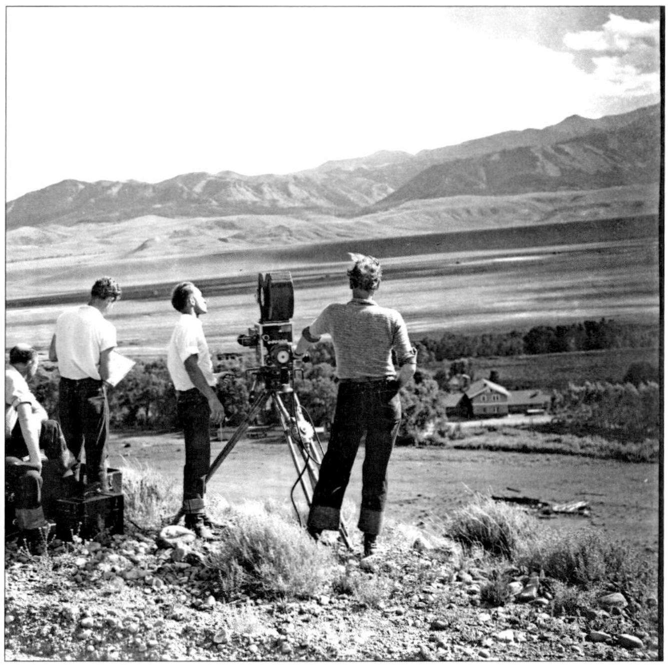

Page 86. Four men with movie camera equipment looking over Pitchfork Ranch.

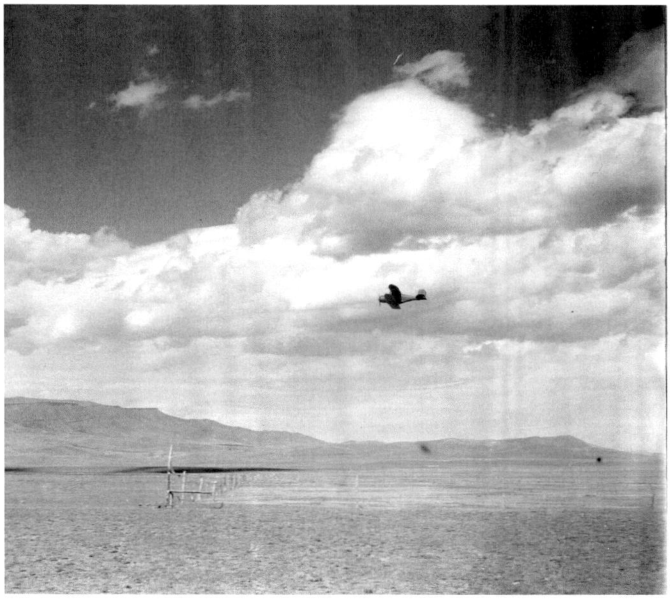

Page 87. A Beechcraft Staggerwing makes a pass over the end of the Pitchfork runway.

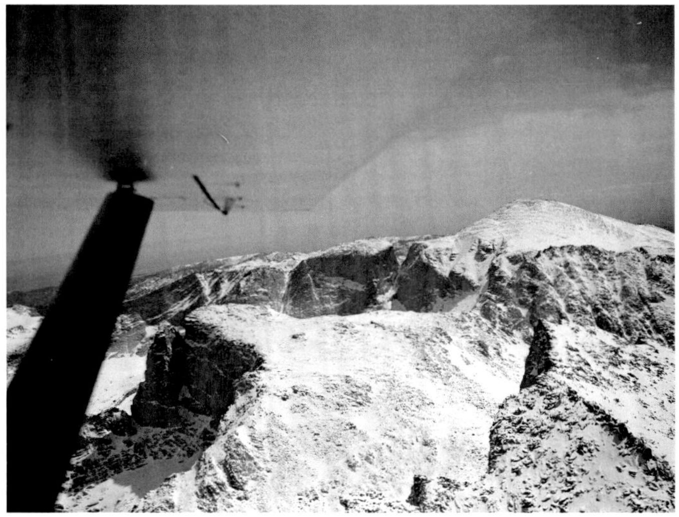

Page 90. Aerial view of snowcapped Gannette Peak in Wind River Mountains with airplane's wing tip and strut in photo.

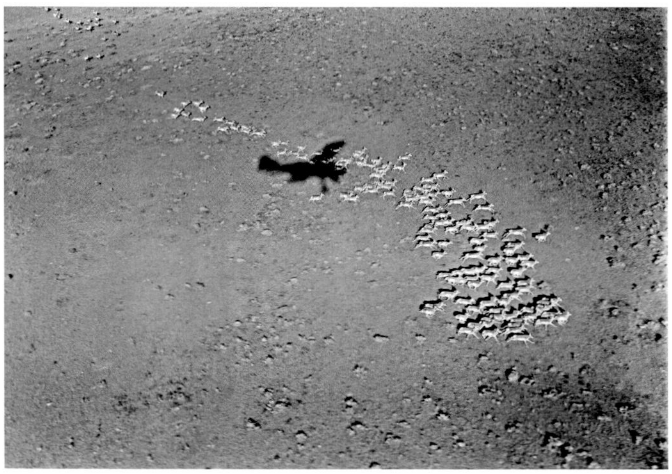

Page 88-89. Aerial view of pronghorn antelope running on Pitchfork Ranch, with airplane shadow on the herd.

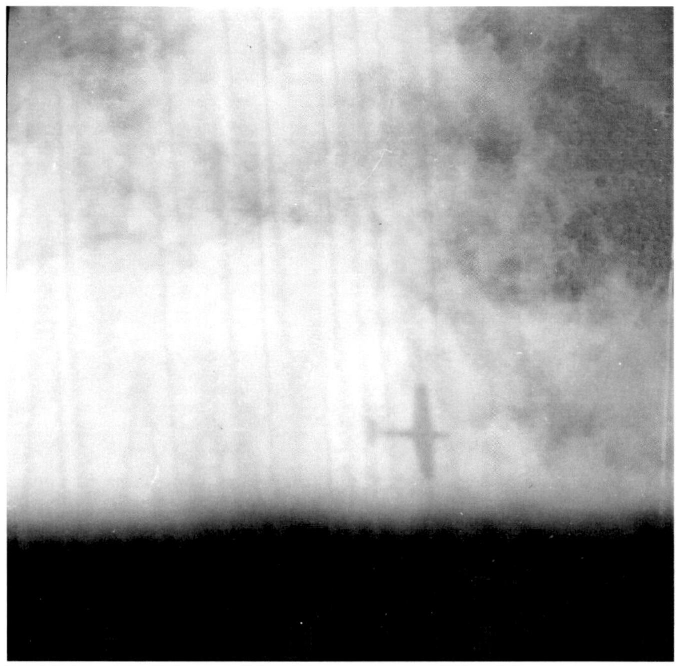

Page 91. Shadow of airplane flying through clouds.

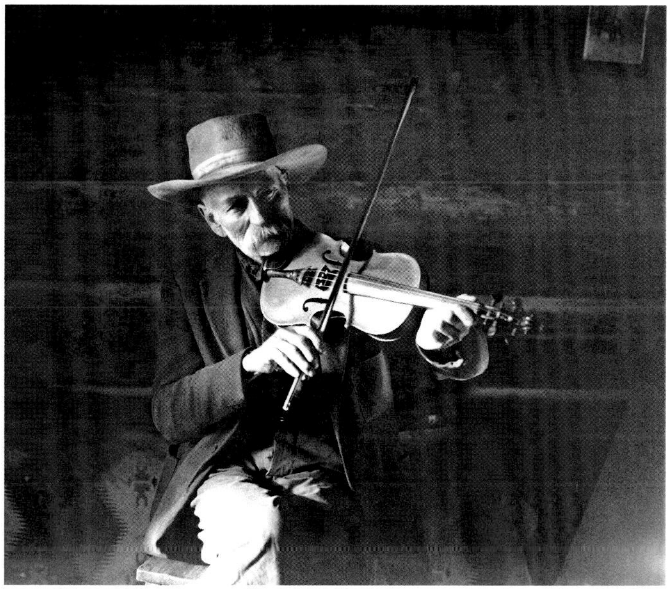

Page 92. William T. Borron sits on a bench and plays the fiddle at Pitchfork Ranch.

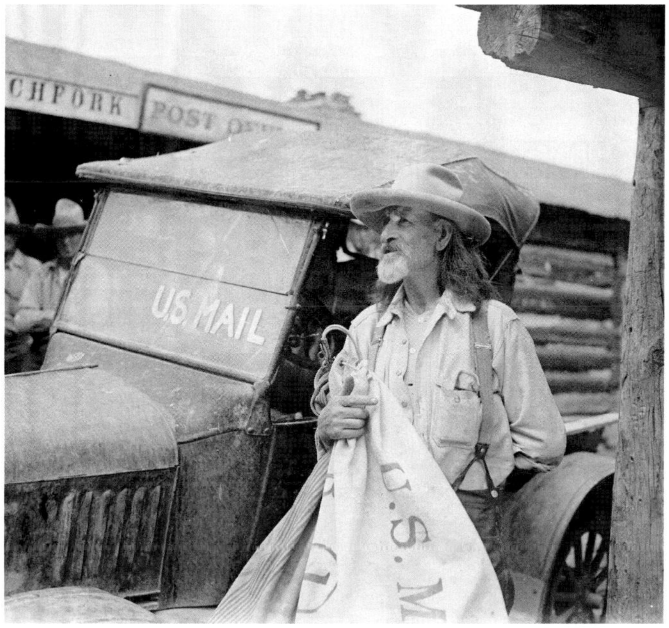

Page 94. Mailman Jack 'Two Dog' Scott delivers a bag of mail to the Pitchfork ranch, near Meeteetse, Wyoming.

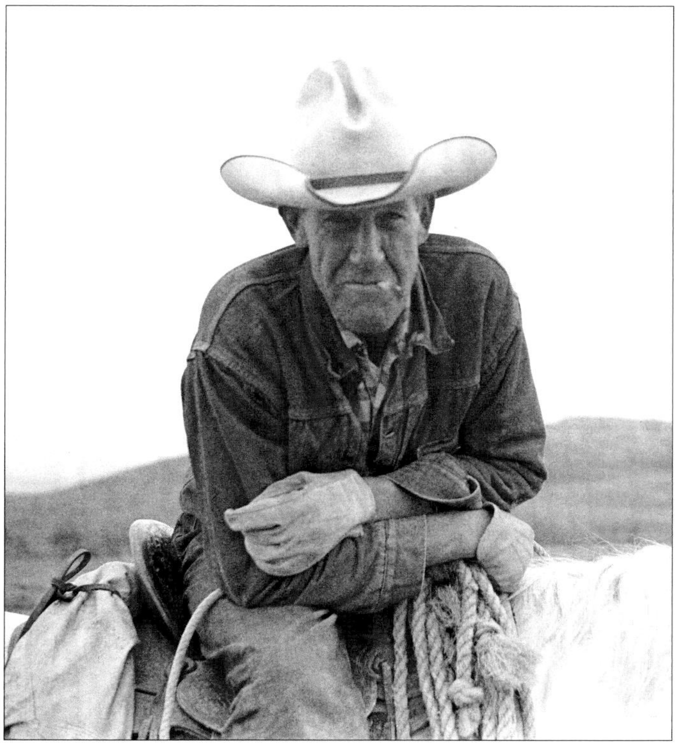

Page 93. Cowboy sits in saddle on a pale horse smoking a cigarette.

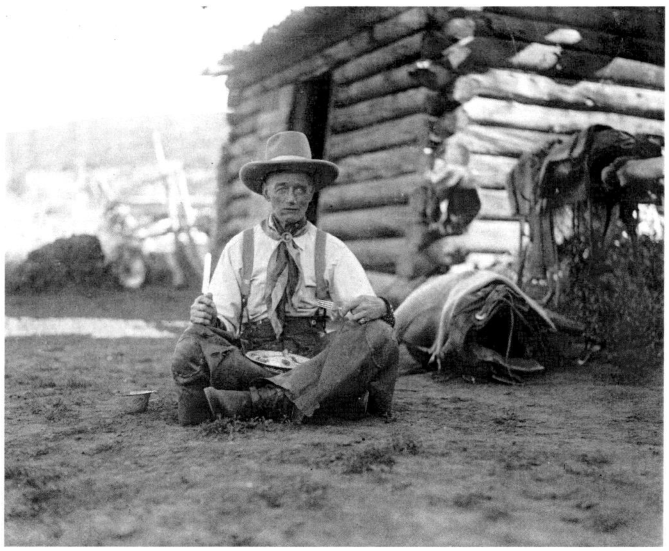

Page 95. Charlie Collins sitting on the ground eating at Valley Ranch, Wyoming.

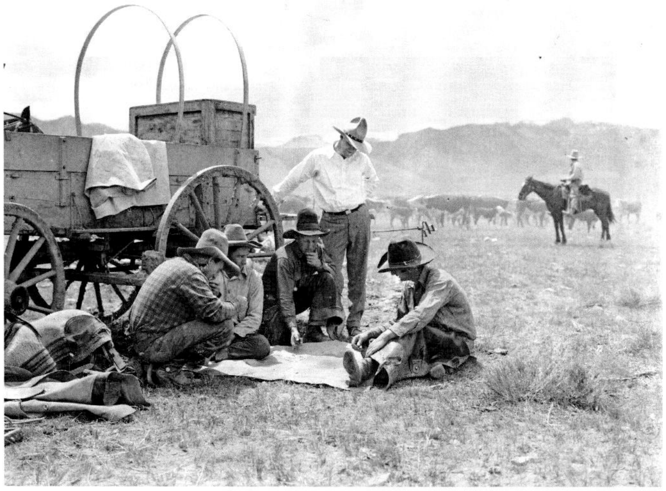

Page 96. C. Jack Rhodes, Sr., Hughie Windsor, Curly Hollingsworth, Mark Windsor, and Dutch Kreal gamble beside wagon on Pitchfork Ranch. Z Bar T brand on wagon and Pitchfork branding iron behind standing cowboy.

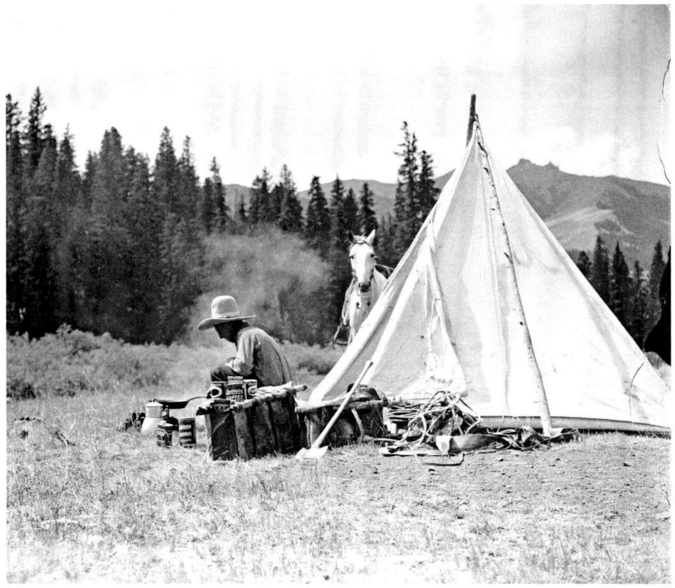

Page 98. Sid Nelson outside in front of his tipi style tent, also known as a sheepherder's tent, at Spring Creek.

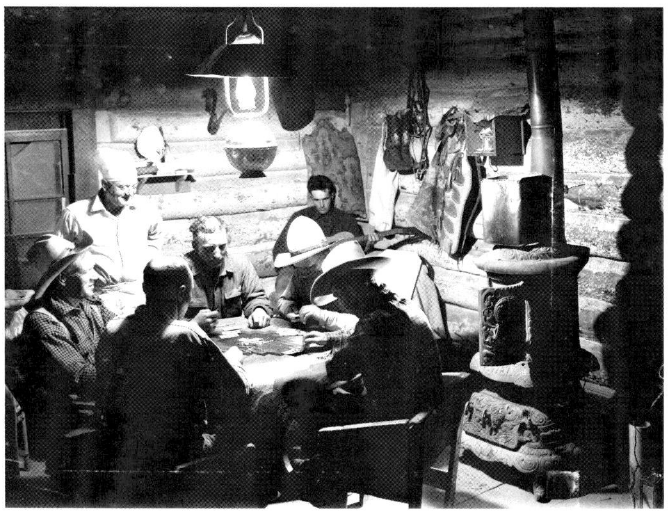

Page 97. Lawrence Todd (Cal Todd's father), Shorty Graham, Harry Thayer (wearing Belden's hat), Curly Hollingsworth, and Burton Avery playing cards in bunkhouse on Pitchfork Ranch.

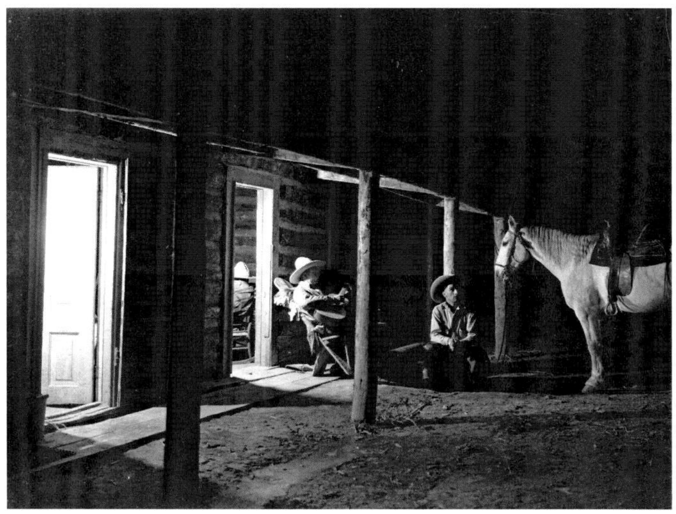

Page 99. C. Jack Rhodes, Sr. (wearing Belden hat), and Hugh Windsor sit in evening by bunkhouse on Pitchfork Ranch playing guitar while a saddled horse waits. Harry Thayer sits inside bunkhouse.

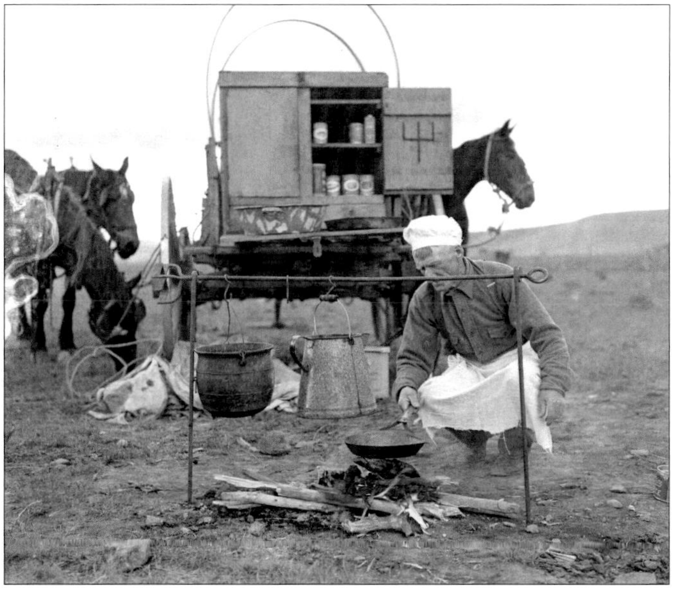

Page 100. Bobby Burns, the mess cook, holds a pan over the fire to cook a meal by the chuck wagon. Pitchfork branding iron holds the pots over the fire.

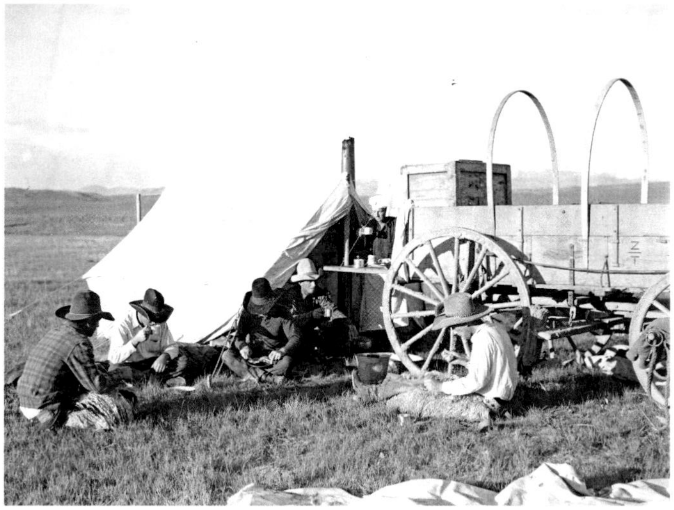

Page 101. Five cowboys gather by a chuck wagon for their meal while a cook stands near the wagon on Rawhide Creek.

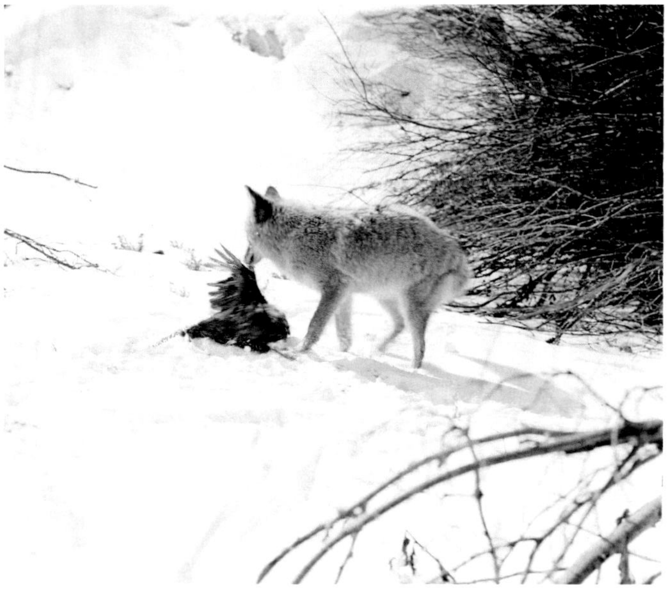

Page 102. A coyote eats a raven in the snow.

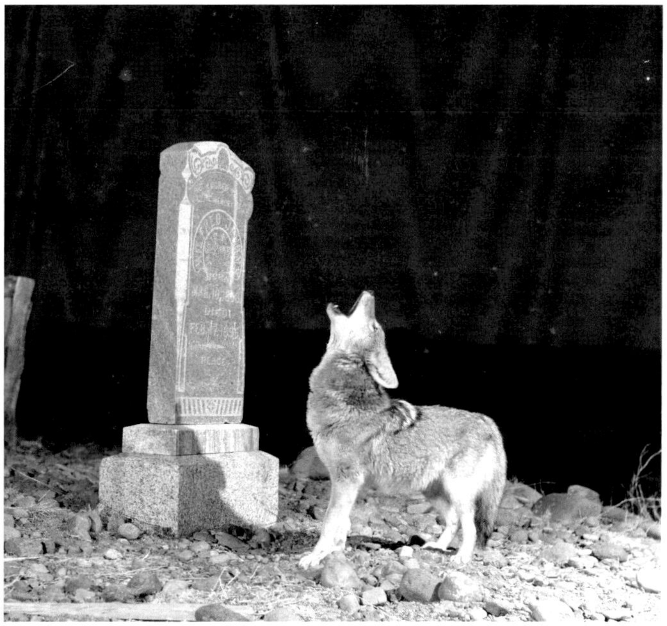

Page 103. Coyote howls beside headstone of Wilfred Jevons near Wood River.

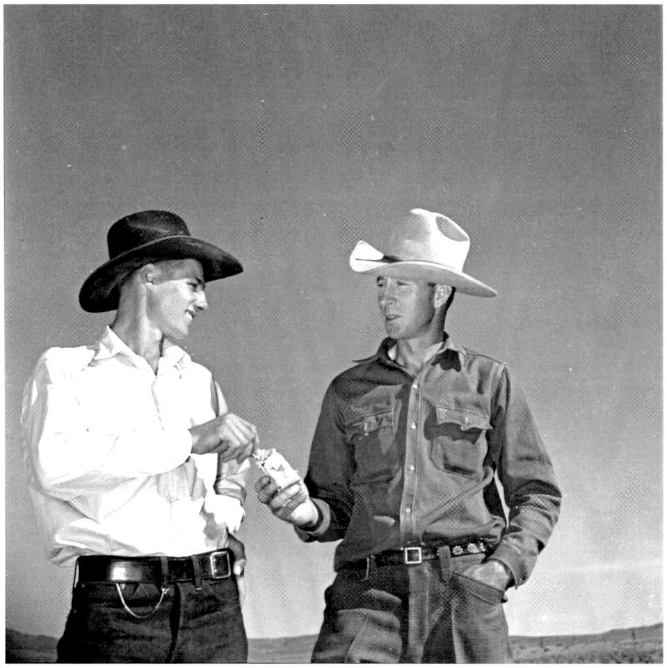

Page 104. One cowboy offering another cowboy a cigarette on Pitchfork Ranch

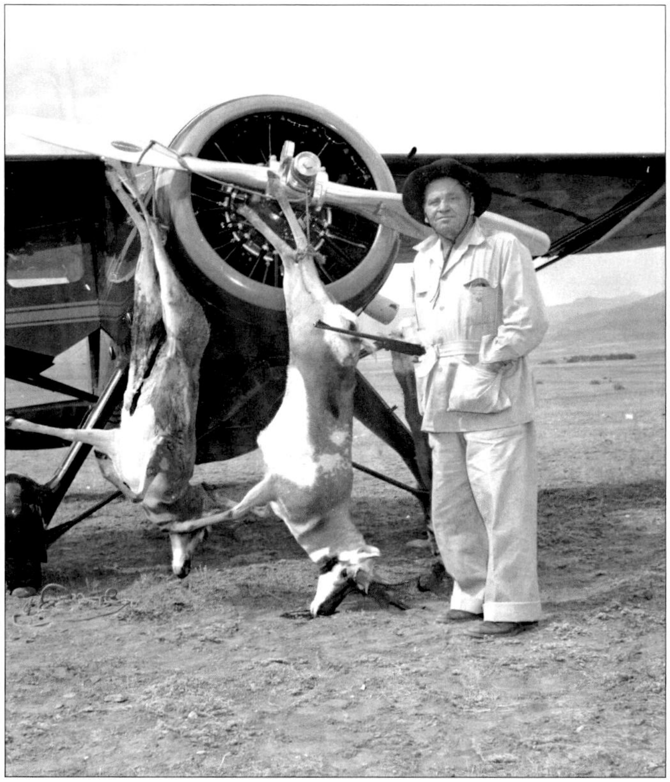

Page 105. Movie actor Wallace Beery with two antelope hanging from his personal airplane on Pitchfork Ranch.

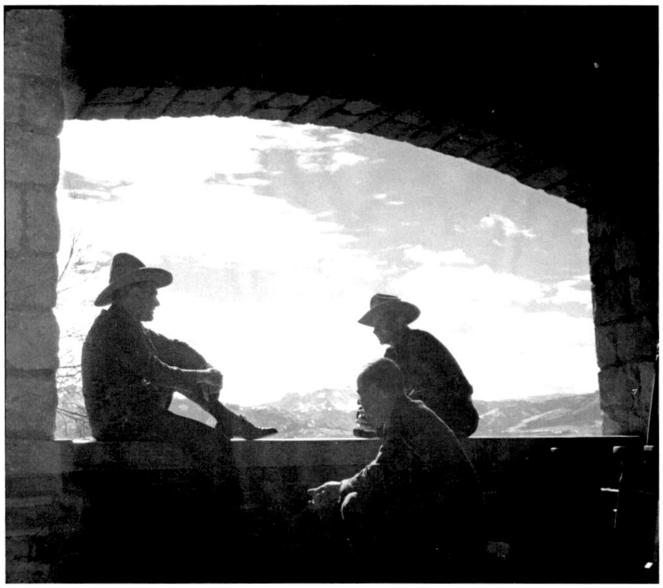

Page 106. Charles Belden on left and friends sitting on porch at main Z Bar T Ranch. Francs Peak in background.

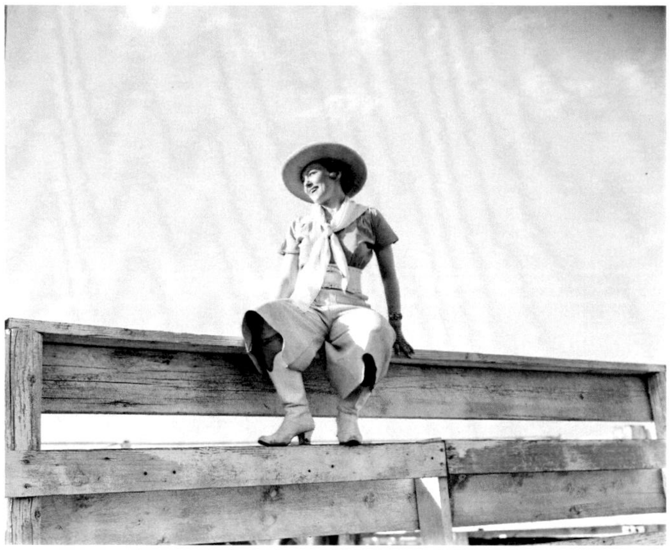

Page 107. Cowgirl sitting on a fence.

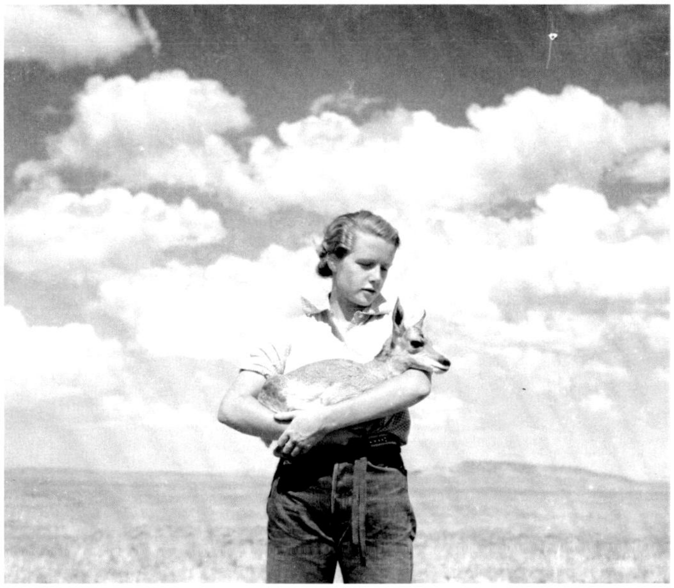

Page 108. Belden's daughter holding baby antelope on Pitchfork Ranch.

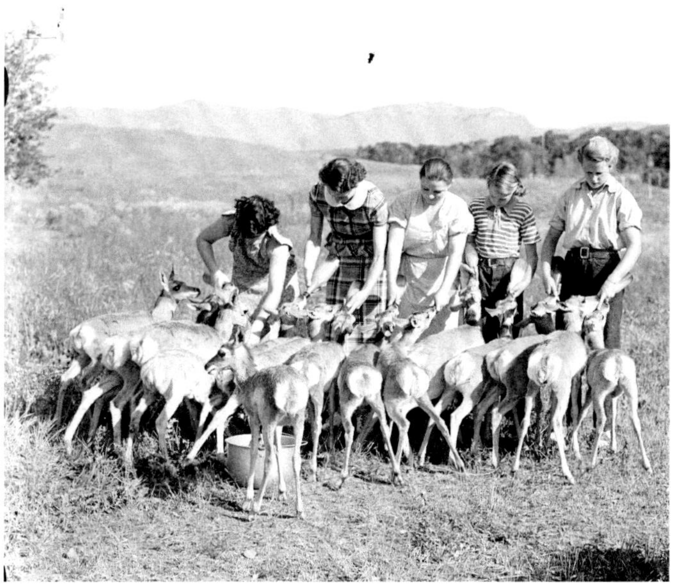

Page 109. Women bottle feeding baby antelope on Pitchfork Ranch.

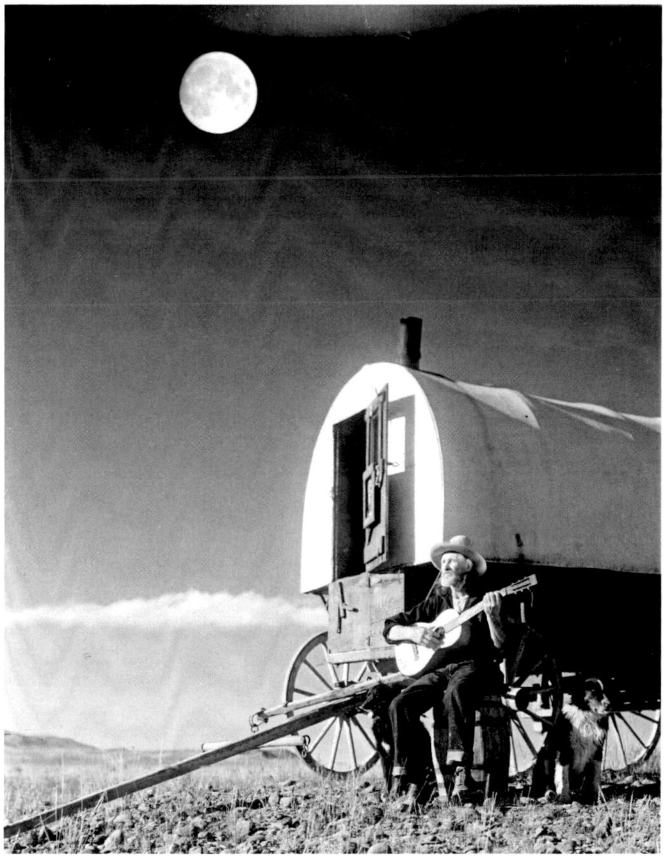

Page 110. Jack "Two Dog" Scott playing guitar beside sheep wagon on Pitchfork Ranch. His two dogs sit next to him.

"To live in the American West is to see a Belden image every day."

—Brooks Roddan